Parental Incarceration and the Family

Parental Incarceration and the Family

Psychological and Social Effects of Imprisonment on Children, Parents, and Caregivers

Joyce A. Arditti

NEW YORK UNIVERSITY PRESS
New York and London

NEW YORK UNIVERSITY PRESS
New York and London
www.nyupress.org

References to Internet websites (URLs) were accurate at the time of writing.
Neither the author nor New York University Press is responsible for URLs that
may have expired or changed since the manuscript was prepared.

Library of Congress Cataloging-in-Publication Data
Arditti, Joyce A.
Parental incarceration and the family : psychological and social effects
of imprisonment on children, parents, and caregivers / Joyce A. Arditti.
p. cm. Includes bibliographical references and index.
ISBN 978-0-8147-0512-4 (cl : alk. paper) — ISBN 978-0-8147-0513-1 (ebook) —
ISBN 978-0-8147-0805-7 (ebook)
1. Prisoners' families—United States. 2. Children of prisoners—United States.
3. Children of women prisoners—United States. 4. Prisoners—Family relationships—
United States. 5. Women Prisoners—Family relationships—United States. I. Title.
HV8886.U5A73 2012
362.82'95—dc23 2011051506

New York University Press books are printed on acid-free paper,
and their binding materials are chosen for strength and durability.
We strive to use environmentally responsible suppliers and materials
to the greatest extent possible in publishing our books.

Manufactured in the United States of America

10 9 8 7 6 5 4 3 2 1

For the journey taken and its costs
For hearts broken and lives lost
All are equal as we wait
Stories told of love and hate
Call us different or oppressed
Behind the fence we did our best.

For Ethan and Alanis with love

Contents

Acknowledgments

The writing of this book would not have been possible without the men, women, and children who shared their experiences with the research community. I am particularly indebted to those families who gave of their time and participated in my own research, which is included throughout the book. They served as an inspiration to write a book that would tell their stories. The world needs to know.

I gratefully acknowledge former and current Virginia Tech students for their assistance with proofreading, references, and appendix: Tiffaney Parkman, Sara Neeves-Bothelho, Chih-ling Liou, Zoe Cornwell, and Kendra Arsenault. Thank you all.

I also thank my editor Jennifer Hammer for her thoughtful comments and suggestions, her sharp wordsmithing, and her encouragement throughout the proposal and book-writing process. Jennifer believed in this project from its inception, and without her this book would not exist.

Finally, I thank my husband for his steadfastness and unwavering belief in my ability to do just about anything, including write this book.

Introduction

A Framework for Understanding Parental Incarceration

Do not weep; do not wax indignant. Understand.

Spinoza (1632–1677)

[People] may be said to resemble not the bricks of which a house is built, but the pieces of a picture puzzle, each differing in shape, but matching the rest, and thus bringing out the picture.

Felix Adler

The visiting area of the jail had a mix of smells: urine, sweat, and desperation. I was instantly reminded of the homes I had visited during my tenure as a social worker, many years prior. The air was close and the room noisy as it was packed with visitors on this early Saturday morning. Children were fidgeting on their mothers' laps, rolling around on the dirty floor, trying to make paper airplanes out of the religious pamphlets they had found in display racks on the wall. There were mostly women and children here today. I tried to push away the thoughts of an earlier visit to this facility, during which I had entered through a different door with the sheriff to tour the holding cells and "pods" where the prisoners spent their days, months, and sometimes years. No fresh air, no sunlight, no privacy, but instead noise, bars, day after day, hour after hour. A human zoo—a place invisible to most except the incarcerated and their captors. So much pain in that place—it overwhelmed me.

There is a reason that prisons are tucked away far from the hustle and bustle of daily life—built in remote towns that need jobs and "industry." Human suffering, whether caused by one's own actions or the actions of others, is a hard thing to confront. No one wants to feel it around them. No one wants to see it. Even this jail went unnoticed in the heart of town, probably because of the lack of windows. The sheriff told me that "he likes it that way." The many jails and

| 1

prisons I had visited were surrounded by fences, wires, and walls: all of it to keep some locked away and the rest of us out.[1]

It is a risk to start a book on parental incarceration with a personal reflection from field notes compiled during a study of the impact of parental incarceration on families. The notes reflect the visceral experience of *being there* and the transformative potential of fieldwork in corrections settings (Arditti, Joest, Lambert-Shute, & Walker, 2010). In doing so I acknowledge the proverbial elephant in the room: human suffering. Prisons and jail are not happy places. Criminologists James Austin and John Irwin (2001) provide a succinct description of the prison experience today:

> Convicted primarily of property and drug crimes, 1.3 million prisoners and another 600,000 jailed inmates are being crowded into human (or inhuman) warehouses where they are increasingly deprived, restricted, isolated, and consequently embittered and alienated from conventional worlds. (p. 90)

Jails and prisons contain a great deal of collective suffering not only on the part of prisoners but also for family members connected with the offender (Arditti, 2003; Arditti & Few, 2008; Sack & Seidler, 1978). Human suffering of this nature, defined as *social suffering*, constitutes

> a collective form of bad luck, that attaches itself like a fate, to all those that have been put together in those sites of social relegation, where the personal suffering of each is augmented by all the suffering that comes from coexisting and living with so many suffering people together…and more importantly, of the destiny effect from belonging to a stigmatized group. (Bourdieu, 1999, p. 64)

Social suffering impacts family, community, and society in both economic and moral terms (Bourdieu, 1999). Spinoza's dictum—*Do not weep; do not wax indignant. Understand*—provides inspiration for this book on parental incarceration. French sociologist and philosopher Pierre Bourdieu (1999) contends that we must take Spinoza's precept to heart if we are to come up with a comprehensive picture of human difficulty and its systemic causes. In that vein, this book represents a scholarly effort to understand.

Of course, like uniquely shaped puzzle pieces, not all offenders are the same, and not all jails and prisons are the same. Some jails and prisons have better conditions than the one described in my field notes, some institutions employ progressive practices, and some provide rehabilitation and opportunities for the imprisoned. Prison may result in unexpected changes for those within its walls. Prison may be a place where a person receives treatment for drug addiction or mental illness for the first time. Prison may stop a violent predator in his or her tracks. Prison may protect those who have been victimized and who breathe a sigh of relief now that the offender is removed from the streets. Yet there is a whole picture here, one that comes into focus when the puzzle pieces are linked—including the piece that constitutes social suffering. The picture is this: prisoners are human beings, many of whom are parents. Children lose parents to prisons and jails, and families change when someone goes to prison. Sometimes these changes help, but very often it seems they hurt not only the offender parent but also the children and others closest to the offender.

This book is meant to achieve two goals. First and most important, it tells the story of parental incarceration by focusing on the imprisoned, their children, and their family members. We know a lot about incarceration rates, crime rates, and so on, but what of the mass of humanity behind bars, as well as those affected on the outside? In this book I put a human face on the numbers and trends in interpreting what science has to say about mass imprisonment; I utilize exemplars, anecdotes, and my own reflections to flesh out interpretation. As much as one might try, it is difficult to be purely objective in the telling of this story because so much is at stake, so many lives are affected, and family adversity of the magnitude that is connected to the incarceration of a parent is very disturbing to witness and document. The research findings are generally not positive, and happy stories are hard to come by. Parental incarceration research is not neutral ground because suffering inspires emotion not only among the researched but also among those who study families in trouble. Qualitative researchers know this only too well. This book is grounded in scientific "fact" per the published research, but in reality these facts are continuously being written and constructed and rewritten (Wonders, 1996). It represents a version of reality in that like other feminist scholars, I acknowledge the "subjective and transitory nature of all truth." The story here is my take on things, a version you can trust, a version aimed at understanding, but it is only one version.

This book joins many other voices to question a criminal justice approach that relies so heavily on imprisonment. While we might all agree that incarceration may be a necessary response to certain public safety threats and injustices, its widespread use creates further safety threats and injustices not only for the public but also for family members of the imprisoned and for the incarcerated parents themselves. A second goal of the book, therefore, is to highlight the reasons for widespread incarceration of parents and the intended and unintended consequences of the imprisonment of offenders, particularly nonviolent offenders, for families. In doing so, I hope the book's contents will inspire critical thinking among its readers and serve as a catalyst to question our nation's current emphasis on punishment in response to an increasingly broad array of activities defined as criminal. A hammer is a good tool, but it can only achieve certain things. We might use it to put a nail in the wall, but it would be of little service in unscrewing a pipe (better to use a wrench). The research presented here demonstrates that the United States relies too much on its hammer and needs to start using other tools. These tools encompass social policy reform aimed at social justice, harm reduction, and the promotion of human development. Imprisonment is an incomplete and often bureaucratic response to human problems that stem from contexts of extreme disadvantage and family adaptations to adversity. As we shall see, "institutional actions can (and often do) deepen and make more intractable the problems they seek to ameliorate" (Das & Kleinman, 2001, p. 2). This book offers a basis not only to ask questions but also to come up with different answers when it comes to dealing with parent offenders and their families—answers that visibly address the underlying conditions associated with criminal justice involvement and embrace core principles of developmental science.

Background

The United States has the highest incarceration rate in the world, having surpassed Russia in 2000 (Mauer, 2006). At the end of 2008, federal and state corrections facilities held 1,610,446 prisoners, reaching all-time year-end highs (West, Sabol, & Cooper, 2009). Additionally, at midyear 2009, another 767,992 offenders were confined to local jails (Minton, 2010).[2] Substantial portions of the nation's prisoners are parents—52% of state inmates and 63% of federal inmates. Bureau of Justice estimates for 2007 indicate that the nation's prisoners report having an estimated 1,706,600 minor children, accounting for 2.3% of the U.S. population under age 18 (Glaze & Maruschak, 2008). One-third of these children will reach the age of 18 while their parent is still incarcerated (Glaze & Maruschak, 2008). Parents of minor children held in the nation's prisons increased by 79% between 1991 and midyear 2007 (Glaze & Maruschak, 2008), and the trend, while slowing (West et al., 2009), reflects the continued and widespread use of incarceration as a crime control strategy in the United States (Austin & Irwin, 2001; Dressel, 1994; Mauer, 2006).

What are we to make of these trends in terms of both crime control and the impact of incarceration on families? With regard to crime control, the relationship between incarceration and crime is a complex one (King, Mauer, & Young, 2005). Historically, the use of incarceration was proportionate to population growth; however, in the last 30 years or so the increased number of people in prisons and jails across the country has far outpaced population growth. Specifically, between 1970 and 2000 the general population rose by less than 40%, yet the number of imprisoned individuals rose by more than 500% (King et al., 2005). Opponents of incarceration interpret this outpacing as one indication of an "overreliance" on incarceration that is excessive, expensive, and damaging to society (Austin, Bruce, Carroll, McCall, & Richards, 2000; King et al., 2005; Mauer, 2006). Yet steady declines in violent and nonviolent crime since 1992–2010 provide evidence for proponents of the increased use of incarceration as a necessary and effective response to crime (FBI 2009, 2010). Recent testimony at a Federal Sentencing Commission hearing by the Department of Justice (DOJ) continues to reflect a belief in the necessity of a "get tough on crime approach" to ensure public safety, although there is an emerging recognition that adjustments may be needed for disparate or extremely severe sentencing guidelines (Testimony of the United States Department of Justice, 2010). In sum, experts disagree regarding the role of imprisonment in reducing crime, although there is some consensus that increased numbers of police and waning crack use are additional factors contributing to lower crime rates.[3] At the very least, a simple causal relationship between incarceration and crime reduction is suspect, with increased prison populations accounting for a portion of crime prevention, but not all of it.

Views about the necessity of incarceration or its purported damage are subject to a wide range of interpretation depending on one's criterion of analysis.[4] As we shall see, a family focus necessitates considerations beyond public safety and crime reduction to include criteria such as child development and health, family functioning, and parental competence. This book takes a "family perspective" that focuses on incarcerated individuals who are parents, and on the impact incarceration has on their ability to parent, as well as the consequences of incarceration on their nonincarcerated family members. Parents who are incarcerated are deeply and often negatively affected by the experience of imprisonment relative to their ability to contribute to the lives of their children, their children's caregivers, and other kin (Hagan & Dinovitzer, 1999). An understanding of family influences has been deemed critical in understanding "a prisoner's life" and an individual's transition back from prison to community (Visher & Travis, 2003).

The core goal of this book is to help meet the growing need of scholars, students, policy makers, and practitioners trying to make sense of the research and to devise evidence-based responses to the results of mass incarceration and its consequences: deteriorating family ties, high recidivism, intergenerational patterns of criminality, and communities where large numbers of parents, particularly fathers, are absent due to incarceration (Herman-Stahl, Kan, & McKay, 2008; Huebner & Gustafson, 2007; Lynch & Sabol, 2001; Western & McLanahan, 2000). Informed by ecological theory and developmental contextualism, this book bring pieces of the empirical literature together in a new way with the hope of more clearly providing an evidence-based foundation for clinical intervention and policy responses. Indeed, psychologists are in the business of intervening with respect to process as many contextual factors are rigid and unchangeable. A focus on process, and in particular parenting processes, provides a fertile avenue for intervention and change.

Most research about prisoners and their families is largely the result of scholars working from either a macrolevel (i.e., societal) perspective within criminology, demography, or sociology, or conversely, from a microlevel perspective focused on individual deviance (Day, Acock, Bahr, & Arditti, 2005). In bringing a *family perspective* to the current literature on parental incarceration, we will consider the nature and quality of parenting as central to the debate, rather than simply a consequence of mass imprisonment policies. It has been said that "the family generally, and parenting specifically, are today in a greater state of flux, question, and redefinition than… ever before" (Bornstein, 2002, xi). Arguably, in the last 25 years, incarceration has emerged as a primary force in the redefinition of parenthood. Parenthood is a life-altering status and experience that naturally involves a focus on children and their development. Parents are charged with protecting their children from harm, preventing adversity, and promoting their children's well-being (Hoghughi, 2004). Children's well-being is inextricably linked to their parents—to their mothers' and fathers' capacity to protect, prevent, and promote. But as journalist Nell Bernstein (2005) points out, parenthood also has consequences for parents in that it involves "giving and responsibility… pleasures, privileges, and profits as well as frustrations, fears, and failures" (p. x). While parenthood may alter lives, so too does imprisonment. Prison confinement is perhaps one of the most radical means of altering experience, changing families, and clearly limiting an individual's ability to "protect, prevent, and promote" his or her children. In this book we will consider the intersection of parenthood and prison. This book is one response to the question: *What happens when the two paths, parenthood and prison, cross?*

What Is a Family Perspective?

> The happiness of any society begins with the well-being of the families that live in it.   Kofi Annan

As reflected by these well-known words from Nobel Peace Prize winner and former United Nations head Kofi Annan, family well-being can be seen as a critical foundation of societal health. However, within the realm of policy-making many policies fall outside the explicit definition of "family policy" and are not formulated with family well-being in mind. A *family perspective* acknowledges the "important role that family considerations can play in a broad range of policy issues" (Bogenschneider, 2002, p. 25). A family perspective involves analyzing a policy or program, in this case, the incarceration of individuals who have offspring, regardless of whether the policy/program in question is explicitly aimed at families. The criterion for such an analysis is family well-being (Bogenschneider, 2002). Criminal justice policy is generally not formulated with family well-being as an explicit outcome. Rather, incarceration-related policy and intervention are more typically aimed at reducing crime and criminality in its myriad manifestations, as well as eradicating certain social ills such as drug use or handgun violence (Donzinger, 1996). A family perspective necessitates examining how parental incarceration affects the imprisoned parent, as well as family stability, the quality of family relationships, and the family's ability to carry out its responsibilities and functions. Central to a family perspective is the issue of parenting: an issue that is not adequately addressed in the literature on parental incarceration, which tends to more often focus on the effects of a parent's incarceration on child adjustment, without due consideration of mediating family processes and offenders' parenting capacity.

In thinking about incarceration, a family perspective centered on parents has great utility. Incarceration involves not only the removal of a parent from a family system and a dramatic lessening or cessation of his or her parenting contributions (Arditti, Smock, & Parkman, 2005; Hagan & Dinovitzer, 1999; Hairston, 1998; Swisher & Waller, 2008) but also the incapacitation of offenders whereby they are psychologically and socially altered as a result of imprisonment (Austin & Irwin, 2001; Haney, 2002; Irwin, 2005). Such alteration can result in reduced parenting capacity during and beyond a period of incarceration for parents who wish to be a meaningful part of their children's lives.

There are several books and reviews that deal broadly with issues pertaining to families and incarceration. Existing reviews tend to either focus in depth on one type of scenario such as the children of imprisoned parents (see, e.g., Hairston, 2007; Murray, 2005; Parke & Clarke-Stewart, 2001; Reed & Reed, 1997), child antisocial behavior and mental health (Murray, Farrington, Sekol, & Olsen, 2009), children with incarcerated mothers (Dallaire, 2007a), or the effects of paternal incarceration on children (Herman-Stahl et al., 2008; Hairston, 1998), or contain overviews of many issues that pertain to parental incarceration but lack an integrative lens, making it difficult, in psychologist Alfred Adler's words, to "bring out the picture."[5] One of the more influential works relevant to thinking about families and incarceration was authored by noted sociologist John Hagan and his colleague Ronit Dinovitzer (1999). The article, entitled "Collateral Consequences of Imprisonment for Children, Communities, and Prisoners," draws from classic theoretical perspectives in criminology and sociology. The authors argue that family is best understood within the larger context of the use of imprisonment "as a criminal sanction," and that growth of imprisonment has tremendous costs in terms of human and social capital. These costs involve repercussions involving the employability of offenders, and the children who must bear the diminished economic and social capital of their families and communities. Most notable here are the deprivations associated with the economic and socialization contributions of the parent as a result of imprisonment.

Perhaps the most important contribution of Hagan and Dinovitzer (1999) was to draw attention to the profound connection between criminal sanction policy and children within the macro disciplines of criminology and sociology. At the time of their writing, an emerging literature was beginning to document the harms children and family experienced as a result of parental incarceration (e.g., Brodsky, 1975; Carlson & Cervera, 1991; Johnston & Gabel, 1995; Sack & Seidler, 1978). In this book we will "dig deeper" in terms of unpacking human and social capital costs by more specifically examining the alteration in parenting functions that incarceration brings via contextual influences and intraindividual (psychological) and relational (interpersonal) processes. These alterations have profound implications for incarcerated parents, their children and intimate partners, and the communities in which they lived and to which they will likely return after their incarceration. Indeed, the effects of poverty and parenting inadequacies on children's development have been well established (e.g., Bornstein & Bradley, 2003; Brooks-Gunn & Duncan, 1997; McLoyd & Wilson, 1991). It is crucial to consider the influential role of incarceration in shaping parenting given its implications for the offender and his or her family.

Theoretical Influences: Ecological Theory and Developmental Contexts

In considering the growing literature on parental incarceration, it is important to employ a "theory" to help identify what is important, why incarceration changes individuals and families, and the resultant outcomes associated with a parent's imprisonment. Theory is an analytic structure that in lay terms helps us to explain something—to put the pieces of a puzzle together and bring out the "big picture." We can apply elements of ecological theory and developmental contextualism as a framework for understanding parental incarceration and its impact on families and children. Both of these theoretical traditions imply interdependence among developmental contexts as well as the stake individuals have in their own development. An ecological framework suggests the importance of environmental contexts and proximal processes in understanding behavior and patterns of adaptation (Cicchetti, 2006). Developmental contextualism focuses our attention on the *relational* nature of human development and suggests that parenting is best understood by examining the changing and reciprocal interactions between individuals and the multiple contexts within which they live (Lerner, Brennan, Noh, & Wilson, 1998).

Ecological Theory

Developmental psychologist Urie Bronfenbrenner's (1979) articulation of nested levels in the ecology of human development is perhaps the most well-known theory that conceptualizes contexts. Bronfenbrenner delimited the macro-, exo-, meso-, and microsystems to draw our attention to the multi-level influences shaping individual and family development. The microsystem is defined as the complex of relations between the developing person (in this case, the incarcerated parent or parent's family member) and his or her immediate settings and interaction over time. Within the microsystem, proximal family relationships are seen as a primary force driving development; thus parental functioning is a critical variable of interest. The immediate question is: How do contexts of imprisonment impinge on, delimit, and define proximal microsystem processes within the confines of the prison environment as well as in the home (Bronfenbrenner, 1995)? Bronfenbrenner is clear that the lives of all family members are interdependent. How a family member reacts to an event or role transition "affects the developmental course of the other family members, both within and across generations" (Bronfenbrenner, 1995, p. 642).

Mesosystems involve interrelations among contexts containing the incarcerated parent—in short a "system of microsystems." Links between prison and home contexts, such as visiting areas, are particularly salient. An exosystem is an extension of the mesosystem in that it embodies other contexts and community factors that influence development; however, these settings do not contain the developing person. This systemic level is particularly important in understanding parental incarceration. For the incarcerated parent, a primary exosystem is the home that he or she left prior to imprisonment and may try to stay connected to during confinement. For the family, a primary exosystem encompasses the specific context of imprisonment for the family member who is incarcerated and the institutional practices associated with the prison setting during incarceration and subsequent reentry of the parent upon release (Arditti, 2005).

Finally, the macrosystem refers to the overarching institutional patterns and cultural prototypes influencing development made manifest through economic, social, educational, legal, and political systemic levels. Macrosystemic influence is of profound importance for the incarcerated parent who is under "state control," and for his or her family given their embeddedness in a broad sociocultural network that stigmatizes imprisonment (Davies, 1980). Stigma intensifies the possibility of risk and has unique disruptive effects for the parents themselves as well as for their family members because of the demoralization and social isolation that come with the prison experience (Golden, 2005; Lowenstein, 1986; Western & McLanahan, 2000).

In sum, from an ecological standpoint, parental incarceration is inherently complex in terms of how it changes the incarcerated parent as well as its systemic effects on families.

Developmental Contextualism

Developmental contextualism is best known as a model of adolescence proposed by developmental psychologist Richard Lerner (1998), which parallels modern life-span approaches to understanding human development. One can see a clear connection to Bronfenbrenner's work given the theory's focus on dynamic interactions between individuals and the "multiple contexts within which they live" (Susman, Dorn, & Schiefelbein, 2003, p. 296). Key concepts of developmental contextualism relevant to understanding parental incarceration are *embeddedness, dynamic interactionism*, and *plasticity* (Susman et al., 2003).

Like Bronfenbrenner, Lerner draws our attention to the multiple influences shaping development, be they biological, psychological, or social aspects of change, and these influences can only be understood *in context*, a state defined as "embeddedness" in the language of developmental contextualism. Contexts of development include "family, peers, and the multiple social institutions that surround the developing individual" (Susman et al., 2003, p. 296).

According to the theory of developmental contextualism, dynamic interactionism is a concept that embodies the notion that processes can be reciprocal and simultaneous. The concept appropriately muddies the causal waters in that biological or genetic influences are no longer considered deterministic; it is particularly applicable in terms of integrating the individual and social aspects of development (Susman et al., 2003). Thus dynamic interactionism implies *agency* and *resilience*, concepts integral to ecological theory (Bronfenbrenner, 1979) in that individuals and collectively families are producers of their own development and can influence, shape, and even *transcend* toxic contexts of development (Brandstaedter & Lerner, 1999; Garbarino, 1995). With respect to parental incarceration, dynamic interactionism suggests the possibility that individuals and family members are not simply "victims" of the criminal justice system but may have diverse responses to imprisonment and adapt to the imprisonment in multiple ways, although admittedly for the prisoner, agency may exist only by degree as the limits of prisoners' agency "are quickly contained and often fiercely policed" (McCulloch & Scraton, 2008, p 17).

Finally, *plasticity* evolves from a focus on context and process in that there is potential for change across the life span via multiple levels of development (Lerner, 1998). The idea of plasticity is particularly important in developing sound prevention and intervention programs aimed at families interfacing with the criminal justice system, many of whom can be characterized as *fragile families* in that they are at greater risk for instability and poverty ("Parental Incarceration," 2008). Plasticity can be the praxis guiding such efforts, and it embodies the idea that "one size does not fit all," and that even well-meaning programs and policies may have unanticipated effects. Thus plasticity suggests that care must be taken in responding to the needs of imprisoned individuals and their families.

Integration

Both developmental contextualism and ecological theory ground a focus on context and process to understand the changes and outcomes associated with parental incarceration. Both theories conceptualize human development in relation to context and the interdependent nature of multiple levels or systems of organization. Bronfenbrenner (1977) described the ecological approach to understanding development as the scientific study of dynamic interrelationships between the changing person and the changing environmental contexts within which a person lives. Similarly, developmental contextualism specifies that biological, psychological, and social contextual levels are fused and constitute the process of developmental change (Lerner, Sparks, & McCubbin, 1999). This fusion or interdependence is of great significance with respect to parental incarceration as it points to multiple connections between contextual levels and the interrelatedness of social problems such as crime and poverty. For example, incarceration can be conceptualized as both an outcome of poverty and a contributor to financial adversity (Arditti, Lambert-Shute, & Joest, 2003; Rose & Clear, 1998; Watts & Nightengale, 1996).

The conceptual influences of both ecological theory and developmental contextualism lead us to pay a great deal of attention to context and process. Moreover, given the notion of "fusion," outcomes are not easily disentangled from the settings and interactions with which they may be associated. That is, context and processes often persist and permeate outcomes, such as adaptation, and cannot always be discretely defined as causal antecedents (Mancini & Roberto, 2009). And while developmental change typically implies a gradual unfolding, there are times of "swift transformation" wherein relational changes occur much more rapidly than normal and are thus associated with unexpected, unpredicted, and ambiguous consequences (Mancini & Roberto, 2009, p. 419). The incarceration of a parent is arguably one of those "swift transformations" for both parent and family. With regard to context, we need to pay particular attention to demographic factors and the disenfranchisement connected to a parent's incarceration as well as to the sociopolitical and physical environment of prison. With regard to "process," we must focus on "intraindividual" or psychological processes, as well as the interpersonal experience of the incarcerated parent. We also need to spec-ify the alterations in parenting identities, roles, functions, and interactions that families make when a parent is imprisoned. Thus family process has an internal (i.e., psychological) *and* relational (i.e., interpersonal) component, and these are best understood relative to the contextual influences associated with parental incarceration. In thinking about outcomes or consequences of parental incarceration, we will examine what the changes brought about by incarceration mean in terms of any adaptations the parent and family make as a result of imprisonment, as well as the implications of primary and sec-ondary losses incurred likely due to the incarceration. It is important to note that the "fallout" associated with parental incarceration, however necessary one might deem imprisonment to be given a certain set of circumstances, does not end when a parent is released and returned home. Thus we must consider the offender's reentry and the family's response to the parent's reen-try as important aspect of the consequences of parental incarceration.

Elements of a Context-Process-Outcome Framework

The blending of the compatible theories of ecological theory, per Bronfen-brenner, and developmental contextualism, per Lerner, supports an integra-tive and systemic interpretation of the empirical research. Comprehensive theory integration in this manner provides a framework for the synthesis of discrete theories and their empirical components into a holistic approach, adapted to account for unique contextual, process, and outcome variables involved in the study of parental incarceration. The application of an integra-tive framework is amenable to all kinds of research—including studies that utilize a different theoretical approach or are atheoretical.[6] It is possible to consider the research collectively and to identify a multiplicity of variables that can be framed as contextual or processual post hoc, with the goal of bet-ter understanding their interdependence and cumulative influence on par-ents and their families. For example, a research study may lack contextual variables or considerations but highlight key processes that when viewed as part of a whole (i.e., the sum of the research) provide a new insight with respect to person-environment interaction. The theoretical approach of this book does not impose itself on the empirical research; rather, the approach allows one to sift through the research on incarceration and bring together an array of ideas and empirical findings into a coherent *whole*. A holistic strategy is advantageous in that it permits the examination of a wide range of research studies, each potentially utilizing varied methodologies and theoretical approaches, within a common framework. A family perspective implies that the whole will tell us something more about parental incarceration than we could glean from examining its parts (in this case, each study; Broderick & Smith, 1979).

Context

There is a growing awareness that development cannot be understood apart from the contexts in which it occurs. Development implies an unfolding, pathway, or change of some sort, and contextual factors play an important role in defining experience—particularly in terms of what constitutes psychopathology or maladaptation (Cicchetti, 2006). Contextual influences may directly or indirectly affect parenting processes and outcomes for incarcerated offenders and their families (Parke & Clarke-Stewart, 2001; Poehlmann, Shlafer, Maes, & Hanneman, 2008). An array of factors have been considered contextual influences. These may be proximal, as in the case of situational or interpersonal influences operating at the microsystem level, or distal, as in the case of meso-, exo-, or macrosystem forces. Context has been understudied, partly because of the difficulty in pinpointing the effects of more distal contextual factors on human development. Such documentation requires cross-fertilization with disciplines that study macro-level phenomena (e.g., demography, economics, sociology; Cicchetti, 2006). And while scholars might specify contextual effects, "rarely do discussions of contexts actually describe what it is about contexts that have a place in human development" (Mancini & Roberto, 2009, p. 8).

Contexts represent a cluster of distinctive characteristics that may constrain or enable, be oppressive or developmentally enhancing, malleable or fixed (Garbarino, 1995; Mancini & Roberto, 2009). For example, the environment and structure of prison visiting rooms (e.g., controlled seating and movement for the inmate; rules prohibiting any physical contact) can be characterized as constrained, oppressive, and fixed, and they powerfully shape family process (Arditti, 2003; Hairston, 1998). Contextual factors associated with cumulative disadvantage, such as a lack of educational attainment or a history of unemployment, have bearing on outcomes, such as family reintegration and the assumption of parenting roles (Uggen & Wakefield, 2005). More distal contextual influences distinctive to U.S. criminal justice policy, such as political disenfranchisement, arguably add to difficulties for ex-prisoners who reenter community and family life (Uggen & Wakefield, 2005). Contextual risk factors pertinent to parental incarceration refer to structural, distal, or macrosystemic factors that impact parental incarceration.

It is important to note that contextual risk factors, those factors that enhance vulnerability or maladaptation, can characterize the *inmate* (e.g., history of substance use, incarceration as an early adult, lengthy sentence, prison overcrowding), the *family* (e.g., young children at home, single parenthood, unemployment), or *both* inmate and family (e.g., deep break policy,[7] stigma). Similarly, protective contextual factors, those factors that ameliorate risk or provide opportunity, such as work-release programs, resource assistance, and mental health services, may benefit the inmate, the family, or both.

Process

A consideration of process implies paying attention to the psychological and interpersonal experience of the incarcerated parent as well as family members who are left behind. Generally process refers to "a course of action, functions, operations, and methods of working" (Mancini & Roberto, 2009, p. 573). A process-oriented approach assumes that person-environment interactions occur in multiple ecological domains over time and "reflects a concern with more than charting…risk factors. The assumption is that risk factors and…outcomes are interrelated due to the action of underlying mechanisms" (Cummings, Davies, & Campbell, 2000, p. 52). Thus a process lens seeks to understand causality by articulating how risk factors set in motion specific processes and mechanisms (Cummings et al., 2000).

Here process encompasses both the intraindividual and the familial level of effect, and these factors may be interrelated. For example, high levels of maternal distress among mothers who are, or who were, incarcerated (Arditti & Few, 2008) may contribute to estranged family relationships and vice versa.

A focus on process, then, lends insight into the complicated social actions through which the family affects the individual (in this case the incarcerated parent) as well as how the individual affects the family. The current lack of a processual understanding has been deemed a serious gap in the research on incarceration and prisoner reentry (Dallaire, 2007a; Uggen & Wakefield, 2005; Visher & Travis, 2003).

With respect to parental incarceration, process is concerned not only with the incarcerated parent's psychological adjustment and intraindividual experience but also with how a parent's imprisonment changes the *relation-*

ships between incarcerated parents and their intimate partners, children, and other family members. Process encompasses important protective mechanisms such as parents' ability to garner social support from friends, family, and institutional systems, as well as the extent to which support needs are being met, or existing support resources are deemed particularly helpful.

From a process lens, one would expect family relationships to be altered by incarceration for a number of reasons. First, *prisonized* parental identities emerge and gain prominence during incarceration. The term *prisonization* is sometimes used to refer to institutionalization in corrections settings and is "shorthand" for the negative psychological effects of imprisonment. Prisonization involves the "incorporation of the norms of prison life into one's habits of thinking, feeling, and acting" (Haney, 2002, p. 80; as derived from Clemmer, 1940). This process of adaptation to the culture of prison society generally implies a loss of agency that has profound implications for parenting (Irwin, 2005). Second, parenting roles are altered because incarceration constrains the enactment of key parenting functions, such as the provision of financial support, discipline, and basic care (Hairston, 1998). Incarceration curtails communication, the offering and receipt of affection, and caretaking. Imprisoned parents may adapt to the unique features of the prison environment in which parenting becomes largely an internal, symbolic process that may be characterized by a great deal of distress (Arditti et al., 2005; Arditti & Few, 2008).

Per ecological theory and developmental contextualism, processes do not occur in a vacuum and are best understood within their context. For example, a primary means of interaction between parents and children during incarceration is institutionalized visitation within the prison/jail facility. Environmental factors and prison policies profoundly shape the quality and nature of family interaction during this time (Arditti, 2005). With respect to prison environments, context is particularly salient and arguably overshadows process pertinent to incarcerated parents and their families given fixed institutional practices and their enforcement. The salience of context extends to probation and parole, whereby the incarcerated individual and his or her family must follow strict guidelines in terms of where and how they live (Parkman, 2009).

Outcomes

Finally, outcomes of interest broadly encompass the effects of incarceration on imprisoned parents as well as on their families and children. Outcomes are consequences connected to the changes that come from "processes of human development and of whatever lurks earlier in a sequence of events, circumstances, or conditions" (Mancini & Roberto, 2009, p. 5). In this case development is intertwined with the contextual factors and processes associated with incarceration and involvement in the criminal justice system.

It comes as no surprise, given the profound situational and experiential alterations associated with imprisonment, that parental incarceration has emotional, social, and economic effects on families and that these effects tend to be deleterious and involve significant losses to both the incarcerated parent and the family (Arditti et al., 2003; Murray, 2005; Murray & Farrington, 2008; Parke & Clarke-Stewart, 2001). With respect to the incarcerated parent's family members, effects can be conceptualized as occurring over time and are also a result of *secondary prisonization* (Comfort, 2008). Secondary prisonization involves the transformation of the nonincarcerated family members' lives—particularly female intimate partners of male inmates—as a result of interacting with the inmate and the correctional system. Changes may result in family members' social life, routine, priorities, and appearance based on their adaptations in response to a parent's incarceration. With respect to the imprisoned parents, outcomes of interest include their psychological adjustment, the quality of their family relationships, and their ability to reenter family and community life after a period of incarceration. The prisoner reentry literature widely documents the difficulties ex-offenders face upon release—particularly in terms of finding employment and dealing with the demands and responsibilities of life on the outside (Lynch & Sabol, 2001; Travis, 2005). Family ties, support, and resource sharing seem to be a critical component of reentry success and reunification of the offender with his or her children (Visher & Travis, 2003).

Risk and Protective Factors

Utilizing a context-process-outcome lens suggests two additional theoretical elements: *risk factors* and *protective factors*. Risk factors can be either static or fixed in that they cannot be changed (e.g., gender, race, in utero conditions affecting development) or else variable (features that can change such as age, or be modified through intervention). In general risk factors are those features or characteristics that contribute to vulnerability or maladaptive psychopathological outcomes (Cicchetti, 2006). Consistent with the notion of interdependence and multiplicity, risk factors tend to co-occur rather than occur in isolation (Rutter, 1990; Sameroff, Seifer, Barocas, Zax, & Greenspan,

1987). For example, mental illness and drug use often co-occur, and these characteristics are together overrepresented among incarcerated populations, presenting a cumulative risk for maladjustment and reentry difficulties (James & Glaze, 2006). Thus attention to multiple risk factors and mechanisms of effect is important (Cicchetti, 2006; Garbarino, 1995).

However, risk factors must be considered in light of any protective factors that the developing individual might experience. Protective factors function to promote competent development and reduce or counterbalance the negative impact of risk factors (Luthar, 2003). For example, in considering parental incarceration as a risk factor for children's academic failure, a high degree of parental school involvement or after-school mentoring may "protect" the child from a lack of success in school and possibly enhance achievement. Thus risk and protective factors are contextual *and* processual. They operate dynamically in shaping human development, at each level of the ecology (i.e., micro, meso, exo, and macro), and in tandem, "transacting with the features of the individual...and the external world" (Cicchetti, 2006, p. 10). Further, resilience and positive adaptation may be manifested differently in children and adults in relationship to different social contexts whether within prison, among peers, in the school setting (for children), or in one's neighborhood (Seidman & Peterson, 2003).

Approach to Selection and Coverage of Empirical Research

In addition to the theoretical influences shaping coverage in this book, the content presented is informed by the empirical research on parental incarceration. I selected largely from empirically based peer-reviewed publications, books, and book chapters that drew directly from the population of interest: incarcerated mothers and fathers, their family members, and in some cases their children. Central to studies drawn upon for this book was a focus on parenting and/or family well-being (criterion for a "family perspective"). Studies dealing with topics related to the issue of incarceration, such as parental arrest, were excluded from consideration.[8] The search process for empirical literature entailed several steps. First, I searched for studies on parental incarceration by examining the reference lists of previous reviews, books, and prior research (including work done by myself) conducted by exemplar scholars (e.g., Austin & Irwin, 2001; Hagan & Coleman, 2001; Hagan & Dinovitzer, 1999; Hairston, 2007; Murray, 2005; Parke & Clarke-Stewart, 2001; Travis, 2005; Travis & Waul, 2003; Western, 2004). Second, I searched electronic databases for published references or government reports utilizing Ebscohost, Google, and Google Scholar search engines and included the following key words or phrases: "parental incarceration," "parents and incarceration," "maternal incarceration," "paternal incarceration," "mothers in prison," "fathers in prison," "parents in prison," "incarceration and children," and "families and incarceration." Databases that were searched included ERIC, JSTOR, PsychInfo, National Criminal Justice Reference Service, Ingenta, BioMed Central, and Heinonline. I refined the search process by adding additional key words pertinent to the book content (e.g., "incarceration and cumulative disadvantage" or "prison overcrowding and mental health"). I then screened titles and abstracts with research assistance from a librarian and a graduate assistant and selected empirical studies that collected information from imprisoned (or previously imprisoned) parents and that had findings relevant for understanding parenting. Given the voluminous number of hits utilizing these methods, criteria for narrowing down studies used in this review of the relevant literature included top hits per database, articles repeatedly cited in reference lists of scholarly research and reviews, and articles connected to the theoretical concepts guiding this book (context and intraindividual and relational family processes). I then constructed three matrices based on the populations assessed (incarcerated/reentry fathers, incarcerated/reentry mothers, or family members/children), which detailed the following information: study type (i.e., quantitative/qualitative, mixed method), design, sample, and study characteristics, theoretical background, contextual factors, processes, and findings/outcomes. I used this information to construct and support the arguments and findings contained in this book. Information about much of the empirical literature on parental incarceration that supported the book content is summarized in Table A1 in the Appendix.

A Note on Methodology

Most studies pertaining to parental incarceration have been characterized as descriptive and based on convenience samples (Geller, Garfinkel, Cooper, & Mincy, 2008; Wilbur et al., 2007). This is largely due to the challenges of conducting research in corrections settings and accessing marginalized and residentially mobile populations (Jucovy, 2003). Indeed, in criminal justice research, sometimes nonprobability samples are "the best that can be done" (Pope, Lovell, & Brandl, 2001, p. 13). While caution is understandably warranted in drawing sweeping conclusions due to questions of generalizability, much of the research, and in particular qualitative studies, pertaining to parental incarceration can be characterized as *purposeful* rather than simply "convenience based." This distinction is important because purposeful sampling implies planning and focused objectives—whereby the logic and power of the approach "lie in selecting information-rich cases for study in depth" (Patton, 2002, p. 230). The use of information-rich cases "yields insights and in-depth understanding rather than empirical generalizations" (Patton, 2002, p. 230).

While probability samples have greater external validity than purposeful samples, researchers generally have to utilize data sets that were not specifically designed to answer incarceration-related questions. Thus critical variables of interest may be excluded, and measures may lack depth or application to issues pertaining to parental imprisonment. Data limitations are particularly noticeable relative to female incarceration and recidivism (Bloom, Owen, & Covington, 2003). For example, answers to the effects of critical variables of interest (e.g., prison programming, variations in relational and community circumstances) on women's postrelease parenting trajectories are "elusive" due to absent or incomplete Bureau of Justice data (Deschenes, Owen, & Crow, 2006). Researchers Kathryn Edin, Timothy Nelson, and Rechelle Paranal (2001) discuss the limitations of data from the Fragile Families and Child Wellbeing Study. The data set follows 5,000 children (of which three-fourths were born to unmarried parents) and their families from 1998 to 2000. In their study of "turning points" in the life course of fathers who have been incarcerated, the authors note that noncustodial fathers, and minority, low-income fathers in particular, are seriously underrepresented in large data sets and that the "underrepresentation problem in most large surveys is so severe that it constitutes something of a crisis" (p. 49). The utilization of these large, quantitative data sets may not provide a complete picture of parenting and often means that processes and mechanisms of effect "remain opaque" (p. 49). Consistent with Edin et al.'s contention that "qualitative data can shed light on these processes" (p. 49), qualitative data are utilized in this book to enhance understanding and inform coverage of parental incarceration.

In addition to purposeful and population-based empirical work, I have also selectively utilized critical reviews and government reports that examined literature or summarized statistical data related to parental incarceration. The coverage here is systematic in that it is characterized by the use of primary empirical sources, an explicit search strategy, a critical appraisal of the literature, and an "evidence map" or quantitative summary (as summarized in the appendix) of exemplar studies that serve as the empirical core of the book (cf. Cook, Mulrow, & Haynes, 1997).

The Use of Exemplars and Case Studies

Throughout this book exemplars and case studies are used to illustrate themes in the empirical literature on parental incarceration. Exemplars and case studies not only illustrate themes but also put a "face" on the parents and children impacted by incarceration. In some cases I draw exemplars from another scholar's qualitative work and note the original study accordingly. I also utilize cases and examples from my own research interviewing caregivers with children visiting a parent at a local jail (Arditti, 2003; Arditti et al., 2003), a qualitative investigation based on interviews with 51 incarcerated fathers in Utah and Oregon (Arditti et al., 2005), and two qualitative studies based on in-depth interviews and follow-up for mothers who were recently incarcerated and released back to their families, children, and communities (Arditti & Few, 2006, 2008). Finally, I constructed "composite" cases based on prisoners and their families who accessed the website "Prison Talk," an online inmate support community. These composite cases are also noted accordingly in the text. Pseudonyms are used for all exemplars and cases regardless of their source.

Summary

What is the experience of incarcerated parents? How does incarceration impact parenting? How far-reaching are the consequences of incarcerating so many parents?

A context-process-outcome framework helps give us the tools to unpack the research and answer these questions in a comprehensive fashion. The framework as derived here is a *theory of interdependence* that points to the connections between one's physical and social environment and one's development, between imprisonment and parenting, and between the offender's experience and family well-being. Interdependent contextual layers and family processes point to lives linked, and perhaps undone, by incarceration. Parental incarceration is the proverbial stone in the pond that, once thrown, sends ripples outward to shore. The incarceration of so many in this country has been characterized as a "massive legal intervention" or "social experiment" (Foster & Hagan, 2007). Arguably, something much larger than a stone has been thrown; the ripples, no longer soft and inconsequential, are now tall waves, which stand to overpower the pond and its environs. A context-process-outcome framework helps to articulate the mechanisms and pathways by which alterations in parenting occur, and how the changes brought about by a parent's incarceration potentially change everything. For example, a focus on context shows us how incarceration intensifies poverty in already disadvantaged households. A focus on process can reveal alterations in how incarcerated parents see themselves that in part ultimately lead to their disengagement from family. In delineating outcomes from this perspective, we see that they do not occur in a vacuum, but that family well-being (or the lack thereof) is influenced by a larger social environment that stigmatizes incarceration, makes it difficult if not impossible to parent from prison, and discourages family members from staying connected to the imprisoned in a way that would enhance development. Indeed, consistent with the introductory quote by Felix Adler, we will identify patterns of risk, resilience, and experience in this volume that link "different but yet matching" empirical findings that, when considered collectively, ultimately portray what it is to be, and to have, a parent in prison. In doing so, a radically different social policy agenda emerges: one that moves beyond mass incarceration and focuses on offenders as *parents* connected to children and families. In line with this focus, this book calls for real reform and programmatic change that is responsive to social inequality and the collective vulnerabilities of the incarcerated and their kin.

2

Context and Processes Associated with Incarcerated Parenting

Mary's Story[1]

Mary turned 40 in prison. She explains that as a child she was bounced around from shelter to shelter because "my mom didn't know what to do with me" and her mother's alcoholic husband, Mary's stepfather, John, "despised me." She recounts: "I was only 12 years old when my mother and her husband would kick me out for things like talking back and smoking cigs and I would spend my nights on the streets until someone's parents or a passerby who would see me sitting in the same spot for days would call authorities who would then take me to a shelter. The shelters would always call my mom and tell her to pick me up, until finally my mom and her husband would kick me out and then call the cops claiming I ran away so that I would be taken to 'juvy.' I spent most of my teenage years in and out of juvy and shelters until at 16 I became pregnant and was placed into a homeless shelter for pregnant teens."

After the baby came, a boy named Toby, Mary seemed to get her act together. She took parenting classes and rented her own apartment with savings from a job she had while pregnant. Her parenting teacher inspired Mary and convinced her that she could be different than her own mother and be a role model for Toby. However, as the demands of raising a child as a single mother and working a low-wage job closed in, Mary slipped into depression and, ultimately, drug use. Her patience with Toby was short, and she was easily upset when he cried, even resorting to slapping him when he wouldn't stop crying as a toddler. With nothing in the way of family support, and with a sense of letting her son down, Mary's depression worsened, and she started missing work, ultimately getting fired. Like many other women offenders, Mary turned to prescription pain medication to feel better, and then to selling her pills to keep her supply coming and make ends meet financially. Ultimately, she was arrested and sentenced for prescription drug fraud. Recently denied parole, Mary has been in prison upstate for 3 years with 3 more to serve. Toby, now

5, lives with Mary's mother and stepfather in the city, about 200 miles from the prison. Mary wonders: What will become of Toby? She worries about how he fares with her estranged parents, and she can do nothing to help him from prison. She is entirely dependent on her mother and stepfather to facilitate contact with her son, and given their poor relationship, it comes as no surprise that Mary has not seen him for 3 years. Mary is frustrated that she has not received any letters or drawings from Toby, despite writing frequent letters to him. She feels like such efforts to communicate with him are in vain and lately hasn't had the energy or desire to write.

Mary sees herself as a failure, both in terms of making her own life work and as a mother. She looks back and wishes someone would have helped her. She still feels helpless and depressed because of the years wasted and feeling unwanted. She thinks it is too late now for her....She thinks maybe Toby will be better off without her.

Mary's story is a sad but all too common one for parents who are in prison. Her life reflects key themes in terms of the context of parental incarceration and the processes that bear on parenting from prison. Mary comes from a background of cumulative disadvantage, in terms of growing up on the streets, poor parenting from her family of origin, and a history of drug use and mental illness. Confinement far from home and her estranged relationship with her mother and stepfather are primary barriers in her ability to sustain her connection to her young son. Mary's poor self-esteem contributes to the unraveling of her relationship with Toby. Her identity as a mother is fragile and negative. Context and processes here clearly work against Mary in terms of her ability to sustain a relationship with her son, and perhaps return to him when she is released. In this chapter, we will go into greater depth regarding the contextual factors, as well as key intraindividual and relational processes, that impact incarcerated parents and have bearing on their well-being and family relationships. Mary's story reflects many of the elements that are discussed in this chapter, and unfortunately, her short biography is consistent with the theory and literature on population-based and purposeful samples of prisoners. We will go below the surface of Mary's life and analyze the contextual factors that are relevant for understanding parental incarceration. We will identify specific individual and family processes that influence parenting scenarios and the quality of family relationships for incarcerated men and women with children.

Incarceration as a Context for Parenting

As we have seen, contexts represent structural and environmental characteristics that may constrain or enable, may be oppressive or developmentally enhancing, and may be malleable or fixed (Mancini & Roberto, 2009). Contextual factors fall into four broad categories: (1) *demographic and structural characteristics (e.g., gender, minority status, family structure)*; (2) *cumulative disadvantage (e.g., poverty, family history, mental problems, substance dependence/abuse, stressful life events)*; (3) *institutional practices (prison regulations and environment)*; (4) *sociopolitical (e.g., stigma, political disenfranchisement)*.

Salient Demographic Statuses

Demographic statuses pertaining to gender, race, and class have received widespread attention within the "mass imprisonment" scholarship—particularly in terms of the ways racism and cumulative disadvantage may propel and keep black men in the criminal justice system (Barak, Flavin, & Leighton, 2001; Pettit & Western, 2004; Shelden, 2000; Western, 2006). Indeed, scholars have pointed out that crime control systems simply reproduce hierarchies of power and inequality derived from social statuses such as race, gender, age, and social class (Barak et al., 2001; Dressel, 1994; Goetting, 1985).[2] Beyond the fact that disproportionate numbers of minority men and women are imprisoned (see, e.g., Mumola, 2000), little is known regarding how contextual statuses specifically shape the parenting experience of offenders with children. Some attention has been given to how demographic factors might impact children's school adjustment and achievement (see, e.g., Cho, 2009a, 2009b). Less is known about the implications of context on the offenders themselves and their family relationships. Using the Fragile Families and Child Wellbeing data, Swisher and Waller (2008) found that recent and past incarceration had a significant effect on how often white fathers saw their children, yet it had a considerably smaller effect for Latino and African American fathers. This finding suggests that there may be racial and ethnic differences relative to parental incarceration and family processes.

Insightful consideration of the implications of race, gender, and cumulative disadvantage can be found in feminist scholarship pertaining to incarceration. Research on battered African American women highlights the difficulties incarcerated mothers face upon release, particularly in terms of finding employment, reunifying with children, and dealing with the conflicting work and family responsibilities of life on the outside (Richie, 2001).

Christian and Thomas (2009) argue that black women are uniquely affected by mass incarceration due to their social location as blacks *and* women. From the standpoint of the offender parent, not only are black women (the majority of whom are mothers) more likely to be sentenced to prison than white or Hispanic women (Sabol, Couture, & Harrison, 2007), but they are more likely to have histories of cumulative disadvantage and victimization, creating pathways to crime that are distinct from that of black men or white women (Christian & Thomas, 2009). Indeed, empirical studies have connected domestic abuse as well as criminalized and fractured domestic networks as distinct pathways into criminality for women in general and for black women in particular (Enos, 2001; Golden, 2005; Richie 2001). Black mothers are also more likely to rely on family and to receive help from their family members during incarceration (Enos, 2001). Christian and Thomas (2009) further argue that black women's experience warrants our attention given their likely connections to incarcerated black men (relative to whites), and the resultant impacts these connections create for already resource-poor women. Consequences of these connections include further marginalization, role strain due to caring for the prisoner and any shared children, and shouldering incarceration-related expenses (Arditti et al., 2003; Braman, 2004).

In addition to the salience of gender and race in thinking about parental incarceration, marital status is an important contextual factor. The implications of marital status are gendered in that, like Mary, mothers are two and a half times more likely than their male counterparts to have been single parents prior to their incarceration (Mumola, 2000). Single parenthood poses unique and profound adjustment difficulties for women in prison, as does ensuring stable and adequate care for their offspring (Enos, 2001; Houck & Loper, 2002). Married fathers are much more likely to have contact and visitation with their family members and maintain family ties than are never married noncohabiting fathers, suggesting the importance of marital bonds in shaping family process during confinement (Clarke et al., 2005). Unfortunately, offenders are at much greater risk than nonoffenders for divorce or separation during their imprisonment (Loopoo & Western, 2005; "Parental Incarceration," 2008; Western, 2004).

Incarceration also seems to connect with a greater likelihood of living alone (rather than with a spouse and/or children) upon reentry, indicative perhaps of weak social bonds after a period of incarceration (London & Parker, 2009). Whether incarceration in and of itself is predictive of a lower likelihood of first marriage is debatable as findings conflict, and the relationship seems to be moderated by a number of variables. One study found a strong relationship between incarceration and a lower likelihood of marriage (London & Parker, 2009), while another revealed little evidence for a persistent relationship between incarceration and the likelihood of first marriage upon reentry for male prisoners (Loopoo & Western, 2005). Still another study found that separation rates were higher for African American fathers who were married prior to incarceration (Western, Loopoo, & McLanahan, 2004). Finally, marital status may also imply something about the level of disadvantage experienced by family members. For example, my colleagues and I (Arditti et al., 2003) noted in our study of 56 caregivers visiting an incarcerated parent with whom they shared children that married caregivers were better off financially than nonmarried caregivers.

Cumulative Disadvantage

Mary's life on the streets as a teenager was unfortunate but not unique. Incarcerated parents and their children tend to come from intense histories of cumulative disadvantage characterized by multiple risks (Foster & Hagan, 2007; Johnson & Waldfogel, 2004; Johnson, 2009; Murray & Farrington, 2008; Phillips, Burns, Wagner, Kramer, & Robbins, 2002; Sampson & Laub, 1997; Thompson & Harm, 2000; Western, 2006). Incarceration further magnifies economic, educational, and social disadvantage for the offender and his or her family (Arditti et al., 2003; Foster & Hagan, 2007; Johnson, 2009; Swisher & Waller, 2008) and is viewed as an "important social fact about the distinctive life course of the socio-economically disadvantaged" (Pettit & Western, 2004, p. 165). We know little about how cumulative disadvantage in justice-involved families connects to parenting. Mary's rejecting, hostile, and disengaged parents fit the limited information we have about family of origin parenting histories among the imprisoned. Male and female inmates recall receiving more authoritarian or more permissive parenting. These parenting styles have been identified in the literature as more extreme (i.e., either too much discipline and control or else no parental monitoring). Further, male and female inmates reported receiving higher levels of corporal punishment, verbal hostility, and nonreasoning than did a noninmate comparison group, suggesting that once established, less effective parenting may be rooted and then transmitted from generation to generation (Chipman, Olsen, Klein, Hart, & Robinson, 2000). One exploratory study of incarcerated fathers reported that one-third had childhoods characterized by extremely traumatic experiences of unresolved loss, parental deprivation, and child abuse (Fairchild, 2009). It can be theorized that these experiences contributed to men's maladaptive attachment representations and undermined their ability to parent and bond with their own children. Similarly, half of 102 jailed California mothers reproduced "cycles of pain" with their own children via harsh disciplinary practices, exposure to intimate partner violence, and their own drug use (Greene, Haney, & Hurtado, 2000). Others have noted that cumulative disadvantage often gives rise to harsh disciplinary practices (see, e.g., Pinderhughes, Dodge, Bates, Pettit, & Zelli, 2000), although there is evidence that among disadvantaged parents, harsh discipline may also coexist with parental warmth (Deater-Deckard & Dodge, 1997) and positive care and advocacy parenting practices (Arditti, Burton, & Neeves-Botelho, 2010). Cumulative disadvantage among families with a parent in prison has been linked to an array of deleterious outcomes such as children's placement in foster care, children's psychological and behavioral maladjustment, and difficulties reintegrating and parenting upon reentry (Enos, 1997, 2001; Phillips et al., 2002; Poehlmann, 2005b).

The work of Susan Phillips and colleagues (2006) has shed light on the role of cumulative disadvantage factors, within the context of parental criminal justice involvement, on parenting. They note in their analysis of child data that in the absence of other explanatory factors, parental involvement in the criminal justice system (CJS), broadly defined as being charged, arrested, or incarcerated, was *not* significantly correlated with reports of inadequate parenting. However, cumulative disadvantage factors such as substance abuse, mental health problems, and low education all significantly increased the odds of parental involvement in the CJS, and two of these factors (substance abuse and mental health problems) significantly increased the odds of both inadequate parenting and family instability.

The research on maternal incarceration and families appears to provide considerable depth with regard to the implications of cumulative disadvantage for the offender parent and her family, pointing to patterns of women's victimization prior to and during their involvement in the CJS (see, e.g., Chesney-Lind, 1997; DeHart & Altshuler, 2009; Enos, 1997, 2001; Golden, 2005; Richie, 2002; Snyder, Carlo, & Mullins, 2001) and high levels of maternal distress (Poehlmann, 2005c), both of which can undermine parenting capacity (Arditti, Burton, et al., 2010; Belsky, 1984). Cumulative disadvantage factors are also a point of consideration regarding the experience of caregivers, most of whom are women and African Americans, responsible for the offender's children (Christian & Thomas, 2009; Comfort, 2008). For prisoners and their families, incarceration obviously interferes with breadwinning, child support, and offenders' provision of resources to help to their families

(Arditti et al., 2003; Geller et al., 2008), particularly upon reentry (Arditti & Few, 2008; Travis, 2005; Visher & Travis, 2003).

In studying incarcerated women, consideration is given to broader indications of cumulative disadvantage (i.e., beyond employment and income), including family history of abuse, past trauma, and relationship disconnections, and these factors seem to contribute to mothers' distress in prison and upon release (Arditti & Few, 2008; Poehlmann, 2005b, 2005c; Richie, 2002; Thompson & Harm, 2000). Regardless of gender, imprisoned populations tend to have histories of more intense cumulative disadvantage and, upon reentry, seem to face sometimes insurmountable challenges to overcoming economic adversity and marginalization given their social exclusion from important opportunity structures such as education or employment (Foster & Hagan, 2007; Travis, 2005; Western, 2006).

Substance Abuse and Mental Health Problems

A prominent feature of the profile of incarcerated parents that has bearing on family life is their drug use. While experts in multiple disciplines generally agree that drug-related prosecutions are largely responsible for the rapid growth of penal populations (see, e.g., Arditti & McClintock, 2001; Blumstein & Beck, 1999; Hagan & Coleman, 2001), there is quantitative evidence that, like Mary, the majority of parents imprisoned, in addition to selling or possession, also *used* drugs prior to their offense (Arditti & Few, 2006, 2008; Edin et al., 2001; Greenfield & Snell, 1999; Mumola, 2000). Bureau of Justice (BOJ) statistics indicate that four out of five parents in state prison reported some type of past drug use, with the majority stating that they had used drugs the month before their offense and often committed their offense while under the influence of drugs (Mumola, 2000). In 2004, the BOJ included measures of drug dependence and abuse for the first time. Based on criteria specified in the *DSM-IV*, 53% of state prisoners and 45% of federal prisoners could be classified as abusing drugs or drug-dependent (Mumola & Karberg, 2006).

Of particular concern are high rates of comorbidity of mental illness and substance dependence/abuse among prison and jail inmates. Mary's self-medication with pain pills as a response to depression is an example of how and why mental illness and drug use co-occur. According to a recent BOJ report (James & Glaze, 2006), not only do a disproportionate number of prisoners report either a history or symptoms (or both) of a mental health problem (56.2% of state prisoners, 64.2% of jail inmates, 44.8 % of federal prisoners),[3] but there are high rates of mental health problems and substance dependence in jails and prisons across the country (41.7% state, 28.5% federal, 48.7% jails). Other studies have found even higher rates of co-occurring substance use and severe mental disorders, with a 72% rate among jail detainees (Abram & Teplin, 1991). Rates of comorbidity are particularly high among women, who report higher rates of mental health problems (approximately three-fourths in both state and federal prisons) and more intense histories of drug use.

The consideration of both mental problems and substance dependency as contextual cumulative disadvantage factors related to parenting is crucial for several reasons. First, parents with mental health problems in state prisons are more likely to receive and serve lengthier sentences than parents without such problems (this relationship does not hold for federal prisoners or jail inmates; cf. James & Glaze, 2006). Second, inmates with mental health problems are more likely to report having parents or guardians with histories of abusing drugs and alcohol, as well as family members who had been incarcerated, pointing to intergenerational patterns of dysfunction (James & Glaze, 2006; see also Phillips et al., 2006). Finally, many offenders (approximately two-thirds in the BOJ data) who report either mental health problems or substance dependence do not receive treatment during imprisonment (Greenfield & Snell, 1999; James & Glaze, 2006), with some studies suggesting even higher rates of nontreatment for women (three-fourths of women in jails; see Teplin, Abram, & McClelland, 1997).

On a positive note, recent evidence suggests that the percentage of drug-dependent/abusing prisoners who have taken part in drug abuse treatment or programs is increasing in both state (from 34% to 39%) and federal prisons (from 39% to 45%; Mumola & Karberg, 2006). Yet even with slight increases in the number of offenders receiving drug treatment, the mental health needs of many offender parents remain unmet, and they are likely to return to their families (which often include kin with the same problems) with significant impairment. The implications of returning home with drug and mental health vulnerabilities include inadequate parenting (Phillips et al., 2006), less successful reentry (Richie, 2001; Naser & Visher, 2006; van Olphen, Eliason, Freudenberg, & Barnes, 2009), multiple incarcerations (James & Glaze, 2006), nonparental care arrangements for children (and particularly for mothers; Hanlon, O'Grady, Bennett-Sears, & Callaman, 2005; Johnson & Waldfogel, 2004; Richie, 2002), and weakened parent-child ties (per mothers, see Arditti & Few, 2008; per fathers' drug use, see Edin et al. 2001).

Institutional Practices

Institutional practices aimed at incapacitation profoundly affect the health and psychological adjustment of the offender parent (Haney, 2002). An array of such practices seem to have bearing on parenting, and their influence is largely indirect. That is, prison/jail conditions and restriction contribute to the offender parent's psychological distress, which, in turn, may contribute to disengagement between the incarcerated parent and his or her children. For example, prison overcrowding is linked with a lack of rehabilitative opportunities, illness, and psychological distress for the incarcerated parent (Haney, 2002; Thornberry & Call, 1983). By directly contributing to the offender parent's distress, overcrowding can be thought of as *indirectly* impacting parenting capacity. Aversive prison conditions and harsh institutional practices (i.e., dirty and crowded facilities, lengthy sentencing, costly phone calls, confinement far from family) serve to discourage the offender's contact with family—particularly with regard to visitation (Hairston, Rollin, & Jo, 2004; LaVigne, Naser, Brooks, & Castro, 2005; Naser & Visher, 2006; Poehlmann et al., 2008). Conversely, more positive, family-friendly environments (via special family program participation) appear to benefit both offender parent and family and make visitation more palatable (Loper & Tuerk, 2006; Snyder et al., 2001). Institutional restrictions precluding physical contact (such as no-contact visits through the glass), generally more common in jails than in prisons, also tend to create a great deal of distress for offenders and their families (Arditti, 2003). Thus visiting conditions and restrictions around contact can be seen as contributing to or mitigating parental distress, and in this manner connect to parenting. Finally, lengthier confinement serves to weaken family ties. A study of 109 incarcerated mothers revealed that the longer women were incarcerated, the more difficult it was for them to maintain their relationships with their children and enact mothering functions (Berry & Eigenberg, 2003). Lengthy confinement also has an indirect pathway of influence though its effect on family stability and the parenting capacity of the nonincarcerated caregiver. For example, lengthy periods of imprisonment are linked to relationship instability for both the offender parent and his or her intimate partner (Loopoo & Western, 2005). Relationship instability and multiple partner transitions then have a demonstrated impact on parenting practices and connect with parental stress, harsh parenting, and decreased literacy-promoting behaviors (Beck, Cooper, McLanahan, & Brooks-Gunn, 2009).

Sociopolitical Factors

Perhaps the most difficult contextual factors to measure involve the sociopolitical climate (Western, 2004). Here qualitative research is particularly apt in that research participants have the opportunity to articulate their perceptions of stigma—including their sense of shame and invisibility (Arditti et al., 2003; Braman, 2004; Braman & Wood, 2003; Lowenstein, 1986; van Olphen et al., 2009). Murray and Farrington's (2008) study of children affected by parental incarceration in Great Britain in the 1950s considered the context of parental separation and compared groups of youth; their findings indirectly tell us something about the sociopolitical environment of incarceration and its implications for families. Parental separation as a result of incarceration (as opposed to divorce or death) was associated with the most psychological risk for boys.

Scholars have argued that "deep-break" policy, that is, criminal justice practices that cut off prisoners from society and family (Nurse, 2002), has transformed prisons from a focus on reentry preparation to custodial containment. Isolated confinement is designed to control massive numbers of prisoners via the rigid enforcement of an extensive set of rules, crowded together within a limited space beyond prison capacity,[4] with limited access to rehabilitative and recreational programs (Gibbons & de B. Katzenbach, 2006; Irwin, 2005; Nurse, 2002; Riveland, 1999). An emerging body of literature addresses the disenfranchisement of the inmate, defined as the deprivation of rights and privileges, during and after incarceration, which serves to marginalize and exclude those going through the prison system from social justice (Austin & Irwin, 2001; Barak et al., 2001; Shelden, 2000). Indeed, incarceration "taints" not only the offender parent but also his or her family members, with a "stigma that never fades" ("Prison and Beyond," 2002, p. 25). Stigma seems to intensify the possibility of risk and has unique disruptive effects for the parents themselves as well as their family members because of the demoralization and social isolation that come with the prison experience (Golden, 2005; Lowenstein, 1986; Western & McLanahan, 2000).

However, it is not entirely clear how stigma and disenfranchisement serve to undermine parenting for offender parents, as there is no research directly examining this issue. We do know that stigma "bleeds" onto family members via their association with the offender; families may in turn avoid visitation or contact with the offender, thus severely limiting opportunities for offender-child interaction during confinement (Arditti et al., 2003; Nurse, 2002). Moreover, disenfranchisement as a result of imprisonment can manifest via the loss of parental rights, an outcome more likely for mothers than fathers, due to their inability to be present for legal proceedings during confinement, and the greater possibility a nonrelative may be caring for their children during incarceration, as well as difficulties obtaining custody after release (Golden, 2005; Hagan & Coleman, 2001; Lee, Genty, & Laver, 2005; Richie, 2002).

In sum, contextual factors are intertwined and create a complex ecology in which the experience of offender parents is influenced by race, gender, structural disadvantage, prison environment and institutional practices, and social stigma (Barak et al., 2001; Western, 2006; Young & Reviere, 2006). These contextual factors often include the accumulation of risks associated with poverty and offender substance use, as well as time- and space-related factors such as lengthy sentences or being housed in prisons far from home, making it difficult for offender parents to stay in contact with their families (Hairston et al. 2004; LaVigne, Naser, et al., 2005; Poehlmann et al., 2008). Contextual factors associated with cumulative disadvantage, such as a lack of educational attainment or a history of unemployment, have a bearing on outcomes such as family reintegration and the assumption of responsible parenting roles upon release (Uggen & Wakefield, 2005; Western, 2004). More distal contextual influences distinctive to U.S. criminal justice policy, such as political disenfranchisement, arguably add to difficulties for ex-prisoners who reenter community and family life (Nurse, 2002; Uggen & Wakefield, 2005). The absence of structural advantage after release suggests multiple risks pertinent to parenting competence that may prove particularly problematic for women, most of whom plan on reunifying with their children and resuming their role as primary caregivers (Greene et al., 2000; Hagan & Coleman, 2001).

Incarceration and Parenting Processes

A consideration of process implies paying attention to the intrapsychic and interpersonal experience of the incarcerated parent, as well as family members who are left behind. Process also encompasses important protective mechanisms such as parents' ability to garner social support from friends, family, and institutional systems (Rutter, 1990). Research on parental incarceration often focuses on child outcomes (see, e.g., Greene et al., 2000, comments), offering limited insight regarding the role of parenting relative to these outcomes.

Mary's story highlights the importance of attending to both intraindividual and relational processes in order to understand parenting within the context of incarceration. Recall Mary's feelings of distress, her sense of not being a "good mother," her lack of contact with her son, and her inability to "coparent" with her mother due to their estranged relationship. Further, healthy child outcomes for Mary's son, Toby, were likely compromised because his caregivers, Mary's mother and stepfather, were not stellar parents. These processes, evident in Mary's biography, are empirically derived from the research and encompass (1) *parental identity*, (2) *parental distress*, (3) *family communication and contact*, (4) *coparenting*, and (5) *caregiver quality and stability*.

Intraindividual Processes

Intraindividual processes encompass the internal life of the offender parent: his or her cognitions, feelings, and motivations (Tesser & Schwarz, 2002). Developmental psychologist Jay Belsky's (1984) articulation of process determinants of parenting highlights the importance of psychological and personality resources for buffering the parent-child relationship from stress.

Incarceration and Parental Identity
Incarceration changes how parents see themselves. Parental identity involves the identity holders' appraisals and aspirations relative to internally held "meaning" standards of parenting (Tsushima & Burke, 1999), as well as their perceptions of how others might view their situation. Young fathers in sociologist Anne Nurse's (2002) study held "meaning standards" of parenting that centered around their vision of a "good father" as a "person who provides guidance, love, and financial support to his children" (p. 73). Burke (1991, 1996) discusses the distress and loss of self-esteem that come when appraisals and behaviors are discrepant. This discrepancy can result from a significant identity "interruption" that interferes with the normal process of identity verification. Distress is magnified in those identity interruptions that are persistent and involve salient social roles (Marcussen & Large, 2003).

Clearly, incarceration constitutes a profound "identity interruption" for a great number of parents. Mothers' distress about "losing their place" in their children's lives as a result of incarceration likely represents their lost identities as mothers (Enos, 1997), as well as their guilt and role conflict about their failure to live up to cultural ideals of a good mother (Arditti & Few, 2008; Berry & Eigenberg, 2003; Poehlmann, 2005c). Mary's sense of failure as a mother reflects her lost identity and guilt. Incarcerated fathers, too, seem all too aware that they are not able to enact typical fathering functions such as providing protection, discipline, and financial care for their children (Arditti et al., 2005). Incarcerated men show evidence of attempting to alleviate distress and resolve identity discrepancy by undermining and downplaying their responsibilities to their children (Clarke et al., 2005). Indeed, it stands to reason that men, in attempting to minimize distress, would repress their fathering identities as a result of confinement (Hairston, 2001). Young incarcerated fathers in particular seem to be at great risk for abandoning fatherhood given that the identity interruption may occur before they have a chance to solidify their role as fathers (Nurse, 2002; see also Edin et al., 2001, who found that older fathers were more likely to try to repair severed bonds with children). Nurse (2002) documents the implications of interrupted fatherhood in her purposeful study of young fathers who had served time in the northern region of the California Youth Authority. Upon release, the majority of fathers interviewed were faced with a great discrepancy between idealized expectations of being "daddy," and children's confused or less than enthusiastic response to the offender's attempt to parent. Incarceration was equated with being "forgotten" by their children, which Nurse concluded led fathers to withdraw from their children after the initial "homecoming." We see a parallel process for Mary in terms of her thinking that her son, Toby, may be better off without her in his life. The perception of being "forgotten" or "losing one's place" relative to one's children runs counter to an optimal sense of parental identity whereby *mattering* to one's children (i.e., perceiving oneself as significant to one's children) is a crucial dimension of parental identity (Marshall & Lambert, 2006).

Identity discrepancy and interruption suggest not only the offender's withdrawal or repression of parental roles and their corresponding behaviors but also a loss of agency (Tsushima & Burke, 1999). Indeed, *prisonized* parental identities emerge and gain prominence during incarceration. These identities are characterized by offenders' helplessness and invisibility with regard to how they see themselves as parents (Arditti et al., 2005; Clarke et al., 2005). Recall that the term *prisonization* is widely used in criminology to refer to institutionalization in corrections settings and is a process identified as acculturating to the norms and customs of the penitentiary (Clemmer, 1940). Prisonization generally implies negative psychological effects and a loss of agency, so that adjustment to the outside society becomes more difficult (Haney, 2002; Irwin, 2005). From a family perspective, a pivotal part of offender adjustment involves the sense of self-worth and competence that comes with parenting. Processes associated with prisonized parental identities seem particularly central to the experience of incarcerated fathers (Dyer, 2007). "You can't be a parent in here" (see, e.g., Roy, 2005) is the common experience articulated by offender parents—a statement that represents the diminished agency that is a hallmark of prisonized parental identities, as well as the inability of the offender parent to align "identity-relevant" perceptions with internalized parenting standards (i.e., what parents "should" be; Tsushima & Burke, 1999).

Parental agency is only possible in systems that are "adaptable, or able to reorganize themselves to counteract disturbance and changes in the environment" (Tsushima & Burke, 1999, p. 175); arguably the prison context, as is the case with most institutions, is anything but adaptable. Prisons can be thought of as "total institutions" characterized by a high degree of social and physical isolation and control over the individuals within the setting (Goffman, 1961). Thus incarceration constrains the enactment of key parenting functions such as the provision of financial support, discipline, protection, and basic care (Arditti et al., 2005; Hairston, 1998). To the extent that these tasks were or continue to be salient for the offender in terms of his or her self-worth, the process of identity verification is thwarted and opportunities for parental agency are significantly curtailed. In sum, interrupted or unverified parental identities can correspond to alterations in parenting roles, a sense of "not mattering" to children, and an overall loss of agency with respect to negotiating relationships with children.

Parental Distress
Sources of parental distress within the context of incarceration are manifold. For example, traumatic experiences and adverse conditions that predate incarceration are linked to emotional pain and psychological difficulties for incarcerated mothers (Greene et al., 2000; Greenfield & Snell, 1999; Hanlon, Blatchley, et al., 2005; Poehlmann, 2005b; Richie, 2002). Distress is also linked to confinement and traumatic separation from children for both mothers and fathers (Arditti & Few, 2008; Braman, 2004; Edin et al., 2001; Poehlmann, 2005c). Thus incarceration likely causes and exacerbates preexisting mental health difficulties for both women and men (Kupers, 1999; Richie, 2001; van Olphen et al., 2009). With respect to mental health, children seem to be a stabilizing force for offender parents (Arditti & Few, 2008; Richie, 2001) and a source of self-worth for even the most vulnerable young mothers. In her ethnography, author Renny Golden (2005) discussed teen mothers who spent time in Albuquerque's Youth Diagnostic and Development Center for incarcerated teens: "What seems to have saved Ann and

Yolanda more than anyone or anything else was their children's births and their own motherhood. For young people taught they count for nothing, a baby's utter need and radical claim on love can teach them something new and precious about who they are" (p. 74). As Ann, one of Golden's interviewees, says, "Everything I do now affects my little girl....It's my daughter that kept me going" (p. 74). The mothers in our case study (Arditti & Few, 2008) echoed similar thoughts and vowed to "get it together" and stay out of prison for their children's sake. But children are also a great source of worry, guilt, and preoccupation for the offender parent. These worries may be due to the weakening of the parent-child relationship during confinement (Edin et al., 2001; Snyder et al., 2001), a lack of parenting competence (Tuerk & Loper, 2006), or fears of a return to "bad parenting" upon reunification (Meek, 2007). Studies on maternal incarceration reveal that during confinement, separation from children is a source of traumatic stress for many women offenders that is characterized by a great deal of emotional pain and guilt (Arditti & Few, 2008; Greene et al., 2000; Poehlmann, 2005b). Limited visitation and phone contact with children were also associated with increased stress, anxiety, and depression among incarcerated mothers (Houck & Loper, 2002; Poehlmann, 2005c). Similarly, incarcerated men with poor father-child relationships during confinement were more likely to be depressed (Lanier, 1993).

Further contributing to the offender's distress is the nature of the losses suffered by the parent and his or her family. Parental incarceration is associated with ambiguous loss (Boss, 1999) and disenfranchised grief (Doka, 1989). Ambiguous loss within the context of parental incarceration leads to uncertain parental roles and painful family relationships (Brodsky, 1975). For many prisoners, incarceration has been described as a "living death"—"the death of the social, the familial, the spiritual" (McCulloch & Scraton, 2008, p. 17). As one inmate parent conveys in a poem to his son: *Because I'm not there, I do not exist"* (Vendlinski, 2003, p. 32, emphasis added). For family members, the living death is a significant and ambiguous loss in that the incarcerated parent is "alive but unreachable" (Jucovy, 2003, p. 2). This living death of the parent can be devastating to families because it remains unclear, indeterminate, and invalidated by the community. The lack of supportive rituals and community verification contributes to parental distress and family difficulties (Arditti et al., 2003; Doka, 1989) and can be far more painful than other types of loss (see Boss, 1999).

Finally, much of the parental distress experienced by offenders with children can be linked to prison life itself. Psychologist Craig Haney (2002) discusses how the offender's prolonged psychological adaptation to prison life and its corresponding deprivations and frustrations—commonly referred to as "the pains of imprisonment" (Sykes, 1958)—result in a diminished capacity to parent. In his classic work in penology, Sykes (1958) argued that retribution demands that imprisonment must be painful. Therefore, prison life is constituted through a variety of physical and social strategies ensuring systematic deprivations designed to punish, coerce, and psychologically intimidate prisoners, contributing to feelings of inadequacy on the part of the offender. These deprivations include the withholding of liberty, goods and services, heterosexual relationships, autonomy, and security. Haney (2002) argues that these "pains" exact certain psychological costs with profound implications for parenting:

> Parents who return from periods of incarceration...cannot be expected to effectively organize the lives of their children or exercise the initiative and autonomous decision making that parenting requires. Those who still suffer the negative effects of a distrusting and hypervigilant adaptation to prison life will find it difficult to promote trust and authenticity within their children. Those who remain emotionally over-controlled and alienated from others will experience problems being psychologically available and nurturing....Clearly, the residual effects of the post-traumatic stress of imprisonment...can jeopardize the mental health of persons attempting to reintegrate back into the free world communities from which they came....the experience of imprisonment has done little or nothing to provide them with the tools to safeguard their children from the same potentially destructive experiences. (p. 15)

The incapacitation that is synonymous with prison confinement is perhaps the most transparent mechanism for the reduced likelihood of ex-offenders taking on family roles after release (Haney, 2002; Western, 2004). Indeed, psychological competence is theorized to be perhaps the most important determinant of parenting (Belsky, 1984); therefore, one can infer that incarceration bodes poorly for offenders in terms of their parenting capabilities. While the prisoner reentry literature widely documents the difficulties ex-offenders face upon release, particularly in terms of finding employment and dealing with the demands and responsibilities of life on the outside (Lynch & Sabol, 2001; Petersilia, 2003; Travis, 2005), very little empirical work specifically examines the ability of ex-offenders to engage in meaningful family roles after incarceration or their parenting capacity during confinement and beyond. Clearly, research is needed that more completely examines how the negative psychological effects on the parent resulting from prison confinement specifically translate into the parenting experience.

Relational Processes

Incarceration profoundly alters family relationships. Confinement curtails communication, the offering and receipt of affection, and caretaking. Incarceration often means that parents miss out on attending key events in children's lives and fail to witness developmental milestones (e.g., a child's walking and talking). Parents' absence during these times weakens both parents' and children's commitment to each other, resulting in severed ties (Edin et al., 2001). Offender parents' embeddedness in prosocial relationships, and in particular family relationships, warrants consideration because these ties can potentially support positive parental identities and allow for the reestablishment of noncriminal relational bonds and roles upon release (Martinez, 2009; Maruna & Roy, 2007). Mary's story exemplifies a worst-case scenario for she lacked support from family and significant others, both as a child herself and as a young mother before her incarceration. One has to wonder how Mary's life, as well as her ability to function well as a parent, might have been different if she had a close network of caring adults and mentors accessible to her. Based on the available literature, critical relational processes pertinent to parenting include family contact, coparenting, and caregiving quality and stability.

Family Contact Processes

Essential to a consideration of relational processes is a focus on contact and family communication processes involving the offender parent. Family contact processes warrant particular attention given the purported links between visitation, family ties, and less recidivism after reentry (Bales & Mears, 2008; LaVigne, Naser, et al., 2005). In general, most offender parents seem to benefit from visitation and want to have contact with their children (see, e.g., Swisher & Waller, 2008; Tuerk & Loper, 2006). During incarceration, tangible forms of contact include phone calls, in-person visits, and letter writing. The different types of contact and with whom the contact occurs (i.e., children or intimate partner) represent the means by which the offender may "do parenting," and each carries distinct implications. Family communication can also be intangible and symbolic. Comfort (2008) describes the process of "presence creation" whereby San Quentin couples "transcend institutional parameters" and communicate by using props, fantasy, and synchronization to "be together" (p. 92). Such efforts are highly imaginative and might include displaying photos (taken in the prison visiting room) of the couple or family at home, putting on familiar clothing that reminds the couple of each other, reading the same books, or participating in the offender's recreational interests outside of prison walls.

Of particular interest is the process of prison visitation, for it is the only means of in-person interaction between parents and children during incarceration, thus representing the most proximal form of contact. It is also the type of contact by which "correctional institutions exert the most control" (Nurse, 2002, p. 37), exemplifying the power of context in shaping family process. For example, evidence suggests that in-person visits during confinement were more critical than contact by phone or letter in predicting positive postrelease family relationships (LaVigne, Naser et al., 2005). The fact that Mary does not see her son during her confinement reduces the likelihood that she will have a quality relationship with him upon her release.

Environmental contextual factors and institutional practices profoundly shape the quality and nature of family interaction during prison visitation (Arditti, 2003, 2005; Comfort, 2008). Visitation rooms clearly are settings that have "coercive influences on behavior" (Scott, 2005, p. 297) given sparse resources, constrained and uninviting environmental characteristics, and explicit and enforced restrictions regarding movement, physical contact, and social interaction (Arditti, 2003; Comfort, 2008; Hairston, 1998). Visitation can connect with loss-related trauma and painful feelings and expose both offender and family members to a "risk situation" fraught with difficulties (Arditti, 2003; Arditti et al., 2005; Arditti & Few, 2008; Sack & Seidler, 1978). In this manner, difficult visitation experiences are a mechanism that potentially *enhances vulnerability* (cf. Rutter, 1990) in that they can lead to distress, degradation, and perhaps the permanent severance of family ties (Arditti, 2003; Brodsky, 1975; Comfort, 2008). On the other hand, to the extent that visitation is "family friendly" and *opens up opportunities* (cf. Rutter, 1990) for meaningful connection for both offender and family members, visitation can be considered a protective mechanism with respect to lessening parental distress and enhancing self-esteem for the offender (Houck & Loper, 2002; Snyder et al., 2001; Thompson & Harm, 2000; Tuerk & Loper, 2006), as well as improving family relationships, parenting skills, and child-centered interaction (Block & Potthast, 1998; Dunn & Arbuckle, 2002).

Coparenting

Theoretically and empirically, a cooperative and functioning coparenting alliance is a "potent family force" (Cecil, McHale, Strozier, & Pietsch, 2008, p. 514) that distinctly explains variability in parental adjustment and involvement, and child outcomes such as behavior problems, anxiety and withdrawal, and interpersonal aggression. The process of "coparenting" stems largely from Salvador Minuchin's (1974) theory of structural family therapy whereby children are believed to benefit from a hierarchy of caregiving adults who function collaboratively, demonstrating solidarity and support for each other. The theory suggests that during times of acute stress children's safety and well-being are better ensured by cooperative coparenting. Research on divorced families suggests that the processes underlying coparenting transcend nuclear family relationships (Ahrons, 1981) and warrant consideration in examining parenting processes in families impacted by incarceration. A recent study by Baker, McHale, Strozier, and Cecil (2010) is one of the few empirical works that examines coparenting among justice-involved families. Among their sample of 40 mothers serving relatively short sentences in a local jail, findings pertaining to the mother-grandmother coparenting relationship were consistent with literature and theory suggesting that coparenting cooperation is beneficial to children. Specifically, analyses derived from observational data revealed that better coparenting relationship quality was related to fewer child behavior problems.

Unfortunately, beyond the Baker et al.(2010) study, there is scant research that directly examines coparenting relationships between offender parents and their children's caregivers. Coparenting research tends to be based on other populations and contexts such as married nuclear households (McHale, 1997), divorce, (e.g., Ahrons, 1981; Maccoby & Mnookin, 1990), family violence (Katz & Low, 2004), and the culture of grandmothering (Goodman & Silverstein, 2002). Much of what we can infer, then, regarding the specific processes that are involved in the development, maintenance, and quality of coparenting relationships has been drawn from other literatures (see Cecil et al., 2008, for a review). The Baker et al. (2010) study is important because it provides new evidence that coparenting processes in "high-risk" families such as those impacted by incarceration are similar to coparenting in lower-risk families (e.g., two-parent families).

For families impacted by incarceration, it is clearly important, then, to maintain broad definitions of coparenting that are inclusive of individuals beyond children's biological parents. For example, incarcerated mothers are much more likely to "coparent" with a relative than are their children's fathers, and this relative is usually a grandmother (Enos, 2001; Hanlon, Carswell, & Rose, 2007). Most mothers plan to reunify with their children upon release, and the reconstruction of the relationships with children's caregivers is a source of great concern. Like Mary, mothers often report a history of troubled family relationships that is difficult to mend (O'Brien, 2001). Vulnerability in caregiver-offender mother relationships can stem from caregivers' sense of shame and disappointment in the offender mother. Caregivers may hold negative perceptions about the mother's relationship with her children, even if the mother herself held positive perceptions about these relationships (Hungerford, 1996). Despite the potential difficulties between offender mothers and their children's caregivers, caregivers who are relatives, and offenders' mothers in particular, will likely do more to keep the offender parent's psychological presence alive for their children than would an estranged spouse or romantic partner (Cecil et al., 2008). Based on coparenting theory and research, as well as research suggesting the importance of family support for offender adjustment (Carlson & Cervera, 1991; Lowenstein, 1986) and reentry success (Visher, LaVigne, & Travis, 2004), it makes sense that strong and collaborative coparenting relationships between offender parents and their children's caregivers enhances parental identity and adjustment during confinement (Enos, 2001) and promotes successful parenting after release (Arditti & Few, 2008). Such solidarity seems relevant for children's adjustment in an array of family constellations and contexts, although research is sorely needed to verify the role of coparenting in families impacted by incarceration.

Caregiving quality and stability. Outcomes associated with the incarceration of a parent involve contextual and process changes that visibly undermine parenting for the offender and less visibly threaten competent parenting for the nonincarcerated caregiver. In thinking about family and child outcomes pertaining to parental incarceration, in addition to contact and coparenting processes, the nature of parenting outside prison walls is of profound importance. A lack of stable and quality parenting on the part of caregivers responsible for the offenders' children links to poor child and family outcomes (Mackintosh, Myers, & Kennon, 2006; Poehlmann, 2005c). Often parenting alterations outside of prison walls occur through the creation of an involuntary single-parent household. While the exact number of single-parent households created via incarceration is not documented, we do know that the growth in single-parent families has been matched by rapid growth in the number of men confined to prison or jails across the country. Since incarceration disproportionately impacts poor young men of color, the growth in the male penal population in recent decades is seen as a strong influence in the formation of single-parent families (Western et al., 2004). The single parent may then experience a great deal of psychological distress, relationship instability, and role strain, thus reducing family well-being (Arditti et al., 2003; Beck et al., 2009; Braman, 2004; Herman-Stahl et al., 2008; Lowenstein, 1986).

Summary

Mary's troubled family background, depression and drug use, and confinement far from home illustrate how contextual factors such as cumulative disadvantage and institutional practices serve to create an overall situation of parental incapacitation. Mary's helplessness to engage with her son during confinement stems in part from her prisonization and estranged relationship with her mother. These contextual factors and processes help us to understand Mary's experience—particularly why she might withdraw from her son, and her ability to reintegrate into family and community life after release. Context and process elements discussed in this chapter can be thought of as threads that will be pulled through the fabric of the book and returned to as we make sense of the literature on maternal incarceration, paternal incarceration, and the effects of a parent's incarceration on families and children.

3

Maternal Incarceration

Allison's Story[1]

Allison Roberts was born January 5, 1981, in a southwest Virginia hospital to Sally and Henry Roberts. She is African American, the youngest of four children, and has three older brothers. Raised by her mother and now-deceased grandmother, in her life history narrative she states: "My father never was a factor in my life: he was an alcoholic and abusive, he continued to make promises that he would never keep throughout my life." Allison did not even meet her father until she was about 12 years old, and she admits—"I was scared of him." Allison's father became incarcerated "again and again." When Allison was 13 her mother became incarcerated as well. Prior to her mother's incarceration, Allison was a good student and was involved in school sports, participating on the softball team, basketball team, and track team. After her mother's imprisonment, Allison "gave up." She explained: "I was without the one who was my life, my role model...my participation in all school activities started to decrease." Despite the fact that Allison almost received a scholarship for softball, she became embarrassed that her mother was in prison and not attending school events. Allison recalled, "Instead of turning to people that cared about me, I turned to the streets, alcohol, started skipping school...I wouldn't even go to practice or games." It wasn't long before Allison became involved in the juvenile justice system. At age 15, she was expelled from compulsory school and, as she put it, "had no one to fight for me to stay in school." Allison became angry and resentful and turned to substances to numb those feelings, acknowledging the hurt she caused her grandmother, who was her guardian during her mother's absence. She was a repeat offender in the juvenile system until age 18, when she was convicted of driving under the influence in the adult courts. Thereafter, Allison received repeated DUI charges, spending time in and out of jail and prison; most recently, she violated her probation by continuing to abuse prescription drugs. Allison, a mother of three, is now serving 6 years in a state prison about 175 miles from her home.

Unprecedented numbers of women are receiving incarcerative sentencing for drug-related offenses, and Allison represents a typical woman in the system. Allison's family background, involvement in the juvenile justice system, and drug use all contributed to the odds of her imprisonment as an adult. Women like Allison now represent the fastest-growing segment of the imprisoned population. Since the majority of female prisoners are mothers, the steep rise in the incarceration of women has been estimated to impact more than a million American children. Female prisoners not only are more likely than men to report having multiple children but also are more likely to report having resided with their children prior to arrest and subsequent incarceration (Mumola, 2000). These facts pose unique and profound difficulties not only for children of incarcerated mothers but also for the mothers themselves in terms of adaptation to prison life and social reintegration upon release. There are a number of important factors to consider in order to understand the dynamics of maternal incarceration and its effect on family process:

- The social and political backdrop fueling the growth of female prison populations
- Family and relationship factors contributing to women's criminality
- Challenges associated with maternal incarceration, including the context and processes associated with child placement and mother-caregiver relationships
- Maternal distress as a core construct for understanding imprisoned mothers' experience and parenting trajectories
- Mothers' reentry

The Steep Rise in Female Prisoners

Female offenders have long been the subject of harsh public opinion, treated as "outsiders" and fallen women who occupy a position very different from the "good woman's" place in society. The dramatic increase in the number of female prisoners within the United States has brought growing attention to the causes and consequences of maternal incarceration. Since 1990, the number of women convicted of felonies in state courts has grown at more than twice the rate of men (Greenfield & Snell, 1999). The *rate* of females under state or federal jurisdiction increased faster than for their male counterparts (4.6% increase compared with 3.0% increase, respectively) from 1995 to 2005. Most women were arrested on relatively low-level and nonviolent offenses (85.1% of female jail inmates were confined for nonviolent offenses). The total number of female prisoners grew 57% (compared with 34% for men) during this same period. The majority of women incarcerated in the United States are women of color, constituting nearly two-thirds of those confined in jails and state and federal prisons. Black females were more than twice as likely as Hispanic females and three times more likely than white females to have been in prison in 2005 (Harrison & Beck, 2006). At midyear 2007, black women continued to be incarcerated and held in custody at higher rates than Hispanic or white women across all age categories (Sabol & Couture, 2008). The racial and ethnic profile of incarcerated women may well represent one of the most dramatic examples of racial disparity in the United States (Richie, 2002).

The incarceration of unprecedented numbers of women who have children is a great point of concern and increasingly part of the conversation about parental incarceration. In 2006, a total of 203,100 women were in state and federal prisons or local jails, accounting for just under 10% of the total U.S. prison and jail population (Correctional Association of New York, 2009). Currently, 1.3 million children have mothers who are under correctional sanction (i.e., confined or on probation or parole).[2] More than a quarter of these children have mothers who are incarcerated (Greenfield & Snell, 1999). Offenders who are mothers warrant our attention, in that the outcomes of their incarceration are profoundly negative and have great bearing on the next generation (Foster & Hagan, 2007; Snyder et al., 2001).

They also warrant our attention in that, like Allison, they often come from extremely disadvantaged environmental and family backgrounds and are further marginalized as a result of their involvement in the criminal justice system. Yet despite the scope and consequences of female imprisonment, women are typically underrepresented at all levels of the criminal justice system (Braithwaite, Treadwell, & Arriola, 2005), including law and criminology research (Golden, 2005). For many incarcerated mothers, their lives reflect a lack of access to opportunity and social justice; thus the context and nature of their criminality are especially important to consider.

Social and Political Context: Criminalizing Mothers' Drug Use

A pivotal issue in thinking about maternal incarceration involves the sociopolitical response to women's relationships with both licit and illicit substances. Licit substances include alcohol and prescription medications; illicit substances are drugs whose use is prohibited by laws and state. In the United States, both licit and illicit substances are scheduled based on their abuse potential as a result of the Controlled Substances Act (CSA) enacted into law by Congress in 1970, whereby the scope and nature of federal drug laws, and police power, dramatically expanded. All scheduled drugs are restricted from nonmedical use. Drugs are scheduled according to five levels, or "schedules," with schedule I substances considered to have the most abuse potential and no medical therapeutic value. Critics argue that the scheduling of drugs has been arbitrary rather than based on medical and scientific fact, and fraught with inconsistencies (i.e., certain schedule II drugs are far more dangerous than certain schedule I drugs.) A central point of controversy involves the placement of marijuana, the most widely used illicit substance, as a schedule I drug.

Women's Drug Use Trends

Before considering how mothers' drug use has become criminalized, one needs to understand trends in women's drug use. There is evidence that drug use among women is widespread and that women may have more intense drug use difficulties than do men (Klee, 2002; Substance Abuse and Mental Health Services Administration, 2009; National Center on Addiction and Substance Abuse at Columbia University, 2006). For example, mothers in state prisons reported having the most serious drug use histories (compared with fathers), with about half of women offenders using alcohol, drugs, or both at the time of their offense (Greenfield & Snell, 1999; Mumola, 2000). About one in three mothers committed their crimes to get drugs or obtain money for drugs (Mumola, 2000).

The apparent intensity of incarcerated mothers' drug use is likely connected to a number of factors, including the tendency of drug-using women to be victims of violence during childhood and as adults (Jacobsen, Southwick, & Kosten, 2001; Klee, 2002, p. 5; Najavits, Weiss, & Shaw, 1997) and evidence that women are using illicit drugs to self-medicate their anxiety, depression, and fatigue (Klee, 2002). Research has uncovered that females are 55% more likely than men to receive prescriptions of abusable drugs from doctors, particularly narcotics and antianxiety medication (National Institute on Drug Abuse [NIDA], 2005). Women seem to be at particular risk for nonmedical use of prescription pain analgesics and tranquilizers (NIDA, 2005; see also Arditti & Few, 2008). When legal supplies of prescription medications are insufficient or unavailable, women will engage in fraudulent strategies to obtain more drugs for use and/or sale. Prescription drug fraud is a common pathway for women's entry into the illicit drug market (Arditti & Few, 2008; Klee, 2002).

The visibility and increase in women's drug use are likely intertwined with increases in the number of single mothers in the United States and around the world. Klee (2002) comments on the overlap of qualities shared by single mothers and drug-using women—notably their economic deprivation, family histories of dysfunction, and social isolation. Other research has documented that illicit drug use and dependence were more common for single mothers receiving welfare than for nonrecipients (Jayakody, Danziger, & Pollack, 2000), suggesting the role of economic deprivation and a lack of employment as contributors to single women's drug use. These factors, coupled with the demands of lone parenting in challenging environmental circumstances, create a scenario that enhances women's drug use and misuse. Given stigma and U.S. drug war policies, the use of illicit drugs and misuse of legal substances is a wide and easy path to prison for a great many incarcerated mothers. Poor, drug addicted women in particular are subject to increased risks associated with using and purveying illicit substances. Not only does buying on the illegal market increase women's risk of overdose and infection, but "they cannot afford to buy substantial amounts of their drug at one time and are subject to finding and buying it more often in small amounts, which…increases their risk of rip-offs, violence, and arrest" (Boyd, 2004 p. 77).

Situating Mothers' Drug Use: Feminist Perspectives

Feminist scholar Meda Chesney-Lind (1986) has been influential in casting attention on the role of social control agencies (i.e., police, courts, prison) in shaping the crime problem and women's criminality, much of which is drug related. She argues that one of the more influential beliefs shaping interpretation of the increase in women's criminality during the 1970s is that women's liberation and demands for equal opportunity were linked with changes in the character and frequency of women's crime. However, she notes that empirical support for the argument linking crime to female emancipation is weak. Feminist perspectives for understanding women's criminality interpret female involvement in the criminal justice system as a result of their deviance from patriarchal standards of female domesticity and subordination (Boyd, 2004). The perceived violation of these norms then contributes to women's criminality due to a double standard of justice for men and women. For example, status offenses (minor noncriminal offenses such as running away or truancy for which only minors can be taken into custody) were punished quite harshly for female juvenile offenders compared with their male counterparts. Further evidence of the double standard includes the role of marital status as well as evidence of obedience to the standards of womanhood via domesticity and motherhood, in effecting lighter or deterred sentences. Chesney-Lind (1986) argues, "Once a female offender is apprehended, her behavior is scrutinized for evidence that she is beyond the control of patriarchy and if this can be found she is harshly punished" (p. 96).

Western ideology of mothering portrays women as self-sacrificing, giving, and pure. This ideal is also based on the assumption that mothers will only use legal drugs in the manner they are prescribed by an "expert" (Lewis, 2002). While patriarchal assumptions about what constitutes a good woman may shape the system's response to female crime, the most profound contributor to the steep rise in the female prison population is undeniably the drug war (Boyd, 2004; Richie, 2001). Critics argue that the punitive focus of contemporary criminal justice policy, particularly incarcerative sentences for nonviolent drug offenses, largely accounts for the rapid growth of the number of female prisoners (Hagan & Coleman, 2001; Snyder et al., 2001). Definitions of femininity and the "good woman" are inextricably linked with the increased focus on and social disapproval surrounding the use of illicit drugs. Female drug use, previously associated with legal drug use by white women for anxiety (e.g., "mother's little helper" during the 1950s), became racialized as cultural formations yielded the "demonized figure of the 'crack mom'" (Campbell, 2000, p. 9). The "crack mom" not only violated norms around social deviance but also represented the most abhorrent social failure with regard to "putting herself first" and giving in to individual desires rather than subordinating those desires to her reproductive status and family roles (Lewis, 2002). Boyd (1999) argues that women of color and poor women (disproportionately one and the same) are excluded from motherhood ideology. Rather, they are perceived as "incapable of nurturing and socializing children," sexually promiscuous, and having one baby after another (p. 9). Mothers who used illicit drugs have been characterized by researchers and the media as immature, out of control, and unfit mothers who pose a risk to their children (Boyd, 1999, p. 10), despite holes in the empirical literature supporting these claims.

Compared with Western Europe, women in the United States seem especially stigmatized for their drug use. UK research psychologist Hillary Klee (2002) attributes U.S. women's stigmatization to a highly punitive response to maternal drug use based on the perceived risks of HIV transmission and/ or drug-induced in utero damage to children. While reactions to women using drugs are universally negative, Klee observes: "Public actions in the U.S. . . . resembled medieval witch hunts in Europe" (p. 4). Indeed, concerns about HIV are not without merit; the burden of this disease falls most heavily on infants of color and their mothers. In the United States, 80% of infants born with HIV are African American or Latino. The majority of these cases are linked to drug use, and about a quarter are linked to sexual intercourse with male IV drug users. AIDS is still a leading cause of death for women of color, and 60% of AIDS deaths are injection-related (Day, 2002). Klee (2002) argues that the stigmatization and "merciless judgment of drug-using mothers by the press, law, and public" (p. 5) have had dangerous consequences, which include women's increasing reluctance to seek out medical services.

Indeed, drug-using women who are pregnant or responsible for raising children have become especially visible as a result of the war on drugs (Campbell, 2000). Women's drug addiction became a bizarre playing field for painting women's growing "equality" with men (i.e., in terms of drug addiction and other problem behaviors) as troubling and subsequently requiring a distinct remedy. In the spirit of developing women-centered intervention, women's dissimilarities from men were inadvertently emphasized, preventing the "further collapse of gender distinctions in U.S. society" (Campbell, 2000, p. 23). Under this formulation drug intervention for women reflected a disturbing form of cultural conservatism.

In addition to the paradox that directing social attention to women's problems with drugs poses with respect to advancing women's rights, the drug war provides a critical context for women to come into contact with the authorities. Consistent with the historical literature on female crime, women continue to engage in predominantly nonviolent and petty offenses. However, these nonviolent offenses have become increasingly drug-related, accounting for the largest source of growth among female inmates (Richie, 2001). The most serious offense for 65% of women in federal prisons and 29.1% of women in state prison was the violation of drug laws (Harrison & Beck, 2006). From the period 1985 to 1996 female drug arrests increased by 95%, while male drug arrests rose by 55.1%.

Mandatory Minimum Sentences and Mothers

The war on drugs has become the stage whereby women, as a result of their "deviance," are confronting a new form of equality unprecedented in any other aspect of their lives: they have become equals to their male counter-parts with regard to sentencing. Any preferential treatment they might have gained from a judge sympathetic to their womanly circumstances as wives and or mothers virtually disappeared under the new sentencing guidelines. The criminal courts became the dispenser of equality beginning in the late 1980s in the context of the drug war via mandatory minimum sentencing.

A mandatory sentence is a criminal sentence established by a legislature that prescribes the fixed minimum length of a prison sentence, thereby limiting the amount of discretion a judge has when sentencing a defendant. New York State introduced the first mandatory sentences of 15 years to life—the infamous Rockefeller laws—for possession of more than 4 ounces of "hard drugs" (e.g., opioids, cocaine). In 1986, Congress enacted federal mandatory minimum sentencing laws, and every state enacted drug-related mandatory laws during the 1980s. The use of mandatory minimum sentencing may well represent the most significant aspect of the war on drugs impacting families today. Mandatory minimum sentences have had numerous unanticipated consequences, but it is generally agreed that their implementation has resulted in an explosion in the size of the nation's prison population and that fixed sentencing has disproportionately impacted minorities and women (Gaskins, 2004). Under this regime, judges are forced to deliver fixed sentences regardless of mitigating factors. For women, those mitigating factors often involved their family responsibilities and in particular the care of minor children.

Further, although Congress intended mandatory sentences to target "kingpins" or those who manage drug distribution networks, only a small percentage of federal drug defendants are in fact high-level dealers. Rather, defendants are typically "low-level offenders" such as drug mules or drug couriers, roles women are most likely to employ (see also United Nations Development Fund for Women [UNIFEM], 2010). These low-level female offenders—the great majority of whom have no prior criminal record—often end up serving longer sentences than higher-level offenders because they have little information to offer prosecutors hungry for convictions. The most culpable defendants are in fact those who have the most information to assist prosecutors, and the most to gain by providing substantial assistance. Such assistance is the only way to reduce a mandatory sentence ("Mandatory Minimum Sentences," 2011).

Family and Relationship Factors Contributing to Mothers Criminality

Women of Circumstance: Caught in the Net with Their Men

The application of mandatory minimum sentencing makes it unlikely that women who have peripheral roles in a drug conspiracy will be able to receive a reduction in their sentence through informant testimony. This is because they generally lack the necessary knowledge about the drug conspiracy to be of much value to the prosecution. Women are subsequently small fish caught in the net with the bigger fish who are the men in their lives. These little fish, who can be defined as *women of circumstance* (Gaskins, 2004), are a new type of drug offender and represent women who were minimally involved in drug crime but punished as if they were the big fish:

> These women are the wives, mothers, sisters, daughters, girlfriends, and nieces, who become involved in crime because of their financial dependence on, fear of, or romantic attachment to a male drug trafficker.... "women of circumstance" find themselves incarcerated and subject to draconian sentences because the men in their lives persuade, force, or trick them into carrying drugs. (Gaskins, 2004, p. 1533)

Under the drug war regime, women are subject to drug conspiracy laws and can be charged with the same offense as the principal conspirator, therefore subjecting them to harsh penalties for drug trafficking.

Within the context of the war on drugs and its corresponding sentencing policies, this form of "gender equality" comes at tremendous cost for women, the majority of whom were responsible for the care of minor children and operated in other worlds that were still arguably inequitable. Gaps in employment still exist; sexism and discrimination are still a part of women's everyday lives, from getting paid less for the same work compared with men, shouldering the burden of child care and domestic work regardless of marital status, and limits on women's access to opportunity. Research has demonstrated that for women who are either underemployed or "overemployed" (e.g., in a job that requires more hours than a woman prefers to work—usually in relation to her family responsibilities), crime becomes a more attractive option (Phillips & Votey, 1984). Thus, women who bear the primary responsibility for ensuring family income, with limited employment options (e.g., poor or uneducated single mothers), are particularly vulnerable in terms of turning to drug-related income sources. Drug-using women are also more likely to engage in sex work or selling drugs to support their addiction than are male addicts (who more often resort to theft and robbery; UNIFEM, 2010).

As we will see, Allison is a woman of circumstance in the sense that her romantic involvement with a male addict named Johnny led her down a road of self-destruction. Her mother's absence and the lack of a positive male role model left her vulnerable to a relationship that would cost her a great deal, including her freedom.

Allison and Johnny

The same year in which Allison was expelled from school, Allison's mother came home from prison. However, it was too late—the daughter was already involved in "the system." Moreover, by that time Allison had become involved with a man 8 years her senior named Johnny, and "from here it goes downhill." Allison writes: "When my mother left, I was a child going toward life with the best intentions to succeed. When she got home, I was headed for destruction." Sally, Allison's mother, tried to keep her from seeing Johnny, but 15-year-old Allison was still angry at her mother for leaving her, and Sally's efforts to control her daughter only made Allison rebel and want to be with Johnny even more. Allison thought Johnny loved her. By the time Allison was 16, Johnny had become physically abusive. Every time he drank, he hit her, about once a month. By the time Allison was 17, she was pregnant. She also took her GED, and in 1998 her first daughter was born. Her beloved grandmother passed away soon after that, and to numb the pain of that loss, Allison turned to her familiar comforts, alcohol and drugs. During this time she was leaving her daughter with her mother a great deal and Johnny became incarcerated. By the time she was 18, Allison received her first DUI and was placed on probation. Soon thereafter, Johnny came back home, and Allison received her second DUI. She also found out she was again pregnant.

Allison tried to change, realizing that she would have two children now who needed her, and she thought Johnny would change too now that they were expecting a second child. She went into a substance abuse program, and for once things seemed to be going well. However, as soon as she had her second daughter, she and Johnny started partying a lot, and he became physically abusive again. When Allison went to her substance abuse support group with two black eyes, her probation officer was notified and became involved, encouraging Allison to leave Johnny. But Allison considered Johnny her lifeline—someone who was there for her when no one else was—a man whom she trusted and loved because "he saw the potential in me."

In spite of her relationship with Johnny, Allison kept trying—working her "program," staying off drugs, and going to school in order to get into a computer technology program. Johnny even went to counseling during this time. Allison was then placed on very low supervised probation, and on some level it seemed that her life with Johnny and the children was finally getting on track. But Johnny didn't like Allison being in school, so she quit. And unfortunately, Allison's migraine headaches were the catalyst for more trouble ahead. Allison recounts that she was prescribed "so many medications I didn't know what to do—they were mine and legal." Johnny started sharing the pain pills with her. Her father, Henry, came back into her life when he was released from prison, and by that time, he had hepatitis C and cirrhosis of the liver. Allison stayed by his side throughout the ordeal until he died in 2003. In 2002, Allison received her third DUI and was given 90 days' confinement in the local jail to be served on weekends. It took 9 months to finish her sentence, but she made it through while Sally and Johnny cared for her children.

Upon her release, and still on probation, Allison joined Johnny in selling drugs and had everything she ever wanted "material-wise." Allison says she has three addictions—money, drugs, and Johnny—and she didn't even know it at the time because she was a functioning addict. She worked, participated in school activities with her children, and was a member of the PTA. She says: "I was there physically but not mentally." In 2004, at the age of 23, Allison became pregnant again with her third child, and it drove her and Johnny apart. She continued to function, working, selling drugs, and using pills. Her life was falling apart, and the pills helped her numb the pain. She knew her children were suffering, especially the middle child, who had been a frequent witness to the domestic violence between Allison and Johnny. Her probation officer (PO) continued to encourage Allison to break up with Johnny, even sending her to a women's shelter for a while "to see what could happen." But she went back to Johnny, who eventually called Allison's PO and told her that Allison was "abusing her medication," thus violating the terms of her probation. Allison's probation was revoked, and she was reincarcerated at a high-security state prison—sentenced to do 6 years and 2 months' time. Allison believes her most recent incarceration has been her "wake-up call" to stop doing drugs. But serving time in the state prison is hard—Allison explains she is often depressed despite the tricyclic medication the prison dispenses to her daily. "You are not a whole person here," she surmises. God is the only thing that makes a difference, and she copes through prayer and writing in a daily journal. Sally and Johnny (who is out of work and on disability), care for Allison's three daughters.

[*At the time of our interview, Allison had already served one year of her new sentence*].

We can clearly see from Allison's story how her involvement in selling and using drugs was linked to her romantic relationship with Johnny. Indeed, Gaskins (2004) specifies a figurative triangle that links women of circumstance, like Allison, to "the male dealers they are romantically involved with, and the drugs themselves" (p. 1535). For Allison and many women like her, criminal drug-related activity is "an uninvited and often unforeseen repercussion of choosing an intimate relationship" (p. 1535). Disconnecting from the male partner's drug business often would entail a willingness to break up the families—something many women are economically unable and personally unwilling to do depending on the perceived importance of the relationship.

Family Disadvantage, Loss, and Intergenerational Cycles of Pain

Regardless of whether mothers are incarcerated due to drug-related activities, like Allison, or other forms of criminality, an examination of their family backgrounds and social environments suggests that mothers involved in the criminal justice system are perhaps the most vulnerable women in the United States (Hanlon, O'Grady, et al., 2005). As for their male counterparts, economic deprivation seems to be a common childhood experience for women offenders (Greene et al., 2000; Hanlon, O'Grady, et al., 2005). For many women, this deprivation may continue into adulthood, as evidenced by a high level of reliance on public aid at the time of their arrest (Greene et al., 2000). Qualitative research revealed that incarcerated mothers also reported a great deal of residential instability while growing up—moving an average of seven times prior to the age of 18 (Greene et al., 2000). Some of this instability can be traced to childhood economic disadvantage; residential mobility also connected to inmate mothers' recollections of their own mothers' multiple relationship transitions that necessitated moving. Women's economic deprivation and lack of financial independence are particularly damaging because their need is great, especially if they are single mothers responsible for the care of children. These women are far less likely than more advantaged mothers to receive child support (Grall, 2006). In many circumstances, the men in their lives (intimates and family members, but not necessarily their children's fathers), also from disadvantaged environments, may be their main source of financial support. Many of these men are engaged in criminal, drug-related activities, which puts women at risk for drug use and/or drug crime as a means of survival.

Intergenerational Patterns

A limited amount of information exists from peer-reviewed journals regarding the family situations of female prisoners, specifically mothers, and their pathways to criminality. Such information is important with regard to better understanding the dynamics of women's criminality, identifying risk and protective factors, and offering intervention to break intergenerational cycles of incarceration. Evidence suggests that mothers in prison are disproportionately victimized as children and have suffered an array of traumatic experiences during childhood. These include emotional, physical, and/or sexual abuse, as well as witnessing violence at home (Chesney-Lind, 1997; Enos, 1997, 2001; Greene et al., 2000; Golden, 2005; Spitzer et al., 2001). In Green et al.'s qualitative sample of 102 mothers incarcerated in central California jails, 2 out of 3 women reported that they had been subjected to physically abusive punishment. Hanlon, O'Grady, et al. (2005) found that the family background of his sample of 167, primarily African American, incarcerated, drug-abusing mothers was the primary risk factor for Brief Symptom Inventory (BSI) severity. The BSI is an instrument that assesses psychological distress and psychiatric disorders. Specifically, "the lack of a structured, nurturing home environment during adolescence" gives rise to problem behavior and associations with "deviant" peers (Hanlon, O'Grady, et al., 2005, p. 71). We can clearly see the process unfolding in Allison's life when she lost her mother to a prison cell.

Much of what we can infer about women's family of origin experiences comes from the qualitative research, which sheds light on their loss histories and their intimate relationships and how these factors may propel women into the criminal justice system. What we can surmise is a complex set of events, experiences, and social networks that expose women to and ultimately involve them in criminal activity. Multiple and unexpected losses such as the death of a loved one or relationship breakup seem to trigger self-destructive behaviors such as binge drinking and drug misuse (Arditti & Few, 2008). Exposure to criminal activity does not make criminal involvement inevitable, but women's vulnerabilities relative to family of origin and relationship difficulties, drug use, and economic disadvantage greatly enhance the likelihood that they will in fact tolerate or perpetrate criminal activity. Allison is a case in point.

Further, drugs and alcohol are often a feature of female inmates' family of origin environment (Arditti & Few, 2008; Hanlon, O'Grady, et al., 2005; Lopez, Katsulis, & Robillard, 2009). Lopez et al.'s (2009) qualitative study of 18 incarcerated adolescent girls (several of whom were also mothers) reports drug use with parents as a common means of spending time with parents and staying close to them. Parental drug use as a feature of incarcerated mothers' family history is important because it is associated with less responsive parenting and mental health difficulties. It seems to be linked with insecure attachments during childhood (Suchman, Pajulo, DeCoste, & Mayes, 2006). Of interest here is how childhood histories of trauma, loss, and drug and alcohol use may be re-created by women, contributing to the conditions and behaviors that lead to their involvement in the criminal justice system (Greene et al., 2000). Further, the replication of family of origin difficulties creates the same vulnerabilities in the offender mothers' children, enhancing the likelihood of intergenerational patterns of risk and incarceration. That is, due to mothers' own incarceration (and in many cases drug-using behaviors), mothers have in effect re-created the family circumstances of their own childhood—their children are now vulnerable to negative influences outside the home, with the family's ability to protect children from such risk seriously compromised (Hanlon, O'Grady, et al., 2005). For example, Greene et al. (2000) note that the parallels between offender mothers' social histories of trauma and abuse and their children's lives "were dramatic and disturbing" (p. 13).

Allison's story is illustrative of how family of origin difficulties, maternal absence, and substance abuse can be reproduced. Her alcoholic father was unavailable to her psychologically and physically and failed to contribute economically to the family, ultimately leaving it in a precarious economic situation. Allison experienced multiple traumatic losses—most profoundly her mother's abrupt exit from her life to serve time, and the death of her grandmother. When Allison was 12, her family foundation crumbled; the dramatic cessation of maternal involvement left her vulnerable to negative peer influences and ultimately to involvement with an older drug-involved male. For Allison's children, a similar pattern emerges. They are subjected to repeated and abrupt separations from their mother, care by a grandmother who has her own troubled history and may be unprepared or unable to deal with the responsibilities of raising three children, and involvement with their own father, Johnny, who has a criminal and substance misuse history. Allison's story illustrates the multiple vulnerabilities that characterize many women who become involved with the criminal justice system. Her pathway to criminality was fueled by abandonment, loss, drug and alcohol use, and an intimate relationship with an older man in the drug trade who caused her great harm. Allison fits the profile of female offenders in that her life was characterized by the presence of depression, intimate violence, and addiction—conceptualized as a "triple threat" to women in terms of their cumulative adverse effect (Arditti & Few, 2008).

Making matters worse for mothers, the prison system is unprepared for the rapid influx of women offenders. Compared with men, women are even more likely to be subjected to overcrowding, harsh conditions, and being placed in maximum-security prisons due largely to the lack of female facilities (Braithwaite et al., 2005). Women, particularly due to their trauma histories, are negatively impacted by routine institutional practices such as strip searches and are subject to harm via staff sexual misconduct (Bloom et al., 2003). According to a recent U.S. Department of Justice (USDOJ) report on sexual misconduct in federal prisons, "prisoners who are victims of staff sexual abuse may suffer physical pain, fear, humiliation, degradation, and desperation, and this harm can last beyond the victims' incarceration. Moreover, because many female prisoners in particular often have histories of being sexually abused, they are even more traumatized by further abuse inflicted by correctional staff while in custody" (USDOJ, 2009, p. i). Despite changes in federal law to crack down on misconduct, reports of sexual misconduct between prison staff and inmates doubled between 2001 and 2008 (USDOJ, 2009), with the most frequent allegations involving criminal sexual abuse between male staff and female inmates. This increase can be only partially explained by increases in the number of inmates and stronger efforts on the part of the Federal Bureau of Prisons to encourage staff and inmates to report abuse. Sociologists Young and Reviere (2006) surmise that "women are punished by far more than simple incarceration; they are punished with overcrowded, exploitive, and unhealthy living conditions" (p. 8). These facts pose unique and profound difficulties for both the children of incarcerated mothers and the mothers themselves in terms of adaptation to prison life and social reintegration upon release.

Indications of intense cumulative disadvantage, troubled family histories, and gender-insensitive institutional practices all contribute to mothers' distress in prison and difficulties upon release (Arditti & Few, 2008; Bloom et al., 2003; Poehlmann, 2005b, 2005c; Thompson & Harm, 2000).

Mother-Child Relationships

Given the incapacitating and socially isolating context of confinement, it comes as no surprise that maternal incarceration is generally linked to the most profound child adjustment difficulties, including school failure, antisocial and delinquent behavior, and higher rates of intergenerational incarceration (Dallaire, 2007b; Huebner & Gustafson, 2007; Murray & Farrington, 2008; Parke & Clarke-Stewart, 2001; Phillips et al., 2002). The more intense consequences (compared with paternal incarceration) that appear to be associated with maternal incarceration are due in part to a number of structural factors. Foremost is the fact that most mothers tend to be primary caregivers prior to their incarceration, thus creating care discontinuities for children (Mumola, 2000). Further, there is a heightened chance that when mothers are incarcerated, children's fathers are incarcerated as well (Arditti, Burton, et al., 2010; Dallaire, 2007b), thus exposing children to increased hardship and the compounded risk that comes with having both parents imprisoned (Beck et al., 2009). Indeed, the most obvious difference between incarcerated mothers and fathers is who cares for the children during the parent's absence. The majority of incarcerated fathers (90%) report that their children were living with their mothers; mothers, on the other hand, report that their children were living with grandparents (53%), fathers, (28%), or other relatives (26%) or in foster care (10%;[3] Mumola, 2000). Prior to arrest and incarceration, women prisoners are more likely than men to report having multiple children and to have resided with their children, and are 2.5 times more likely to have been single parents than their male counterparts (Mumola, 2000). Imprisoned mothers are also at greater risk for the termination of parental rights as a result of incarceration (Hagan & Coleman, 2001).

Incarceration as a Context for Maternal Distress

In thinking about the question of how incarceration influences the family lives of already vulnerable mothers, it is important to consider the importance of maternal distress as an explanatory construct, establishing a pathway of influence. This pathway begins, as we have seen, with the accumulation of disadvantage experienced by most incarcerated mothers. Disadvantage histories in conjunction with the incapacitating effects of the incarceration itself contribute to women's psychological, relational, and situational distress. While the consequences of this distress may reverberate in many aspects of a woman's life during and after incarceration, consistent with a family perspective, children may bear the brunt of the distress in terms of how both cumulative disadvantage and maternal distress impact their mothers' parenting. Indeed, family stress theory posits, "The primary mechanism through which contextual stressors impair parenting is parental psychological distress" (Kotchick, Dorsey, & Heller, 2005, p. 449).

A rich body of empirical literature has demonstrated that psychological distress mediates the link between cumulative disadvantage and harsh, inconsistent parenting (McLoyd, Aikens, & Burton, 2006). We can expand on the theoretical and empirical conceptualization of psychological distress by broadening the notion of parental distress to include relational and situational elements as well. This combination of factors is defined as maternal distress. Maternal distress is defined as mothers' discomfort with their ability to protect children from harm, prevent children's adversity, or promote children's well-being (Arditti & Grzywacz, 2011). Maternal distress is important because it is implicated in the risk of physical and psychological harm in children. These harms to children can occur via mothers' less effective parenting, and in particular their failure or inability to protect children from maltreatment perpetrated by mothers' intimate partners. Specifically, maternal distress has been implicated in less empathetic parenting, harsh disciplinary practices, and child abuse (see Feshbach, 1986; Shahar, 2001). In the most extreme circumstances, left untreated, maternal distress can be a factor in mothers' murdering their children (Oberman & Meyer, 2008). Maternal distress is also central to the experience of a child witnessing his or her mother's assault (Little & Kantor, 2002). This conceptualization of maternal distress is based on grounded theorizing resulting from an analysis of mothers' experience after a period of incarceration (Arditti & Few, 2008) and empirical verification of maternal distress among low-income single mothers whose children experienced some form of parental incarceration (maternal, paternal, or both; Arditti, Burton, et al., 2010).

A growing body of evidence implicates maternal distress in an array of deleterious outcomes such as harsh parenting and developmental problems for children (e.g., internalizing or delinquent behavior; Feldman, 2007). Maternal distress is usually conceptualized in psychiatric terms and is typically equated with negative psychological states such as depression (Arendell, 2000; Kinsman & Wildman, 2001), comorbid depression and anxiety (Feldman, 2007; Klebanov, Brooks-Gunn, & McCormick, 2001), or persistent negative affect (DeGarmo & Forgatch, 1997). Conceptualizing maternal distress as a predominantly intrapsychic mood state is problematic, particularly when it is applied to understanding mothering in contexts of incarceration, in that it overly "medicalizes" the experience of maternal distress (cf. Barclay

& Lloyd, 1996). A medicalized concept is one in which an everyday issue is transformed into a medical problem (Conrad, 1992). Locating maternal distress as an individual "medical problem" holds the mother personally responsible, confines explanations to the biomedical or psychological domains, and prevents analysis of the contextual and relational realities of parenting, thus contributing to a deficit, stigmatizing, "person-blame" discourse. Feminist scholars argue that medicalization is a facet of social control of women. That is, pathologizing distressed mothers can be viewed as a means though which patriarchal family norms and stereotypical ideals of motherhood can be imposed on women in order to regulate their behavior (Boyd, 1999, 2004). Maternal distress is best understood *in context* relative to mothers' disadvantage, their loss regarding how their incarceration has affected their relationships with their children, and their concerns regarding their children's well-being and care during their absence (Arditti & Few, 2008). By utilizing a construct grounded in women's lives, it is possible to more fully understand their family lives and subsequent parenting trajectories.

Sources of Maternal Distress
Obviously, incarceration hampers mothers' ability to protect their children from harm[4] (see, e.g., Hanlon, O'Grady, et al., 2005) and enhance their children's well-being. Separation from children is believed to be the most damaging aspect of women's imprisonment (Bloom et al., 2003), both for the mother herself and for her children.[5] Research documents the multiple barriers associated with maintaining healthy mother-child relationships during imprisonment and upon reentry (Bloom & Steinhart, 1993; Costa, 2003; Hagan & Dinovitzer, 1999). Primary among these barriers is mothers' loss of contact with their family members and children. Compared with men, many women have lost touch with their families and ultimately face even greater adjustment challenges with respect to reintegration (Bloom et al., 2003).

Less than one-fourth of all incarcerated women receive in-person visits (Mumola, 2000), and mothers are less likely to receive visits than incarcerated fathers. This is likely due to the barriers and restrictions associated with visits, the greater likelihood that a women's prison will be located in a remote rural area, and the shifting and uncertain care of children that characterizes families impacted by maternal incarceration (Hagan & Coleman, 2001; Greenfield & Snell, 1999). During incarceration, other tangible forms of contact between women and their families include phone calls and letter writing. Phone calls and letter writing to children have been found to be beneficial for incarcerated mothers in terms of enhancing attachment and their sense of parental competence (Poehlmann, 2005c; Tuerk & Loper, 2006), as well as maintaining relationships with other family members (LaVigne, Naser, et al., 2005).

Women's perceived failure to live up to cultural ideals of motherhood also contributes to their distress. These ideals romanticize parenthood; women are expected to provide "unconditional love, to be nurturing and self-sacrificing, instinctively providing the best care for the children" (Lewis, 2002, p. 32). Sociocultural conceptions of adulthood emphasize the primacy of motherhood for women's social self (Simon, 1992), thus rendering incarcerated mothers highly vulnerable to psychological distress given their absence from home and inability to enact mothering functions. Incarceration along with the conditions and/or behaviors that may have brought a woman into the purview of the criminal justice system (e.g., illicit drug use, theft) are antithetical to motherhood ideals. This gap—between "the good mother" and the reality of an incarcerated woman's life—is a source of ambivalence, guilt, and disempowerment. The stereotype of the perfect mother is "particularly pernicious for those struggling to mother in abject poverty or in other extreme conditions...with minimal support" (Lewis, 2002, p. 39). This stereotype not only is harmful for mothers but also can prove deadly for their children. For example, deep conflicts about motherhood have been an issue for troubled mothers who have enacted the most unthinkable form of harm to their children—that of taking their children's lives (Oberman & Meyer, 2008). When mothers are seen as less than perfect, they are regarded as abnormal and deviant. Many incarcerated women, regardless of the reasons that led to their imprisonment, are arguably struggling to mother under the most extreme and stigmatizing circumstances. It stands to reason that the gap between internalized ideals about the good mother and their self-perceptions gives rise to distress and feelings of inadequacy, suggesting that maternal identity is prominent (i.e., associated with strong emotions per Stryker, 1980) for many women during their confinement. Indeed, empirical research shows that incarcerated mothers tend to feel extremely guilty about being away from their children (Arditti & Few, 2008; Poehlmann, 2005c).

Mothers and Reentry

At some point the majority of female offenders finish serving their time and are released back into the community. Most of those who are mothers plan on reunification with their children. The issue of mothers' reentry is of great concern in thinking about parental incarceration, since women are more likely than their male counterparts to have been children's residential and primary caregivers prior to confinement and hence more likely to plan on resuming parenting responsibilities upon their release. Women account for approximately 11% of successful discharges from parole and 8% of unsuccessful discharges; 45% of women for whom parole supervision ended in 1996 were returned to prison that same year or absconded. A three-year follow-up study revealed that for women discharged from prisons in 11 states, an estimated 39% were reconvicted and 33% were returned to prison (Greenfield & Snell, 1999).

Unfortunately, beyond recidivism rates, data limitations are particularly notable relative to female incarceration and reentry (Bloom et al., 2003). For example, answers to the effects of critical variables of interest (e.g., prison programming, variations in relational and community circumstances) on women's postrelease reentry and parenting trajectories are elusive due to absent or incomplete Bureau of Justice Statistics data (Deschenes et al., 2006). Once again, purposeful, qualitative studies serve as a foundation for understanding women's experience. Consistent with the definition of purposeful research, Richie (2002) argues in her grounded theory analysis of women's reentry experience based on a series of qualitative projects that while small samples may not be randomly assigned or yield statistically significant results, the women in her work represent the demographics and conditions experienced by incarcerated women in the United States. Other qualitative studies of reentry mothers also demonstrate that their samples are purposeful and yield themes consistent with past research (e.g., Arditti & Few, 2006, 2008).

The literature suggests that women who are incarcerated face particular barriers that worsen their prison experience and elevate its negative impact on their lives and families. This scenario has been described as "troubled motherhood" (Brown & Bloom, 2009, p. 317), given the poor conditions that impact reentry mothers' maternal experience prior to prison. When women are returned to disenfranchised neighborhoods without any appreciable work history, coupled with limited access to community health resources, their chances of successfully integrating are seriously compromised. For example, substance abuse treatment is seen as critical to women's successful reentry (Richie, 2002). With many incarcerated women possessing histories of chronic and debilitating substance abuse problems, it comes as no surprise that relapse is "one of the most salient factors in women's recidivism" (Richie, 2001, p. 371).

In addition to substance abuse problems, intense histories of cumulative disadvantage and the stigma and disenfranchisement that result from incarceration potentially render women in the criminal justice system the most vulnerable of women. Women tend to come home with the same problems they had prior to incarceration, and in many cases incarceration intensifies any vulnerabilities that already are present (Brown & Bloom, 2009; Richie, 2002). Evidence suggests that the parenting situations of reentry mothers were troubled before their incarceration, including a disproportionate involvement with child welfare services. In a recent qualitative study, nearly a quarter of the 48 participants had records of previous investigations for child maltreatment (Brown & Bloom, 2009). Further, when mothers are arrested and incarcerated, there is a greater likelihood of children being entangled in the legal offense. For example, they are likely to witness their mother's arrest; the issue of the child-mother relationship after prison is complicated "when children are swept up at the time of arrest for being in the wrong place at the wrong time" (Brown & Bloom, 2009, p. 318). As a result, women suffer a great deal of guilt and shame.

The intensifying effects of incarceration are particularly apparent with regard to mental health difficulties, further challenging women's ability to reenter and successfully renegotiate motherhood. While institutional and legal practices aimed at incapacitation negatively affect the psychological adjustment of all offenders (Haney, 2002; Young & Reviere, 2006), one can surmise that incarcerated women are particularly vulnerable to these effects due to their disproportionate trauma histories, their potential exposure to sexual harassment while in prison, and the possibility that even acute, major psychological problems may not have been diagnosed in prison (Richie, 2002). Research demonstrates that, like substance abuse, serious mental health needs are unmet upon reentering family and community life after incarceration (Arditti & Few, 2008; Richie, 2002). This is a great point of concern given that mental health difficulties are a strong predictor of recidivism (Warren, 2007). Yet, mental illness is grossly overrepresented among incarcerated women (Braithwaite et al., 2005); a 2004 study found that 73% of women (compared with 55% of men) in state prisons nationwide had symptoms of a clinical diagnosis of mental illness and/or were receiving treatment from a mental health professional in the past year (James & Glaze, 2006).

Intersectionality, Reentry, and Employment

In addition to the challenges that may connect with any unmet mental health and treatment needs, reentry mothers must face the challenges associated with not only finding but also sustaining legal employment, often in conjunction with reunification with children. In this way mothers are distinct from many men reentering the community who may not bear the primary responsibility of parenting children. Many reentry mothers are dealing with the multiple demands of employment *and* caregiving responsibilities with very little in the way of financial resources or support from children's fathers (Arditti & Few, 2006, 2008; Brown & Bloom, 2009). While scholars emphasize the critical importance of meaningful employment for successful reentry, surprisingly little information exists about the employment experiences of former prisoners. Moreover, what research does exist focuses on male inmates and their employment patterns prior to and after incarceration. Findings and recommendations tend to be framed within men's experience with very little attention to mothers' special needs (see also Solomon, Johnson, Travis, & McBride, 2004). Gender is not generally part of the discourse here, likely due to women's historical invisibility within the criminal justice system as well as the far greater numbers of men affected by imprisonment. Certain generalities pertaining to employment would likely apply to women such as the disruptive and incapacitating effect that incarceration has on one's employment prospects (Pager, 2003; Petersilia, 2003; Richie, 2001). For example, compared with other stigmatized groups such as welfare recipients and individuals with a GED, employers are least willing to hire those individuals who were incarcerated (Holzer, Raphael, & Stoll, 2002).

In thinking about mothers' reentry, the concept of intersectionality helps frame their experience. Intersectionality typically denotes the ways in which race, class, and gender shape women's lives (Hooks, 1984), and it has been applied to a range of issues (e.g., rape, domestic violence), including their employment experience (Crenshaw, 1991). Intersectionality suggests that the issues women of color face cannot be understood by looking at the dimensions of race, class, and gender separately but rather by exploring how these dimensions *intersect*. For example, one of participants in our mothers' reentry study follow-up (Arditti & Few, 2008), a nurse's aide named Linda, commented about the burden of being *both* African American and an "ex-con" in terms of finding employment. Linda believed that the *intersection* of race and felon status was the reason she could not get hired. She explained: "It was bad enough to be an ex-con, when she [the interviewer in Linda's recent attempt to get a nurse's aide job] saw I was black too, I could tell on her face there was no way I would get the job." Linda's lack of desirability in the job market contributes to her disempowerment and feelings of helplessness (Arditti & Few, 2008).

Female prisoners are especially likely to hold multiple memberships in various "stigmatized groups"—even when compared with their male counterparts—given their social locations as women and as mothers. For example, in a study conducted by me and my colleague (Arditti & Few, 2006), several of the 28 women in our sample were also welfare recipients at one time, had a GED or no high school diploma, and had primary responsibility for their children since their release. Thus, in addition to the typical barriers incarceration poses for employment, women's caregiving responsibilities, to kin and to their own children, and children's response to their mothers' attempts to reclaim motherhood pose additional challenges (Brown & Bloom, 2009). Qualitative evidence suggests the women who were incarcerated had unsteady histories of employment and school attendance and lacked the necessary training to obtain a legal and stable job (Richie, 2002). Women are likely to depend on family members, who themselves may not have adequate resources, and on public and community agencies (Arditti & Few, 2008; Brown & Bloom, 2009; Richie, 2002). As resources become exhausted, and good faith efforts to secure jobs are without success, the lure of illegal means of generating income becomes more attractive.

Churning or "reentry cycling" is a problem for all ex-offenders and particularly pernicious for women due in part to their location in overlapping systems of discrimination and subordination. Allison had been in and out of detention all her life, and unless there are dramatic positive changes in herself and in her family life, her prospects for staying out of prison seem dim. In addition to being classified as an ex-felon and subject to structural disenfranchisement (e.g., loss of voting rights, loss of access to certain types of public resources such as student aid) and stigma, incarcerated mothers are often marginalized via their *motherhood* (responsible for the invisible work of child care and family caregiving), their *drug use, their mental health difficulties, their color*, and *their poverty*—including their need for and histories of welfare assistance. Women's intersectionality suggests a great need for research and intervention that responds to the overlap that results from reentry mothers' membership in a multitude of stigmatized groups. Crenshaw (1991) elaborates on the links between intersectionality and manifestations of power, noting that "power is exercised . . . through the process of categorization. . . power to cause that categorization to have social and material consequences" (p. 1297). Indeed, it is easy to argue that the lack of services and resources for reentering prisoners, and policy and programs addressing the unique needs of mothers are part of the consequence of their intersectionality.

Sue's Reentry Story

Sue is a single mother of four children, one of whom she lost track of during her incarceration. She continues to search for this child, likely located with an estranged paternal grandmother across the state. She has a daughter Sheri aged 10 and two young twin sons who were 2.5 years old at the time of my visit to her small apartment. Sue, a follow-up participant in the mothers' reentry study,[6] was one of the few women in our project who successfully completed her probation. But as one familiar with the literature might suspect, Sue had multiple and conflicting demands between working, parenting, and staying out of trouble. On the surface one might qualify her as a reentry success: she had full-time employment, housing, and child care. After spending a little time with Sue, one came to realize she also had a lot on her plate—perhaps more than she could deal with. First, Sue had a history of depression and angry outbursts, had at one time been treated with medication to control mood, but did not take any prescribed meds now because she "didn't like the way it felt." Given the limitations in her health care, it is easy to understand why she would make decisions about medication without the benefit of a qualified doctor or therapist to assist her in those decisions or offer some alternatives. Like any mother with small children, and certainly as a single mother, it is understandable that Sue would get frustrated with her twin boys' demands for attention—particularly when she comes home from her office job (which she hates but must keep) exhausted and tries to fix dinner. "They crawl up my leg and cry Mommy, Mommy—I just have to hit them to get them to mind..." As a former protective caseworker, I see the red flags—Sue engages in harsh physical disciplinary practices, and I can imagine that without proper mental health care and support, these practices can easily escalate into abuse.

It's hard to be a single mom. It's not easy to work all day and come home to take care of three children solo, two of whom are active 2-year-old boys. Sue's mother is dead and her father is a progressed alcoholic who she insists was "good to her" despite her frequent trips to the bars with him as a child. I worry about her isolation and her moods and her occasional binge drinking with her girlfriends to "relieve stress." Incarceration toughened Sue up even further and created a great deal of strain with her daughter, who shows signs of anxiety and trauma from her separation from her mother.

As I leave Sue's apartment, I worry about her and her children. My instincts tell me she will end up back in prison. I hope I am wrong.

Sue is African American, a never-married single mother, has a long record, and has previously been on welfare. She has a dense intersectionality; collectively the marginalization associated with Sue's social and economic location weighs heavily against her ability to successfully reintegrate. As illustrated in Sue's case, justice-involved mothers often represent the most vulnerable of low-income, single-mother-headed households, if not prior to then certainly after their release from prison (Arditti, Burton, et al., 2010). Indeed, it has been demonstrated that incarceration contributes to the deterioration of preexisting marital or intimate ties between offender mothers and their male partners (who are generally the father of at least one of their children (Arditti & Few, 2008). Further, the disadvantaged circumstances in and around offender mothers' lives influence their parenting practices, which subsequently bear strongly on their children—particularly upon their release. Maternal incarceration results in emotional, financial, and social suffering for offspring, and more often than not, mother-child relationships are "beyond repair" after incarcerative sentences (Travis, Solomon, & Waul, 2001).

Relationships between mothers who have been incarcerated and their children may be "beyond repair" largely due to mothers' distress, their lack of parenting competency, and their sometimes detached, estranged relationships with their children. Lengthy sentences and institutional practices, which detract from consistent and meaningful contact with children, enhance this possibility. Some level of detachment seems necessary to cope with difficult or estranged mother-child relationships. Indeed, consider the words of this mother who after incarceration told us, "I just can't cry anymore, I can't think about my children anymore" (Arditti & Few, 2008, p. 311).

Estrangement from children is a very real outcome associated with a parent's imprisonment and is generally more keenly experienced and painful for mothers who were likely primary caregivers prior to their incarceration (Mumola, 2000). Indeed, the "fall from grace" is often harder for women with children than for men. Brown and Bloom (2009) argue that the idea of parental authority is an essential aspect of maternal identity in the working-class families most likely to be impacted by incarceration:

Discipline and its functions, such as monitoring, accountability, advising, and handing out sanctions, are as much a part of motherhood as love and caring. For women whose incarceration occasioned long-term separation, this aspect of motherhood, like others related to emotional bonding, is likely to become fragmented. Conviction, incarceration, and absence have eroded parental authority in both its moral and practical dimensions…. Her stature as a moral leader in the home has been irrevocably discredited…she has lost the moral rectitude that is culturally central to motherhood. (p. 326)

Again, the erosion of "parental capital" (Brown & Bloom, 2009, p. 326) likely begins before prison; however, incarceration intensifies children's difficulties as well as mothers' ability to help (Brown & Bloom, 2009; Golden, 2005).

Summary

Allison's and Sue's stories illustrate that incarcerated mothers are perhaps "the most vulnerable women in the world." Their vulnerability stems not only from their criminal history and experiences pertaining to incarceration but also from their intense histories of intergenerational disadvantage, victimization, and marginalization in multiple social spheres. Mothers' vulnerability is intensified within the context of current drug war practices and social norms that idealize motherhood yet demonize women's difficulties, such as drug use and drug selling, that are intricately connected to their life circumstances and relationships. Given women's typical role as primary caregivers to their children prior to incarceration, relationships with children are characterized by a great deal of emotional distress. Taken together, these factors create significant barriers to healthy reunification with children and to successful reentry after release from confinement.

4

Paternal Incarceration

Charlie and Merle: Stories of Broken Ties

Charlie is 41 years old and is 5 years in on a 15-year federal sentence for larceny and possession of cocaine with intent to distribute. Prior to his sentence, during his litigation, he was held 2 years in a local jail, close to his home. He and his family did not have the resources to post bond. After 7 years of confinement and more to go without the chance of probation or parole, his two daughters, aged 18 and 12, feel lost to him, as does his wife of almost 20 years. Part of the problem is that Charlie is now serving his time at a medium-security prison in Oklahoma. It is about 120 miles from his home, not too bad compared with some of the places he has heard about from the other guys. For the first year of his sentence in Oklahoma, his wife had faithfully brought the children to see him one weekend a month. They stayed overnight at the Holiday Inn Express so they could see him both Friday evening and all day Saturday. Charlie also spoke frequently with the children by phone, exhorting them to do well in school and "listen to their mother." However, since his first year in Oklahoma, visits have become less and less frequent—trailing off to virtually nothing—and phone calls are far and few between. He hasn't seen his family for almost a year now. Charlie gets it. His wife is tired. His kids would rather be with their friends. He doesn't blame them but still feels rejected and depressed. He was unable to attend his older daughter's high school graduation this past spring. His daughter is angry at him for leaving her and will not write him or take any phone calls.

Merle's son Billy was just 7 when Merle went to prison. They were close then. Merle met him at the bus stop after school almost every day to walk him home while Merle's girlfriend, and Billy's mother, Tammy, worked as a maid at a nearby hotel. Merle had thought one of the advantages of his marijuana business was that he could work from home and be there for Billy while Tammy worked during the day. Big mistake. Merle was charged with a continuing criminal enterprise and has served 8 years toward his 20-year sentence. Tammy has moved on with a new man, who has family in Sacramento. They decided to move there together in the hope of securing better jobs and having child care for Billy. Merle is at the federal corrections institute (FCI) in Michigan and has not heard from either Tammy or Billy since they left. He has no address or phone number. At first, the pain was gut-wrenching. Now, he has learned to mentally detach to cope with the pain of Billy's absence from his life. He has taken his pictures of Billy down from his wall, and when asked by other inmates if he has children, Merle simply responds with a brusque "no." [1]

Both Charlie's and Merle's stories highlight contextual and processual concepts that are critical to understanding the implications of incarceration for fathers. Based on a review of the empirical literature, we can identify four areas of concern, all of which are reflected in Charlie's and Merle's stories:

- Incarcerated fatherhood and paternal identity: the high price of feeling helpless
- Father involvement: constraints and efforts to father behind walls
- Pivotal challenges: contact and coparenting
- Father-child ties and reentry

Because of their incarceration, Charlie and Merle are relatively helpless in terms of staying in contact with their children. Like most men in their situation, they are dependent on their children's mothers to receive visits. Yet, institutional practices such as lengthy sentences and being housed far from home have contributed to the unraveling of each man's relationships with his children and intimate partner. Charlie's wife, worn out by the responsibilities of raising two girls on her own, does not have the time, money, or energy to make the long trek to visit. The girls are dealing with their own demons—particularly his older daughter, who resents his absence and sees him as a ghost of the father she once knew. Merle's situation is also common. He is out of the loop, and now that Tammy has moved on, the only way he can cope is to completely withdraw. He feels helpless and does not really identify with being a father. In fact, Merle cannot even remember the last time he was able to really "do something" for Billy.

Profile of Incarcerated Fathers

Despite political rhetoric bemoaning "fatherless America," [2] family disruption connected to incarceration of fathers has received minimal empirical exploration. Recently, growing attention has been given to incarcerated fathers, driven in part by an increasing awareness that their confinement links to growing numbers of single-mother households (Edin et al., 2001; Western et al., 2004) and negative child effects (Parke & Clark-Stewart, 2001). The record prison population has resulted in an unprecedented number of incarcerated men; 54% of these men are fathers. It is estimated that approximately 744,200 fathers are held in prisons across the country (Glaze & Maruschak, 2008). This figure does not include fathers confined in jails, as far less is known about the characteristics of fathers in the jail population. Given the large number of inmates in local jails (750,581 as of midyear 2007), their consideration is warranted as we think about incarcerated fatherhood and its implications for men, children, and families (Herman-Stahl et al., 2008). As we have seen, while the rate of increase of mothers in prison has been more rapid than for fathers, by far, men constitute the largest population of parents in prison, reporting a total of 1,559,200 children (mothers reported 147,400; Glaze & Maruschak, 2008). The average incarcerated father is aged 32 (with black and Hispanic men typically younger than white men per Sabol & Couture, 2008), and has 2.1 children with multiple partners who reside in more than one household (Arditti et al., 2003; Hairston, 1998). Forty-two percent of fathers in prison report living with at least one of their children, often the youngest one, prior to their incarceration (Arditti et al., 2003; Glaze & Maruschak, 2008). Since 1991 the number of children with a father in prison has grown by 77%. Similar to demographic trends pertaining to the prison population as a whole, fathers in prisons are more likely to be persons of color: 4 in 10 fathers are black, 3 in 10 are white, and 2 in 10 are Hispanic. Of the 1,559,200 children with a father in prison, 46% are children of black fathers (Glaze & Maruschak, 2008).

Recent data from the Fragile Families and Child Wellbeing study suggest that incarcerated fathers differ in significant ways from the general population of fathers. Incarcerated fathers are more likely to be violent, African American, less educated, and prone to drug and alcohol abuse, and to have poor relationship skills (Carlson & McLanahan, 2002). Fathers in prison disproportionately come from impoverished urban neighborhoods (Clear, 2007; Clear, Rose, & Ryder 2001; Travis, 2005). They come from families characterized by intergenerational patterns of criminality and have a history of involvement in the criminal justice system (Carlson & McLanahan, 2002). Similar to the general prison population, drug offenders are heavily represented among incarcerated fathers (Mumola, 2000), with black men generally receiving longer sentences for these offenses than white men (Meierhoefer, 1992). Most incarcerated fathers report incomes well below the poverty line, with 53% earning less than $12,000 in the year before their incarceration (Mumola, 2000). However, more than half of fathers in prison report that they were the primary source of financial support for their children, with approximately 46% of men residing with their children prior to their confinement (Glaze & Maruschak, 2008). It should be noted, however, that many fathers who enter prison have not been able to demonstrate that they could support their children before prison and are seriously hampered in their ability to do so upon reentry. For example, recent national estimates suggest that in 2005, incarcerated fathers accounted for 16% to 18% of the $107 billion in child support arrears; on average those fathers with a child support order owe about $10,000 at the time of incarceration (Katzenstein & Shanley, 2008). Another recent study evaluating reentry programming found that nearly all the fathers in their sample (about 92%) reported owing back child support, with most of the respondents owing more than $5,000 (Lattimore, Steffey, & Visher, 2009).

The concentration of large numbers of fathers, mostly poor, relatively young African American males (Nurse, 2002), in correctional institutions bears heavily on the families of these men and helps in part to explain the incidence of cumulative disadvantage among families impacted by paternal incarceration (Arditti et al., 2003; Hairston, 2001). The loss of any financial support coming from fathers prior to their incarceration further compromises the economic survival of affected households (Arditti et al., 2003; Hairston, 2001). The decreased physical presence of males in the home and community shifts an enormous economic and child care burden to women.

Situating Incarcerated Fatherhood

The demographic profile of incarcerated fathers provides some context for their life histories and evidence of cumulative disadvantage. The concentration of African American fathers in prison suggests structural inequities in men's lives prior to incarceration, as well as their treatment by the justice system. These facts help situate our analysis of incarcerated fathers. Beyond their demographic characteristics, incarcerated fathers are impacted by the limits of their confinement and the stigmatized context of their "nonresidence" relative to their children. These limits include being housed in facilities far from home and institutional constraints imposed by the prison setting. For example, geographic distance from family members, transportation and financial barriers, lack of child-friendly visitation contexts, and harsh, disrespectful treatment by correctional staff all impinge on meaningful contact between fathers and their children during confinement (Arditti, 2003; Hairston et al., 2004; LaVigne, Naser, et al., 2005; Naser & Visher, 2006). Thus fathers cannot be understood apart from the prisons that hold them and the parenting activities they believe are constrained as a result of their imprisonment.

Here it is useful to distinguish between fatherhood and father involvement. Fatherhood typically pertains to a man's motivations to perform the fathering role and his internalized thoughts, images, and role identity. Based on this definition, fatherhood is an "intraindividual" construct with paternal identity as a central point of focus. Father involvement typically refers to a man's behavior as he enacts the paternal role; it is a relational construct in that concern centers on his engagement with his children and the enactment of fathering functions (Day, Lewis, O'Brien, & Lamb, 2005). Both fathering identity and father involvement are important. Identity theory posits that father involvement will vary as a function of the importance with which a father views his role (Pleck, 1997). Men's parenting and identity work in prison are uniquely shaped by a coercive power that substantially regulates and redefines who they are as fathers (Roy, 2005); this redefinition of a man's fathering identity has implications for his involvement with his children during confinement and upon release.

From Father to Inmate: Identity Shifts and Incarcerated Fatherhood

Men's involvement in the criminal justice system creates a conflict between their identities as inmate and father (Tripp, 2009). The process of *prisonization* underlies these conflicting identities. As we have seen, prisonization involves the individual's inculcation of the prison subculture so much so that preprison identities "fade" and the prison identity of "inmate" ascends (Clemmer, 1940; Schmid & Jones, 1991). These identities may be manifold (i.e., employee, friend, husband) and can be strong or weak. The importance of a particular identity relative to a person's self-concept can be thought of in two ways: as "identity salience" or "identity prominence" (Stryker, 1968). The more *salient* a particular identity, the more constant behaviors attached to the identity are enacted across time and situations (Thoits, 1991). Salient identities are adopted readily in diverse situations; nonsalient identities are deployed in very few situations (Nuttbrock & Freudiger, 1991). Identity prominence refers to the "feeling strength" of an identity. Here, identities are ranked with regard to the feeling or emotion associated with them (Stryker, 1980). Further, difficulties or interruptions in a role identity will cause distress to the extent an individual is invested in the identity, since "ongoing problems threaten a valued aspect of self" (Simon, 1992, p. 26). As the inmate identity gains salience, it seems that the fatherhood identity decreases in salience (Dyer, Wardle, & Day, 2004). That is, because of the constraints of the prison environment, there are few opportunities to invoke the fathering identity and multiple opportunities to invoke the inmate identity within the context of confinement. Research seems to support this point—fathers may sever ties with their children (Nurse, 2002), downplay their responsibilities to their children (Clarke et al., 2005), or go through a dormant phase (Arditti et al., 2005), all of which suggest a lack of salience. In Merle's case, we can clearly see how the absence of opportunities to father after incarceration, particularly in contrast to who Merle was as a father prior to confinement, has contributed to his withdrawal and view of himself as no longer having a child.

The inmate identity that results from prisonization is one kind of survival strategy in navigating the world of prison. The development of an inmate identity has been theorized as a means to cope with the deprivations and pains of imprisonment (Sykes, 1958). Inmate identities are composed of criminal thinking and ideation, and acceptance of the negative interpersonal consequences of crime (Walters, 2003). Prisonization and the transformed identity that results have bearing on fatherhood and also undermine social reintegration upon release (Walters, 2003). For example, Charles Terry (2003), a convict scholar (i.e., a former prisoner who now studies criminology) who explores the intersection of addiction and prisonization, reflects on how his inmate identity overshadowed his self-concept and contributed to his recidivism: "My perspective had become a reflection of the overregulated, upside-down, violence-prone, hypermasculine, and extraordinarily routinized lifestyle common to such institutions. Much of what I believed, including my conceptions of self, others, good versus bad, and right versus wrong, mirrored the norms and values of that peculiar setting" (p. 3).

Inmate identities are rooted in cultural ideals that equate economic capacity as a core attribute of masculinity (Whitehead, Peterson, & Kaljee, 1994). In contexts of limited opportunity, racism, and economic inequality, African American men in particular may formulate a "hustler identity" as a consequence of employment and economic difficulties. Hustling is a complex identity of money-making activities that include a willingness to work long hours, hold multiple jobs, take risks to yield maximum profits, and take advantage of whatever economic opportunities are available even if they are illegal (Whitehead et al., 1994). The hustler identity gives a man respectability and solidifies his masculinity. It signifies his status and ability to provide for his family (Whitehead et al., 1994), which are essential components of what it means to "be a man" (Arditti & Parkman, 2011). The formulation of a "hustler" identity on the outside, indicative of a man's social status on the streets, may also be transferred to some extent in the prison setting relative to garnering resources and contraband during confinement. That is, hustling while in prison can potentially give a man dominance because he possesses more valued objects than other inmates (Austin & Bates, 1974).

In addition to the influence of any criminal or "hustler" identity predating incarceration, it is also theorized that imprisonment itself challenges a man's masculine identity and that imprisoned men may cope by exuding an exaggerated masculinity (Phillips, 2001). A heightened display of masculinity may serve a protective function so that the inmate appears "tough" to peers, thus minimizing the potential of victimization; however, this inmate identity, perhaps useful in surviving prison, is antithetical to the father identity. Inmate identities are a result of isolation from society and family and necessitate some distancing from outside ties. For example, Tripp (2009) describes how several fathers participating in his qualitative study seemed to cope with jail by "accepting one's position as an inmate, and acknowledging one's separation from…connections and relationships 'out there'" (p. 41).

While identity salience theory suggests the invocation of inmate identities over fatherhood identities, it is less clear to what extent fathering identities are, or remain, prominent for incarcerated men with children. Evidence suggests that father identities may be somewhat dormant during incarceration, but they do not necessarily disappear. Rather, fathering identities alter. For some men, a "prisonized" paternal identity emerges and gains prominence (Arditti et al., 2005; Dyer et al., 2004). This prisonized identity is characterized by feelings of distress, helplessness, and a profound lack of control (Arditti et al., 2005). The alteration in identity is involuntary, in that incarceration involves stripping a man of his fathering identity. Consider this excerpt from one of the participants in our study of incarcerated fatherhood (Arditti et al., 2005), separated from his wife at the time of the interview. He is clearly upset as he shares this story with the interviewer: "Her [his daughter's] mom makes reference to me as 'Rusty' when it comes to her and…I don't appreciate that. Anytime my daughter's with me, she'll call me Daddy. But when she's with her mom, she'll call me Rusty" (p. 276). For many incarcerated men, prison means going from "Daddy" to "Rusty," shifting to the margin of the family, and accepting an ambiguous role without definition.

This shift seems to invoke strong emotions suggestive of a *prominent*, albeit prisonized, paternal identity.

Indeed, many male inmates express concerns and fears about their ability to return to family roles outside of prison walls (Nurse, 2002; Schmid & Jones, 1991; Tripp, 2009). Incarcerated fathers seem particularly likely to doubt their parenting competence (Houck & Loper, 2002). Men's description of incarcerated fatherhood largely centers on their helplessness, regrets, and difficulties of being a "good father" (Arditti et al., 2005). One father serving a stint for an assault conviction comments, "[I regret] not being a good father while in prison. I'm not really helping at all." Another father who had already served several years time reflects: "I know that it really doesn't count behind four walls to make an attempt to be a father to someone. I don't think that's a father, I think that's a cowardly move" (Arditti et al., 2005, p. 275).

Imprisonment and "Responsible Fathering"
Defining oneself as a "bad" father or, as in the previous case, as a "coward" occurs not only as a result of any tension that might arise between conflicting father and inmate identities per Tripp (2009) but also in relation to cultural images and prescriptions of what constitutes a "good" father" (Day et al., 2005). The vision of the good father is composed of cultural ideals such that fathers should be active, involved, and responsive in the care of their children (Lamb, 2000). Specifically, a consensus is emerging that good fathers are *responsible* fathers, implying a moral benchmark of evaluating a father's behavior, suggesting that some fathering behavior can be judged as "irresponsible." From this perspective, responsible fathering means establishing paternity, being present in the child's life (even if divorced or unmarried), sharing economic support, and being personally involved in the child's life in collaboration with the mother (Doherty, Kouneski, & Erickson, 1998).

A hallmark of a responsible fathering framework involves the primacy of children's needs and fathers' moral obligations to provide financial, emotional, and physical care for their children, all of which are seriously or completely curtailed by imprisonment. Additionally, some men go to prison only to miss the birth of their child, posing a great challenge to responsible fathering. Responsible fathering is a referent by which many men define their experience of incarcerated fatherhood. The crux of this internalized referent is that good fathers are at the very least available and present in their children's lives. For example, this 42-year-old incarcerated father equates his absence with child neglect: "To me, it is obvious it is neglect because I'm not there. I am not available to my children." He likens his confinement to abandoning his daughter: "I'm locked away and can't be there for her" (Arditti et al., 2005, p. 276). Another dad in prison expresses a similar sentiment in discussing the changes that incarceration brought to his previously close relationship with his daughter: "In the beginning we were close—all the way up until the age of eight or nine...but after...getting myself in trouble [going back and forth to prison] I guess she kind of gave up on me....*I am not a bad dad*—they tell me they love me and everything, but it is just that I am not always there for them when they really need me around" (Edin et al., 2001, p. 12, emphasis added). Thematically, men seem all too aware of the implications of "not being there" for children as illustrated by one father's lament: "I am not there all the time.... though I want to be and it hurts me and it upsets me....I missed all that time with R (his son) when he was an infant. He was born...last year and he didn't know who I was" (Edin et al., 2001, p. 13).

It is likely that many fathers are contributors in their children's lives prior to their incarceration (Hairston, 1998). However, research examining the nature of fathering prior to imprisonment is scarce. Lattimore et al. (2009) found that half the fathers in their sample of nearly 1,700 parolees reported that they had primary care responsibilities for the 6 months prior to their incarceration. My own reimmersion in a data set assessing imprisoned fathers in Utah (Day, Acock, Arditti, & Bahr, 2001) suggests that approximately half of the 51 participants reported close relationships with their children before and during imprisonment. Further, fathers reported spending considerable time with their children prior to imprisonment, and that time was linked with perceptions of being a "good father" before and during imprisonment. Incarcerated men tend to father children in multiple relationships; for example, fragile family data suggest that more than 60% of the men in the sample who reported multipartner fertility had also served time in jail (Logan, Manlove, Ikramullah, & Cottingham, 2006). This trend suggests a complex pattern of residence, parenting, and father involvement for men with incarceration histories.

Fathers with children in multiple households are spread thin; previous work on nonresident low-income fathers indicates men who form new families may have less involvement and paternal investment with children from earlier relationships (see Furstenberg & Cherlin, 1991; Carlson & Furstenberg, 2006; Manning & Smock, 1999). Father-child ties are especially fragile in families impacted by incarceration that may experience lengthy periods of paternal absence. In a rare study that considers these issues and how they bear on parenting, Modecki and Wilson (2009) interviewed 50 incarcerated African American fathers in custody (in jail) in central and northern Virginia. Using a series of vignettes to assess men's parenting practices revealed several interesting findings. Lower education, longer time served, and having children from multiple mothers were all associated with preferences for more restrictive and less responsive parenting practices.

Research pertaining to incarcerated men's parenting practices and upbringing (i.e., Chipman et al., 2000; Modecki & Wilson, 2009) suggests several possibilities with regard to incarcerated fathers. First, one can cautiously infer that incarcerated men received authoritarian parenting in their families of origin and reproduce these parenting strategies with their own children (this deduction is based on their preferences for restrictive parenting in the vignettes). Second, men with a history of incarceration may pose an additional risk to children to the extent that they will enact restrictive discipline, and this restrictive discipline is a negative force on the family. This final point is debatable given research that suggests that harsh discipline characteristic of low-income parents can also be viewed as adaptive—particularly in dangerous neighborhoods where children's obedience may be necessary for their survival (Russell, Mize, & Bissaker, 2002). Some insight regarding the nature of father-child relationships before arrest and imprisonment is provided by a study of fatherhood and incarceration drawn from repeated in-depth interviews with 90 low-income noncustodial fathers with a history of incarceration or some form of involvement with the criminal justice system (e.g., arrest only; Edin et al., 2001). A portion of these men, labeled the "severed ties group," maintained contact with their children prior to arrest. They had established a bond with at least one of their children, which involved either residence or a pattern of regular visitation and financial support.

Incarceration also presents a significant obstacle in men's provision of financial support through informal agreements with children's mothers. Informal agreements include in-kind assistance such as child care, cash, or goods to the family outside the purview of legal regulations and the courts. Many low-income fathers prefer to offer in-kind support directly to mothers and children (Waller & Plotnick, 1999). For many families, these informal agreements would have been made if men had not been confined (Swisher & Waller, 2008). For example, caregivers reported that their children's fathers had provided financial support and/or child care to their children prior to incarceration, regardless of legal marital status (Arditti et al., 2005). Thus there is some evidence of "responsible fathering" (in terms of financial provision and time spent with children) among populations of men with criminal justice involvement prior to arrest. As for Charlie and Merle, for these men who were involved in their children's lives, incarceration "proved devastating to their ties with their children and children's mothers" (Edin et al., 2001, p. 10). Indeed, reinspection of a data set drawn from incarcerated fathers in Utah and Oregon (Day et al., 2001) reveals a similar theme: men who consider themselves "good fathers" are more likely to view incarceration as creating problems for their families than are men whose fathering identity is less positive. Further, incarceration generally means that fathers will miss out on key events and milestones in their children's lives, such as when Charlie was unable to attend his daughter's high school graduation. Involvement in everyday and milestone events serves to preserve parental bonds and signals to others that men intend to engage in responsible fathering (i.e., support the child emotionally and financially). "Missing out" weakens men's commitment to their children, and "father" becomes a shadow identity—taking a backseat to other more salient identities and roles enacted in prison.

In sum, qualitative studies reveal what men say about fatherhood. "It's hard to be a father in here" seems to be the predominant sentiment of incarcerated men (Arditti et al., 2005; Roy & Dyson, 2005). By and large, the core experience of incarcerated fatherhood is helplessness stemming from men's inability to carry out fathering functions they recall engaging in prior to their imprisonment (Arditti et al., 2005). Men's distress concerning how they see themselves as "bad fathers" suggests that fathering is still prominent (i.e., evokes a strong feeling state), but it may become less so as time elapses and ties between fathers and family members weaken.

Fathering and "Possible Selves"
Fathering identity is shaped by men's sense of failing their children and family members and their eroding investment in fatherhood. Past, present, and future also have an impact on how fathers see themselves: "Fathering only made sense relative to what a man used to be or do, or more commonly *what he hoped to be upon release*" (Arditti et al., 2005, p. 277, emphasis added). For many men, "doing time" is just that, and attention is directed toward what one hopes for in the future. Identity processes demonstrate that incarcerated fathers formulate identities based on cultural norms about responsible fathering, as well as who they were as fathers before incarceration. One is only a "bad father" insomuch as one considered himself a "good father" prior to imprisonment.

Some evidence suggests that incarcerated fathers tend to hold a futuristic orientation about fathering as well as their father referent from the past. That is, central to incarcerated fatherhood are men's expectations and images of reunification with their children upon their release. The importance of these expectations and aspirations for the future can be seen in a "possible selves" theoretical framework applied to the study of incarcerated men (Meek, 2007). Possible selves are "positive and negative images of the self already in a future state" (Oyserman, Brickman, & Rhodes, 2007, p. 479). These future representations are based on an evaluation of traits, abilities, and circumstances derived from representations of the self in the past and present (Meek, 2007). The notion of a possible self describes the incorporation of future goals into the self-concept (Markus & Nurius, 1986) and is helpful in thinking about the impact of incarceration on fathering. Roy is a 31-year-old father with seven children who is serving time. He articulates his possible self: "I really want to be there for my kids and help out as much as possible, and I'm willing to make the sacrifices necessary to be there for them as much as I can. Whatever hoops I got to jump through I'm willing to jump them" (Arditti et al., 2005, p. 277). Another father, Jason, expresses similar hopes, saying that upon release he wants to be "the best father...I can be....I can't wait to get back out and spend more time with them" (p. 278). Similarly, Meek (2007) found that a hoped-for "good dad" self was a central element of men's goal for the future.

Some scholars (e.g., Day, Acock, et al., 2005) have suggested that fathers, particularly those awaiting release, have unrealistic expectations about their relationships with their children and may find themselves disappointed in their attempts to realize their "good dad" self. Qualitative research suggests that fathers may idealize their relationships with their children and "spend time in prison building up expectations for their own behavior after they are released" (Nurse, 2002, p. 85). Men may then share these hopes with their children and with their children's mothers. This futuristic, possible self of a dedicated "family man" can become a burden after release as men face the "weight of unmet promises" made to children and their children's mothers (Nurse, 2002, p. 84).

Father Involvement

The nature of father involvement behind walls is highly constrained and limited to what is experienced during visits or via letters and phone calls (Arditti et al., 2005; Nurse, 2002). In a qualitative analysis of incarcerated fatherhood, my colleagues and I (Arditti et al., 2005) found little evidence that fathers had opportunities to display affectional or behavioral aspects of involvement. Men in this study provided thick description regarding their inability to have contact with their family member or to help their family, and being "out of the loop" with regard to knowing what was going on with their children. In describing their lack of involvement with their children, emphasis seems to be placed on men's lack of capacity to carry out fathering functions such as protection, support, guidance, and discipline. These functions are seen as essential elements of how one enacts the fathering role (Arditti et al., 2005). Another father in the study did what he could to stay involved while in prison but judged these efforts as inadequate: "When I came to prison I started writing, sending handkerchiefs, beanies, socks…and it's like, this doesn't pay the bills" (p. 279). Frustration regarding men's inability to discipline was a focal point in this study. For example, an incarcerated father of four told interviewers: "They [his children] get a lot of emotional support from me, that kind of stuff, but as far as parenting goes, I don't play that role; I don't discipline them.…I'm incarcerated" (p. 278).

As we see in Charlie's and Merle's cases, the lack of physical "face-to-face" contact with children is an important contributor for fathers' inability to stay involved with their families and feel close to their children. For example, correlational analyses suggest that incarcerated men who received more frequent visits reported feeling close to and appreciated by their children (Day et al., 2001). However, some fathers report *not* wanting to see their children while in prison because it makes it harder to "do the time" (Edin et al., 2001), they feel ashamed to be so "down and out" (Arditti et al., 2005; Edin et al., 2001), or they recognize the difficulties visitation causes their children (Arditti et al., 2005). Some fathers willingly cut off contact with family from the outside (Arditti, 2005; Edin et al., 2001) because it "makes your time hard…worrying about what's going on out there" (Edin et al., 2001, p. 15). Several men also viewed cutting off visits as evidence of their care for children. That is, some fathers worry that contact will negatively impact their children because of the visitation conditions themselves or the behaviors that fathers engaged in that brought them to prison in the first place. For example, drug use was an issue for a father who was uninvolved with his son prior to incarceration and who had no contact with him during his 5-year confinement: "I haven't seen him since he was five years old. I know where he goes to school; I know where he lives. But it's because I'm using drugs—or I was using drugs—it was better for me to stay away. It wouldn't have been fair to him" (Arditti et al., 2005, p. 279).

Jerome's Story: Opportunity as a Context for Father Involvement[3]

As with mothers, institutional practices seem critical in fostering parental involvement as well as fathering identity. As we have discussed, contextual factors enable or constrain the unfolding of processes linked to one's ability to parent. The empirical literature highlights the highly constrained nature of most prison visitation environments as well as the challenges parents have staying connected to their families and children. Jerome's story provides a rare counterview:

> I've been locked up since before my son Jehar was born. After two years, by following hundreds of rules, I got to go on "family reunion visits" with my wife. We could spend a whole weekend together alone. When I found out my wife was pregnant, I was happy but nervous about being a father from prison. But Jehar is a true blessing. He brightens my days. Now he is 7...he is a really nice child. (Green, 2008, p. 8)

On the one hand, Jerome's positive outlook and involvement with his son, Jehar, has a lot to do with his ability to overcome his tough childhood and construct a fathering role that he can feel good about. Jerome explains:

> Even though I'm locked up, I'm trying to give Jehar what I didn't have as a child—a dad in my life....I needed someone to show me love and affection. Instead I received the opposite. I feel sure about myself as a father, because I know I'll never do what was done to me as a child. I know beating is not the answer....I treat my son like a...prince. I tell him he's very smart, loved, and blessed. I encourage him to do his best. My son seems confident in his actions. (Green, 2008, p. 9)

What else distinguishes Jerome's story from more common fathering scenarios such as Merle's or Charlie's cases? One factor clearly involves the family visitation practices at the state institution where Jerome is confined. Jerome describes the opportunities offered at the prison where he is serving time:

> Twice a year we have weekend visits, staying together as a family [with his wife and son] in a trailer. It feels good to be a full-time parent for 40 hours. My son and I play outside...we bake cakes and cook a decent meal. I get to

see Jehar sleep....I make him hot tea. I spoil him but I also discipline him while we're together.

In warm weather, the prison holds picnics and families come and spend a nice day. There's gifts, games, decent food, dance contests. It's a day when Jehar and I can run around and have a ball. (Green, 2008, p. 9)

While the parting is bittersweet, Jerome's ability to engage in day-to-day fathering functions such as caregiving, affection, discipline, and play provides continuity and a strong foundation for his relationship with his son. Without these opportunities, most fathers end up like Charlie and Merle. Jerome's institution is unusual given its liberal family visitation practices, which clearly serve as a "protective factor" and reduce the risk of father-child disengagement, an all too common outcome for incarcerated fathers.

Pivotal Challenges: Coparenting and Relational Conflict

We have seen how institutional practices and fathering identities are critical factors shaping men's fathering in prison. Perhaps one of the most important family processes determining whether fathers will remain engaged in their children's lives involves their coparenting relationships with the children's mothers. Coparenting has generally been defined as how a mother and father support or undermine each other in their parenting roles (Maccoby & Mnookin, 1990). As we have seen, it typically is conceptualized and studied in contexts of father nonresidence such as divorce. In the divorce literature, coparenting is an important process because it bears on men's involvement with their children (Ihinger-Tallman, Paisley, & Beuhler, 1993), with more cooperative relationships linked to nonresident fathers having more frequent contact with their children (Sobolewski & King, 2005). Recent findings from the Fragile Families data set indicate that parents' ability to work together in rearing their children across households has been found to keep even the most vulnerable, unmarried nonresident fathers connected to their children (Carlson, McLanahan, & Brooks-Gunn, 2008).

Coparenting is also seen as an important process that directly influences paternal identity (Rane & McBride, 2000) and may even moderate the influence of paternal identity on involvement (Ihinger-Tallman et al., 1993). Despite the lack of research that examines how coparenting bears on incarcerated fatherhood and father involvement during confinement, theoretically it makes sense that these processes will impact imprisoned men and their families. Of particular interest is the fact that fathers are influenced heavily by the views and attitudes of their partners or—in the case of imprisonment—the mother(s) of their children. Mothers seem to powerfully influence a man's fathering identity and how competent he sees himself to be, and to ultimately shape the nature of his involvement with his children (McBride et al., 2005). A rare confirmation that this theoretical premise likely holds for imprisoned fathers comes from my reanalysis of prison data: those incarcerated men who saw themselves as "good fathers" also reported friendlier and more cooperative relationships with their children's mothers than men who viewed their competence as fathers more negatively (Day et al., 2001).

Coparenting in contexts of nonresidence is challenging. Even in situations of nonresidence that do not involve imprisonment, many parents find it difficult to engage in cooperative coparenting after separation (Sobolewski & King, 2005). Coparenting necessitates the redefinition of power boundaries in the family. The crux of such change in situations of divorce involves parents, mostly fathers (as a result of nonresidence), needing to accept the loss of control over aspects of their children's lives (Emery, 1994). Evidence suggests that renegotiating relationships after separation or divorce is not an easy task; relationships between men and their ex-wives are often hostile and antagonistic (Arditti & Allen, 1993; Arendell, 1995). Incarceration obviously equates with men's loss of control over the care and upbringing of their children. Given the involuntary nature of incarceration on the part of the offender, this loss of control seems to be hard for fathers to accept—and possibly more difficult than in other contexts of nonresidence. This greater difficulty stems from men's complete and total reliance on the mother of their children to facilitate contact. The redefinition of power in contexts of father nonresidence due to prison puts control singularly in the hands of children's caregivers, who more often than not are their mothers. Men's ties with the women with whom they share children are uncertain and fragile (Brodsky, 1975; Roy & Dyson, 2005). Incarcerated fathers are all too aware that in most cases, unless a relative steps in, mothers hold all the cards with respect to their involvement with their children. Jerome's ability to stay connected to his wife through weekend family visits is both unusual and yet critical in maintaining their intimate union. Family visits provide a forum through which Jerome and his wife can cooperate and parent Jehar together. In the absence of these kinds of opportunities, intimacy between fathers and their children's mothers tend to wane, and coparenting is not an option.

Maternal Gatekeeping

The quality of coparenting intimate relationships is particularly important for incarcerated fathers due to the female partner's *gatekeeping* function relative to children. Intimate partners who also have responsibility for the care of children (generally the mother of at least one of the children) usually unilaterally control the offender's access to his or her children (Arditti et al., 2005; Edin et al., 2001; Roy & Dyson, 2005). The idea that mothers control fathers' involvement is referred to as "maternal gatekeeping," which has been defined as mothers' general reluctance to relinquish family responsibility, their rigid and differentiated conceptions of family roles, and their desire to validate their own parenting identity as more important than that of fathers (Allen & Hawkins, 1999). Researchers often look to maternal characteristics to explain gatekeeping. For example, low levels of trust, high levels of hostility toward the father, and mothers' dissatisfaction with men's fathering suggest pronounced gatekeeping and lower levels of father involvement (McBride et al., 2005; Parke, 2002).

The context and consequences of men's imprisonment provide fertile ground for conditions conducive to maternal gatekeeping. Intimate relationships tend to break down as a result of imprisonment, with low levels of trust, estrangement, and disappointment characterizing such relationships. One father in Edin et al.'s (2001) study, Mark, talks about the lack of trust between him and his daughter's mother:

> We was going to get back together: marriage and everything. But she wasn't totally honest….she kept trying to creep around…I suspected it [the mother's clandestine relationship] so I did find out and she still denied it and from that point there it was just like a thing, "I can't never trust you now."…
> If I wouldn't have got locked up…it would have never happened. (p. 16)

Family scientists Kevin Roy and Omar Dyson (2005) also found that for the incarcerated fathers in their qualitative study, most intimate relationships moved through cycles of hope and distrust over time.

Gatekeeping in the prison context has been characterized as the "babymama drama." Roy and Dyson (2002) explain: "Babymama drama was a process of negotiation of men's roles as fathers. It reflected a risky balance of conflict and support between incarcerated fathers and their former or current partners" (p. 296). One father in the study talks about his "babymama drama" that involved his partner's betrayal: "I had the feeling that she [was cheating on me while I was in] prison. I kept asking, and she didn't tell me. I kept writing . . . and didn't get no more letters. You know when you're in a relationship and they're lying. I thought, 'Why in the hell am I doing this?'" (p. 300). The loss of a trusting connection with his children's mother dashed this father's hope of reconnecting with his children.

The Least Angry Mother

In several qualitative studies, fathers have reported feeling that their children's mothers discouraged their involvement with their children and would not facilitate contact due to deteriorating family ties, confusing and conflictual intimate relationships, and an absence of commitment on the part of men's intimate partners (Arditti et al., 2005; Edin et al., 2001; Roy & Dyson, 2005). The young incarcerated fathers in Anne Nurse's study (2002) also traced their success in maintaining ties with their children to the quality of their relationships with the nonincarcerated custodial mother. Nurse's (2002) description of the limits on father-child contact imposed by the California Youth Authority provides an interesting example of how context collides with coparenting processes and determines the level of contact young fathers might have with their children. Institutional practices and policies profoundly shape the extent of offender parents' contact with their children during imprisonment. In addition to the usual institutional culprits constraining parent-child contact (e.g., lack of transportation and resources for travel on the part of the family, being housed far from home), the fathers in Nurse's study (2002) had another constraint: they were only permitted to choose one girlfriend to put on their visitor's list.

> A man who has children by several women can list only one [visitor] in the "girlfriend" or "wife" category. Since mothers are the primary people bringing children to the institution, inmates must make a choice about which of their children they want to see. I asked one young man what he had done when faced with this choice. He told me that *he chose the mother who was least angry with him.* (p. 39, emphasis added)

The young father in the preceding example is intuitively aware that his chances of contact depend on a harmonious relationship with his child's mother. "The least angry mother" is the mother more willing to facilitate contact and less likely to "gatekeep."

The "one-girlfriend" rule is a problem on several levels. Most obviously, it keeps some men from seeing their children, because inmates are forced to make a choice about which children they want to see. Second, on the rare occasion that men can make changes to their visiting list, "switching women" may end up alienating more than one mother, with a man further risking the loss of contact with children. Finally, Nurse (2002) discovered that the one-girlfriend rule was a problem for men whose girlfriend was not mother of his children. Given the choice of seeing one's girlfriend or seeing one's child, few men can resist seeing their girlfriend. Inmates may try to arrange having a relative (such as their own mother or grandmother) bring the children, but again, this strategy is contingent on the mother's willingness to allow her child to visit the institution without her.

Consider, for example, the words of this father who, divorced from his child's mother, explains the reason he believes he could not see his son while in prison:

> If my son wants to visit me, and the majority of my family thinks it's a good idea, and I think it's a good idea, he tells me over the phone he wants to see me, but yet because his mother doesn't agree, basically there's no way he can come without her consent, so it can't be done....I believe it's a control issue. (Arditti et al., 2005, p. 282)

As illustrated by this father's account, regardless of who might be willing or available to bring the child to visit, mothers remain gatekeepers and may prohibit or discourage visitation for an array of reasons. Further, it is important to note that these reasons may go well beyond mothers' angry feelings, mistrust, or disappointment with the offender. Mothers' gatekeeping may stem from real concerns about the negative effects of the visitation experience on the child (Arditti, 2003; Arditti et al., 2005). Policies similar to the one-girlfriend rule are widespread in prisons and jails across the country given the typical limits imposed on the number and eligibility of visitors on an inmate's visitation list. One can see how such practices, coupled with the tenuous quality of the relationships between men and the mother(s) of their children, would serve to diminish father-child contact—contact deemed critical in maintaining family ties.

Mothers' New Relationships

Further complicating matters for fathers is the great likelihood that the mother(s) of their children may form new romantic relationships (Edin et al., 2001; Nurse, 2002). Fathers are discouraged by their children's mothers' new partners who were perceived as threatening or undermining men's status as parents (Nurse, 2002; Roy & Dyson, 2005). Interviews with paroled fathers suggested that new partners for either the mother or the father could determine a man's involvement with his children (Nurse, 2002). Jealousies and tensions often characterize these relationships: fathers may not get along with boyfriends, and mothers may actively discourage their involvement. Fathers may also withdraw from their children as a result of guilt or shame that another man has become central in their children's lives because they themselves were unavailable during confinement. Hostility between the mother and a father's new girlfriend can also serve to discourage father involvement during confinement and beyond.

Sometimes, as in Merle's case, mothers' new relationships are also coupled with children having to physically relocate (Roy & Dyson, 2005). My colleagues and I noted several instances of relocation in which fathers did not know where their children were or how to contact them. Jimmy was confined in Oregon for 40 months, 180 miles from his son and twin girls. He explained: "I've only seen them [the twins] once…because their Mom took off with some dude" (Arditti et al., 2005, p. 280).

These new relationships create fear and distress for the father during confinement, some of which may be well-founded in situations in which children are being abused. Indeed, recent research has demonstrated the degree to which father surrogates, such as a mother's boyfriend in the home, increase the risk of child maltreatment (Radhakrishna, Bou-Saada, Hunter, Catellier, & Kotch, 2001). Incarcerated fathers are helpless to enact protector roles and are unable to shield their children from perceived or real harm that might befall them at the hands of mothers' new partners. Fathers' reports of children witnessing violence between the mother and her new partner, or their child being victimized by the new partner, are not uncommon in qualitative studies (Arditti et al., 2005; Roy & Dyson, 2005). This father in my study told the interviewer that he believed that a boyfriend was abusing his daughter: "I would never let somebody harm my daughter if I was out there.…But, you know, there ain't nothing I can do now" (Arditti et al., 2005, p. 279).

In sum, while the empirical evidence in qualitative studies is remarkably consistent in terms of the difficulties imprisoned men have in terms of verifying a healthy fathering identity, enacting fathering behaviors, and maintaining ties with their children, there is also evidence of men's efforts to "father behind bars." These efforts are largely symbolic and implemented through letter writing and phone calls. These forms of contact are a means to demonstrate care for children and emotionally support the mothers of their children. Most men have a sense that their imprisonment has been hard on the mothers (Edin et al., 2001) and may attempt to coparent or discipline by phone, exhorting children to "listen to their mother" (Arditti et al., 2005). It should also be noted that there are cases in which mothers are extremely loyal to their incarcerated partners and make extraordinary efforts to facilitate their children's contact through in-person visits, the provision of financial resources for phone calls, and symbolic efforts to keep the fathers' memory alive in the home (Arditti et al., 2005; Comfort, 2008; Roy & Dyson, 2005).

Implications of Father-Child Ties for Reentry

The most recent BOJ report estimates that 735,000 prisoners were released in 2008 (West et al., 2009). The great majority of these prisoners are men who will return to their communities and families. Unfortunately, many of these same men will return to prison. For example, in a study of 15 states, two-thirds of state prisoners were rearrested and more than half went back to prison within 3 years of release (Langan & Levin, 2002). Parole violators accounted for approximately one-third of prison admissions in 2008 (West et al., 2009). Decades of research on prisoner reentry has documented the multiple challenges associated with reentry. Primary among them are finding housing and employment and complying with the requirements of one's probation or parole (Petersilia, 2003; Travis, 2005). Men's histories of disadvantage and the stigma attached to having served prison time contribute to the difficulties ex-offenders have in making it on the "outside."

In general, men's family life is of interest largely because of its purported link with crime desistance, which is the termination of criminal offending or "going straight" (Travis, 2005, p. 266). There is general support for the link between parenthood and desistance. For example, married men who reside with their wives and children after release tend to have a more successful transition (Visher & Travis, 2003). Further, men with large, close family networks also seem better able to desist from crime than parolees with fewer bonds (Bahr, Armstrong, Gibbs, Harris, & Fisher, 2005).

Central to the desistance process is the establishment of a "new identity" whereby the offender sheds his or her identity as a law violator and embraces a "civic identity" characterized by law-abiding behavior and positive social ties. One can see how fatherhood is an important, albeit understudied, context for men to reconstruct their identities. The availability of fathering opportunities after release is likely critical in establishing prosocial identities after confinement. How do men with prisonized identities make this transformation? Is it possible to shift back from the margins of fatherhood? For men with continued ties with children and the mothers of these children, the journey in renegotiating a fathering role is certainly easier (Edin et al., 2001). Unfortunately, there is not much in the research that speaks specifically to how men make fathering transitions and the extent to which father-child relationships foster desistance and successful reentry. In a broad sense, reentering offenders employ a process called a "redemptive script" (Maruna, 2001), and this process is viewed as central to desistance. The script involves reconceptualizing oneself, basically rewriting history, and coming up with a new narrative, a clean view of oneself, based on what one hopes to become. Self-change must occur first, and this is an internal, cognitive process (Paternoster & Bushway, 2009). Making a willful decision to break with the past and all it entails (criminal activity, "wild peers") is critical and foundational to subsequent shifts in identity and preferences for the offender. Only then can the offender father work toward something "positive in the future and steering away from something feared" (i.e., reincarceration; Paternoster & Bushway, 2009, para. 7). A "possible self" that is rooted in responsible fatherhood can be an important blueprint not only for desistance but also for reestablishing, or perhaps establishing for the first time, father-child bonds after confinement.

Given the incapacitation that is synonymous with prison, and the sense of powerlessness that is a hallmark of prisonized paternal identities, living the redemptive script one may create for oneself with respect to fathering is daunting. For example, men's lack of self-esteem and personal power in prison can translate into efforts to control family upon release (see Travis, McBride, & Solomon, 2005). These control efforts can result in conflictual and even violent relationships with intimate partners (e.g., Hairston & Oliver, 2006) and likely limit fathering opportunities or, certainly, undermine the quality of father-child relationships. It is unknown what the exertion of control or authority, stemming from prisonization, might mean for men's relationships with their children. For example, men's expectations concerning how children should behave and respond to them as parents may collide with reality (Nesmith & Ruhland, 2008). Coupled with men's histories of authoritarian parenting (Chipman et al., 2000) and hypermasculine inmate identities established during prison, many reentering fathers may lack the tools and knowledge to construct a functional fathering self.

Despite the potential problems that may arise from a father's disempowerment, central to the ex-offender's redemptive script is a rethinking of who he wants to be as a father after release. Thus barring contraindications such as family violence and child maltreatment, it seems especially important for men to have opportunities to father after release to establish and verify paternal scripts. Men's relationships with their children become part of the new story for a man in terms of his crime-free identity, and it would make sense that vital father-child relationships serve to anchor a commitment to desist from crime. A father will be more successful in self-change if he has a specific and realistic strategy both to reach that goal and to avoid the kind of person he does not want to become (Paternoster & Bushway, 2009). For some fathers, the fear of incarceration, in conjunction with active fathering opportunities, acts as a powerful deterrent to criminal activity and may actually "reverse" a father's criminal career trajectory and bring him back into the formal economy (Edin et al., 2001). One father (in Edin et al.'s study) who lived with his youngest child and his child's mother contributed financially to the household from his earnings at a low-wage job. His comments illustrate how a father identity can anchor desistance: "Without the kids I'd probably be a dog. [Being a father] has stopped me from doing something real stupid" (Edin et al., 2001, p. 28).

Another dad from Edin's study, when asked if he would consider selling drugs again, demonstrates how having children is pivotal to his ability to steer away from criminal activity:

[No], I want to *keep it clean* and that is the hardest thing. I could do that and probably make three times over [what I'm making now]. But I don't think that it would make me a better person....I would be bringing an environment around my child that I just do not want. (Edin et al., 2001, p. 28, emphasis added)

An analysis of 51 parolees (the majority of whom were men) provides further support for the notion that father-child relationships link to desistance (Bahr et al., 2005). While being a parent was not related to parole success, success was related to the quality of parent-child relationships. The authors conclude that "maintaining and developing parent-child bonds helped these paroles adjust to life outside of prison" (Bahr et al., 2005, p. 261). Thus it is not simply the act of fathering but also the quality of father-child ties that seem to matter with regard to desistance. Indeed, fathers who defined their relationships with children as "close" were more likely to consider their incarceration as problematic than were fathers who reported less involvement prior to their incarceration (Day et al., 2001).

Taken together, the evidence suggests that fatherhood, and more specifically active father involvement, makes incarceration more "costly" for men. One of the cornerstones of desistance theory is that the costlier incarceration is, that is, the more a person has to "give up," the more likely it is an offender will desist (e.g., Maruna, 2001; Sampson & Laub, 2003). We can predict that upon release, Jerome will have a better shot at successful reentry than either Merle or Charlie. Jerome's relationship with Jehar is a strong incentive to desist from crime. Indeed, as Jerome's story demonstrates, it is not just fatherhood in and of itself that gives men enough reason "to keep it clean"; rather, it is the *quality* of those relationships with children, the sense that one's presence and actions will *matter* to one's children, that may make the difference in terms of desistance.

Summary

Context and processes intertwine to shape incarcerated fatherhood as well as the nature of their involvement with their children during confinement. Jerome's, Merle's, and Charlie's stories illustrate how institutional practices constrain or enable fathering identities and men's engagement with their children and significant others. Because of their typically disadvantaged backgrounds, the lack of positive male role models in their own childhood, and the disconnection with family that comes with confinement, incarcerated fathers may lack a strong and positive fathering identity. How men see themselves as fathers is altered through prisonization and men's corresponding sense of helplessness and isolation. Men's sense of disempowerment, coupled with hustler "tough guy" inmate identities, runs counter to responsible fathering and functional family relationships. Empirical and anecdotal evidence suggests that children are important to many incarcerated fathers. Father-child relationships can anchor a desistance from crime after confinement and serve as the basis of a "new start" for men, based on a decision to break from the past and construct a new way of life. As we saw in Jerome's case, contact with children during prison as well as active fathering opportunities are critical in terms of developing and maintaining a positive, sustainable fathering identity. Jerome felt "sure about himself as a father," and this sense of confidence and empowerment can only come with the ability to engage in day-to-day fathering activities and cooperate with children's caregivers during confinement. As illustrated by Merle's and Charlie's situations, and exemplars from the empirical data, perhaps the greatest challenge for fathers in prison is dealing with conflictual and confusing intimate partner relationships. Cooperative coparenting relationships with children's mothers are critical in men's ability to access their children during prison and after their release.

5

The Effects of Incarceration on Families and Children

It is busy on the "Prison Talk"[1] website today. There are numerous postings by children with incarcerated fathers or mothers, parents with incarcerated children, husbands with incarcerated wives, women who share children with incarcerated men, and incarcerated parents themselves. Thousands and thousands of postings speak to the experience of the offender, as well as how incarceration affects those family members closest to the offender. To understand the implications of parental incarceration, one only has to read the stories of those who are most affected. Men, women, grandparents, and children all post on the various forums dedicated to supporting the families of those with an incarcerated loved one.

Shari is a young mother who solicits advice from the virtual support network regarding the stress associated with bringing her young son to visit his father in prison. Her 3-year-old son, Shane, born after his father went to prison, gets bored within 15 minutes of arriving. "There's nothing for him to do," Shari laments. Shane ends up getting "into trouble" with his dad and mother, who become irritated with him because they have no toys or distractions to offer Shane in the stark visiting room. The boy's father and Shari worry their visit will be terminated if Shane does not sit still and behave. Shari signs her post: "Holding it down since 1-16-2009."

Two young women who grew up with their fathers in prison discuss the importance of being honest about having a parent in prison:

Kim, now a psychology student in college, defines herself as a "reasonably secure person," despite the fact that she has had a father in prison since she was just a year old. Although Kim and her father have been through tough times, she remains very close to him. She credits her close relationship with her father to both of her parents and pays homage to her mother's honesty regarding the circumstances of her father's imprisonment. Kim respected the fact that her mother "took calls from my dad" and facilitated the relationship even when the parents were not speaking. Kim advises others: "No lies no matter what." In Kim's view, children are smarter than they are given credit for and deserve to be told the truth. Kim also cautions others not to use terms such as "locked down" or "in the hole" with children. She remembers hearing these terms herself as a child and imagining the worst: her father chained to a wall or inside a deep cavity within the prison. As a university student, Kim wants to help other children who have an incarcerated parent and has become a "Big Sister" for a local mentoring program.

Fifteen-year-old Zoe recalls the confusing experience of her father's arrest and what it was like to visit him in prison as a younger child. She remembers watching TV in the living room on the evening when the police came to her house, knocked the front door down, and took her father away. After a sleepless night, Zoe thought that if she wore a pretty dress and "looked cute," the police would let her daddy out of jail. The ensuing visits to the prison left her scared and confused because "everything was so gray and isolated." She would get particularly frightened when the prison guards spoke firmly to the other inmates. Zoe forgives her father for his drug dealing, but she shares that she "will never forget." She notices that even now, 8 years after her father's arrest, she is anxious around authority figures. She admits: "My chest hurts and my palms sweat" whenever the police come into her high school with the K-9 unit for routine locker checks.

Others, like Ron, seek advice from the online group on how to deal with their intimate relationships:

Ron's wife, Rene, is serving time for prescription drug fraud. He is working two jobs to try and make up for the loss of income that Rene used to earn as a nurse. Ron is raising the couple's two sons, aged 8 and 13, by himself. He pays child support for a third child from a previous union who does not reside with him. During the day, Ron works construction and then later, he does the night shift at a security firm. His mother, confined to a wheelchair, does her best to help with child care after school, but she often complains about her grandsons' "wild behavior" and her inability to control their whereabouts. When they are not with their grandmother, the children spend a lot of time alone, particularly late at night when Ron is working. It is not an ideal situation, and it is getting increasingly difficult to make ends meet. Ron worries about the effects of the boys "going without." For example, the boys cannot play soccer this year because Ron lacks the money to cover the cost of uniforms, shoes, and registration. Lately, Ron has been feeling stressed out because Rene keeps requesting more prison commissary funds.[2] The couple started with a set amount, but

Rene now complains it is not enough. He is trying to send more— Ron knows commissary is not cheap. Rene claims that she and her bunkies are trying to buy commissary food and avoid the "prison junk" as much as possible. But he worries that she is spending the money on other inmates. He is already sending her $75 a month. Prison commissary fees, along with Rene's legal bills and the gas and lodging costs associated with weekend visits to the women's prison, are taking their toll on the family's finances. Ron is having trouble providing for his growing sons' needs and recently has missed a month or two of child support. Working more is not an option. Rene is angry at Ron for "disrespecting her" by not sending more money, and lately their phone calls and visits have been conflictual. Ron asks the online group for advice regarding how he should handle the situation with Rene.

As we can see from the preceding case exemplars, there are profound emotional, social, and economic effects on the family members of the incarcerated. While much has been written on the effects of incarceration on children, consistent with a family perspective, in this chapter we can achieve a broader view by considering the entire family as the unit of analysis and focus on the contextual and processual pathways by which parental incarceration impacts families. Our purpose is not to reproduce a detailed review of child outcomes; there are several excellent pieces of scholarship examining consequences of incarceration with respect to child effects (e.g., Murray, 2005; Parke & Clarke-Stewart, 2001). Here, a family focus is not only mindful of child effects but also inclusive of the experience of caregivers charged with the responsibility of parenting the incarcerated person's children.

We can organize a discussion on families in the following manner:

- Distinguishing between primary and secondary effects
- Traumatic separation and ambiguous loss
- Family contact and communication processes
- Family strengths and resilience

In addition to a focus on the incarcerated parent, a holistic approach necessitates a consideration of how a parent's incarceration impacts the family members he or she leaves behind. With respect to the effects of parental incarceration on families, it is important to note that a substantial proportion of publications specifying these effects are in fact reviews or summaries, mostly with regard to the impact on children (e.g., Parke & Clarke-Stewart, 2001; Murray, 2005; Murray et al., 2009). While there is considerable overlap with regard to the information conveyed in various reviews about the effects of parental incarceration on families, new insights may be gleaned by reconsidering the primary empirical research within a context, process, outcome framework and looking to see what questions remain unanswered.

Critical Questions

Two critical questions emerge with regard to the effects of parental incarceration on families/children. The first is: *How much of the impact is due to changes associated with incarceration, rather than a result of incarceration itself?* Family effects resulting from the parent's incarceration itself can be thought of as *direct, or primary, effects.* Family effects resulting from the changes associated with incarceration, such as economic disadvantage or a lack of parenting stability, can be thought of as *indirect, or secondary, effects.* Both are important to consider with regard to child and family outcomes associated with incarceration.

Most studies are not designed to answer the question of indirect or direct effects. In other words, it is unclear whether parental incarceration is the cause of family problems or a "risk marker"—that is, a symptom of other family problems and social conditions. Longitudinal studies, which can potentially yield answers with regard to causality, are inadequate with respect to answering the preceding question because they generally rely on secondary data that contain little information about family or developmental processes (Murray et al., 2009; Poehlmann, Dallaire, Loper, & Shear, 2010). A secondary analysis of an Australian birth cohort study is a case in point regarding the difficulty researchers have in sorting out direct and indirect effects and the lack of good data over time (Kinner, Alati, Najman, & Williams, 2007). The findings of this study provided some evidence that dysfunction is unique to the children of prisoners. Most of the relationship between mothers' reports of paternal arrest and imprisonment and poor youth outcomes could be accounted for by risk and disadvantage markers such as socioeconomic status (SES), mothers' substance use, maternal anxiety and depression, and level of parental supervision (Kinner et al., 2007). However, even after controlling for these risk markers, paternal arrest was still associated with boys' externalizing behavior (i.e., supporting a direct effect from parental arrest to child outcome). Externalizing behaviors tend to be defined as overt and disruptive and can involve the violation of societal norms, the destruction of property, and harm toward others (Kell & Price, 2006). The study points both to the importance of cumulative disadvantage and maternal behavior in shaping child outcomes within the context of imprisonment and to the unique disruptive effects of parental arrest for boys. However, data limitations were significant. Analyses were based on only one-third of the original sample, thus underestimating the effects of father's imprisonment on youth outcomes. Further, the data did not provide important information about the nature, timing, and duration of paternal imprisonment as well as fathers' behavior in the home.

In addition to data inadequacies and difficulties sorting out effects, the unique impact of parental imprisonment on children is difficult to discern because family changes, particularly with regard to parenting, are embedded in context and tough to disentangle. That is, it is difficult to understand these processes apart from the setting in which they occur. With regard to understanding the effects of parental incarceration on children, Parke and Clarke-Stewart (2003) argue:

> Incarceration is not a single or discrete event, but a dynamic process that unfolds over time…[and] requires considering the short-term effect of the parent's arrest and the removal of the child from the parent, the impact of the parent's unavailability to the child during incarceration, and the effects…of reunion after the incarceration period. (p. 199)

Thus considering events preceding arrest and circumstances surrounding the incarceration is critical in thinking about the impact of parental incarceration on children. Subsequently, most findings pertaining to how parental incarceration, *in and of itself*, affects children and families are not definitive due to design or data inadequacies, or merely because the incarceration is embedded in a myriad of tangible and intangible experiences that create impact on children (Murray et al., 2009).

Perhaps a more manageable question is whether child effects are directly due to the *separation from/unavailability of* the incarcerated parent or more broadly to the phenomena of parental incarceration itself. Using retrospective data from the United Kingdom, Murray and Farrington (2008) attempt to address this question. Their analysis suggests that the loss of a parent as a result of incarceration appears to be distinct and more developmentally prohibitive for boys than other types of losses, giving credence to the argument that separation as a result of parental incarceration uniquely and negatively impacts children. Other studies of child effects resulting from parental incarceration provide additional support for this view. For example, based on an examination of young children in 3,000 urban families, not only did paternal incarceration have significant and damaging consequences for the socio-emotional well-being of children, but these effects were stronger than other forms of father absence (Geller, Cooper, Garfinkel, & Mincy, 2010).

Intriguing information about the source of child effects among families impacted by parental incarceration comes from the reports of 73 randomly selected inmates of a federal minimum-security prison (Fritsch & Burkhead, 1981). Incarcerated mothers and fathers were asked to describe the acting-out (i.e., externalizing) and acting-in (i.e., internalizing or inner-directed behaviors causing emotional distress) behavior of their children. Statistically significant associations between parental incarceration and child adjustment revealed that fathers were more likely to report having problems with children "acting out" and mothers were more likely to report children "acting in." However, these relationships only held provided that children were *aware* of their parent's incarceration. When children believed their parent to be away for some other and socially acceptable reason (e.g., being at school, working, in the hospital), these significant relationships disappear. The authors conclude that it is not the parental absence per se that results in behavior problems for children *but absence in conjunction with imprisonment.* On some level seeking to disentangle the effects of parental separation on children from the effects of incarceration is not as important as understanding that an array of variables determine how well children and nonincarcerated family members respond to the incarceration of a parent. This is good news because (1) it suggests a great deal of *plasticity* in that outcomes depend on the configuration of a wide range of factors, and (2) these "configurations," as well as the outcomes associated with them, can change over time as a function of human development.

A second critical question that emerges in the literature on parental incarceration is: *What types of protective and promotive factors improve outcomes for children with an incarcerated parent?* An age-specific resilience model of parental incarceration emphasizes factors that either protect (defined as moderators that have a positive effect under stressful conditions such as family prison visits) or promote (defined as factors that promote positive development under nonstressful conditions such as quality caregiving; Poehlmann & Eddy, 2010). The model is an important step in highlighting the possibility of diverse responses to adversity within the context of parental incarceration. Much of what we can infer about protective and promotive factors comes from other literatures and theorizing aimed at high-risk children who experience adversity such as poverty or parental substance abuse. Yet, an emerging basis for conceptualizing the role of resilience and family strengths is located, if not somewhat buried, in the literature on parental incarceration as well. A special effort must be made to reexamine that literature with an eye toward uncovering resilience processes.

Effects of Parental Incarceration on Children and Families

The available research has indicated the largely negative effects of incarceration on offender parents, children, and spouses or intimate partners such that family health declines, child adjustment is compromised, poverty intensifies, and family relationships deteriorate or cease altogether (Arditti et al., 2003; Carlson & Cervera, 1991; Geller et al., 2008; Johnson, 2009; Murray & Farrington, 2008; Osborne & McClanahan, 2007; Phillips et al., 2006; Trice & Brewster, 2004; Wilbur et al., 2007). A particular area of concern pertains to the connections between parental incarceration, mental health difficulties, and behavior and school problems in children. Joseph Murray and colleagues (2009) conducted a meta-analysis of 16 empirically rigorous studies investigating the effects of parental imprisonment during childhood (the studies examined both children of the incarcerated and imprisoned parents). Parental imprisonment was connected to poor mental health in children and a trend toward antisocial behavioral outcomes for children after parental imprisonment, even after controlling for covariates. Similar conclusions were yielded by a study of 3,540 children (in 2,348 different families) in 1997 (Johnson, 2009). Children who experienced parental incarceration at some point during childhood were more likely to exhibit externalizing problems (i.e., aggression, deviance, "acting out") and internalizing problems (i.e., intraindividual, psychological problems such as depression). Similarly, parental incarceration tends to undermine children's school success by contributing to dropout, absences, school failure, and disciplinary infractions (Hanlon, et al., 2005; Trice & Brewster, 2004).

Other risks predicting mental health and school outcomes in children include not only parental incarceration but also parental characteristics associated with incarceration such as parents' antisocial behavior and criminal history, as well as minority status. Johnson's (2009) analysis included measures of fathers' history of criminality and deviant behavior. Yet, even controlling for these factors, parental incarceration still predicted child behavior and school problems, giving credence to the argument that a parent's incarceration has direct impact on children. Further, parental incarceration was *not* associated with child behavior problems if confinement occurred prior to the birth of the child, suggesting the unique impacts incarceration has for families despite a priori conditions of cumulative disadvantage. And as we would expect given racial disparities in parental incarceration rates, black children are more widely affected by a parent's incarceration (Johnson, 2009).

While the data might be compelling, caution is still warranted in drawing firm causal conclusions about the impact of parental incarceration on families and in particular children. Most studies are systematically biased due to the challenges of studying justice-involved families. For example, many studies may overestimate the effects of parental imprisonment on children because they do not control for child behavior and parental criminality prior to incarceration (Murray et al., 2009). We can cautiously infer from the data that the emotional, social, and economic effects of parental imprisonment are unique from the separation itself or the disadvantage that accompanies incarceration (Arditti et al., 2003; Braman, 2004; Johnson, 2009; Murray, 2005; Murray & Farrington, 2008).

Children's Loss and Trauma

Trauma is perhaps one of the more visible and long-lasting primary effects of parental incarceration. With regard to children, it is generally seen as a result of parental separation due to arrest and/or incarceration.[3] Child trauma is of central importance because one can think of many behavior and mental health problems as stemming from the trauma associated with the arrest and imprisonment of a parent. Zoe's story at the beginning of the chapter illustrates a common trauma scenario for children with an incarcerated parent. Her case reveals how the sudden loss of her father, as well as her subsequent "scary" experiences during visitation in the prison setting, may underlie her anxiety around police officers and her sense of "not being able to forget."

An Unclear Loss

Social-psychological theories of loss and trauma emphasize that our greatest losses, such as the loss of a parent or spouse, become social losses—of interaction, companionship, love, and the "human touch" (Harvey, 2002, p. 4). The loss of a parent to incarceration can be thought of as an *ambiguous loss*, defined as an unclear loss in that a loved one is missing either physically or psychologically. Ambiguous loss results from situations of not knowing if a person is "dead or alive, absent or present, permanently lost or coming back" (Boss, 2004, p. 237). Ambiguous loss differs from ordinary loss in that there is no certainty that the person will come back or return to the way they "used to be." There are two types of ambiguous loss (Boss, 1999). In the first type, people are perceived by family members as physically absent but psychologically present. This type of loss is experienced by the family outside the prison setting, in that the incarcerated parent is not physically present but may be psychologically present in the home. Examples of psychological presence might be that the family still sets a place at the dinner table for the imprisoned parent, puts on the parent's favorite TV show every evening, or leaves the imprisoned parent's voice on a phone answering machine as if he or she is still there. In the second type of ambiguous loss, a person is perceived as physically present but psychologically absent—a potential experience one might have while visiting at a corrections setting or, arguably, upon the parent's reentry into family and community life. In other words, any family member, but particularly the offender, may be physically present but psychologically absent, or in Boss's (2004) words, "a different person" due to his or her own pain connected to imprisonment. Dissociation (i.e., going outside one's body), a common symptom of traumatic stress, is also indicative of the second type of ambiguous loss (physically present but psychologically absent).

The trouble with ambiguous loss is that it lacks resolution: "Typically [it is] a long-term situation that traumatizes and immobilizes, not a single event" (Boss, 1999, p. 24). Such a definition is consistent with developmental theorists' argument concerning the unfolding of parental incarceration impacts over time. Clearly, when we think about the effects of parental incarceration on children and families, the theory of ambiguous loss helps us to situate the fact that we are not dealing with an ordinary "clear-cut" loss—clear-cut in the sense that the loss is commonly defined and understood, and marked by visible bereavement rituals. Unlike other contexts of loss such as death or illness, loss of a family member because of incarceration seldom elicits sympathy and support from others (Schoenbauer, 1986).

Disenfranchised Grief: A Funeral No One Attends
The uncertainty and pain that are the hallmark of ambiguous loss are compounded by hostile, disapproving, or indifferent social attitudes pertaining to the loss of a family member through imprisonment. Kenneth Doka's (1989) ideas about disenfranchised grief provide conceptual meat for understanding the inner lives of families who are disrupted by incarceration. Disenfranchised grief is defined as occurring when persons experience a loss that is not or cannot be openly acknowledged, publicly mourned, or socially supported. Disenfranchisement can occur for several reasons, such as when

the relationship is not recognized, as in the case of ties between the bereaved and deceased that are not based on socially sanctioned or publicly recognized kin ties (e.g., gay partners). This is a likely possibility for many families impacted by incarceration and is most applicable to lovers and friends of the prisoner who are connected by informal bonds rather than legal or blood-kinship ties. Disenfranchisement is also characteristic of losses that are not openly recognized and not defined as socially significant. This may include "highly charged losses" that do not fit socially approved categories of loss, but rather generate feelings of shame and embarrassment and contribute to "secret-keeping" (Werner-Lin & Moro, 2004), Incarceration is one of those circumstances in which the reality of the loss itself is not socially validated and in which family members may collude to maintain secrets about the loss (e.g., lying to children regarding their parents' whereabouts). Furthermore, parental incarceration is a significant and ambiguous loss whereby the object of the loss remains physically alive but treated as dead (Sudnow, 1967). Indeed, incarceration represents the social death of the loved one, and surviving family members may experience a profound sense of loss. The death feels complete, yet the loss cannot be publicly acknowledged because the person is still biologically alive. It can be likened to going to a "funeral that no one attends" (Arditti, 2002) or, in the words of one visiting caregiver, "a death without a body" (Arditti, Joest, et al., 2010). This field note entry about a grandmother who was bringing her imprisoned son's children to visit at the jail poignantly illustrates the invisibility of the family members' grief:

> She [i.e., the grandmother] brought up…that it was like the family was in mourning—they were grieving but had no body and couldn't really grieve in public because going to jail is not acceptable. You are supposed to hide this fact, but if they had died then they could grieve publicly and get the support needed. But when someone goes to jail and you lose them from your daily life, almost like a death, you cannot grieve out loud, you have to grieve silently or else risk shame. (Arditti, 2003, p. 128)

The inability to grieve publicly means the parent is likely mourned in isolation, denying family members critical support from other family members or community (Werner-Lin & Moro, 2004).

Another reason for disenfranchisement involves situations in which the characteristics of the bereaved disenfranchise their grief. This is often the case for young children who may be perceived by others as having little comprehension of or reaction to the death of a significant other (Doka, 1989). In the case of a parent's social death resulting from incarceration, the failure to recognize children's grief is even more probable, and children may be particularly invisible with respect to their loss.

Traumatic Separation

The theory of ambiguous loss also helps us to frame child and family trauma as it occurs as a result of a parent's incarceration. The issue of child trauma is critical in thinking about the child effects of parental incarceration due to the relationship between trauma exposure and later adjustment or pathology (Pynoos, 1993). As with all child trauma experiences, trauma pertaining to the imprisonment of a parent is complex and multilayered and involves the management of intense physiological and emotional reactions. Some experts characterize children's experience in the context of parental incarceration as "enduring trauma," composed of ongoing and repeated stressors that serve to impede development (Myers, Smarsh, Amlund-Hagan, & Kennon, 1999). Noted scholar Jeremy Travis and colleague Michelle Waul (2003) utilize general principles in the literature on child development and trauma to hypothesize how children experience the incarceration of a parent. In doing so, they draw two conclusions that have bearing on the issue of primary or direct effects: (1) children always experience the loss of a parent as a traumatic event, and (2) children have greater difficulty coping in situations characterized by uncertainty (p. 16). The authors provide an important foundation in thinking about child trauma and child outcomes, although they note, "No research studies have parsed out the effects of loss of a parent due to incarceration form other stressful and traumatic circumstances that also generally characterize the lives of these children" (p. 17). Indeed, there is a paucity of research available using designs and analytic techniques that would permit a certain answer to whether trauma is due to the effects of the loss itself or other circumstances associated with the loss. However, as discussed previously, there is intriguing evidence to suggest that it is the "other circumstances" (i.e., stigma) associated with the loss *in conjunction* with the incarceration that produced negative effects on children (Fritsch & Burkhead, 1981).

Research utilizing purposeful samples[4] of justice-involved families provides empirical evidence that the loss of a parent due to incarceration is in fact traumatic and can be characterized as ambiguous and uncertain. For example, a comparative study of 36 children of incarcerated mothers found that one-third of the children in the study displayed symptoms of posttraumatic stress disorder (PTSD; Kampfner, 1995). PTSD symptoms included difficulty sleeping and concentrating, depression, emotional expressions of fear, anger and guilt, as well as flashbacks and nightmares. Compared with a control group of 36 children with a similar high-risk background whose mothers remained at home, children with incarcerated mothers demonstrated sustained and vivid recalls of traumatic events even after 2 to 3 years of separation. The study author reported a striking difference between the two groups of children: "Many children of incarcerated mothers reported having no emotional supports; they could not identify people...with whom they could talk about their mothers. This [lack of support] was not true of children in the control group" (Kampfner, 1995, p. 94).

Like Zoe, some children affected by incarceration also witness their parents' arrest—an experience seen as enhancing the likelihood of PTSD (Kampfner, 1995) and emotional maladjustment (Dallaire & Wilson, 2010). Although very little evidence exists documenting the prevalence of children who witness their parent's arrest, the available information suggests that this occurrence is not unusual. Estimates vary from 20% of children (Covington, 1995; Johnston, 1992) to rates approaching 84% (Kampfner, 1995). A recent inquiry among parents in New Mexico state prison revealed that 32% of mothers and 26% of fathers reported their children witnessed their arrest (Nolan, 2003). Children may have multiple experiences of witnessing arrest within their families, compounding the potential for intense child trauma. For example, elevated PTSD symptoms were most prevalent among children (already in the child welfare system due to maltreatment reports) who witnessed a family member's arrest and also had a recently arrested parent (Phillips & Zhao, 2010). Witnessing parental arrest is highly context specific and may also involve witnessing a parent engage in criminal activity. The arrest scene may involve violence, verbal altercations with police, and the use of weapons (Dallaire & Wilson, 2010).

Witnessing parental arrest not only disorients and upsets children but can evolve into a hatred or, as in Zoe's case, create a fear of the police and authority figures. Nell Bernstein's (2005) journalistic exposé highlights the trauma that results from parental arrest and describes how typical arrest practices unnecessarily victimize children. She argues that arrest practices are a first indication of how little children matter to the institutions that lay claim to their parents: "With appalling regularity, young people describe being left to fend for themselves in empty apartments for weeks or even months in the wake of a parent's arrest" (p. 14). Children may witness repeated arrests or come home from school only to find a parent gone and "draw their own conclusions" (Bernstein, 2005, p. 14). Given these kinds of scenarios and the empirical evidence, it seems clear that parental unavailability due to arrest, and ultimately incarceration, presents specific difficulties for children.

Further empirical support of the link between parental incarceration and trauma was revealed in a recent mixed methods study (Bocknek, Sanderson, & Britner, 2009). The 35 school-age children who participated in the study demonstrated a high prevalence of posttraumatic stress, high rates of both internalizing and externalizing behaviors, and school difficulties. The demographic profile of the children in this study paralleled national data (i.e., mostly children of color with a father in prison, living with their biological mother), adding further credibility to the results. Approximately 77% of the children interviewed had clinical posttraumatic symptom scores (via the Child Report of Posttraumatic Symptoms [CROPS]), and scores were correlated with youth self-report of withdrawal (the measure of internalizing behavior) and delinquency (the measure of externalizing behavior). The findings from this small data set were enriched via in-depth qualitative interviews. Qualitative descriptions poignantly illustrate the nuances of child trauma and how it might link with various outcomes in children's lives: "Jeremy, age 10, reported that he had not attended school in over a year. He stated that this was because he was afraid of the security guard. His mother added that she doesn't make him go anymore and that he will have to repeat the third grade" (Bocknek et al., 2009, p. 328). Another child in the study, Eduardo, aged 12, also had to repeat a grade. He exhibits symptoms of posttraumatic stress and spends his time at school alone and in the back of the classroom. His social worker reported that when Eduardo is "frustrated or upset, he becomes unresponsive and covers his head with his hands" (Bocknek et al., 2009, p. 328).

Through qualitative interviews such as these, the painful feelings children have as a result of their parents' incarceration and their efforts to avoid the intensity of those feelings are revealed. During one interview, one child who had a good relationship with his nonincarcerated mother became so upset when discussing his father that he put his head inside his shirt. When the interviewer asked what he could do when he feels sad, the child explained he tries to keep his mind off of it, or else keeps his anger inside (Bocknek et al., 2009). Other markers of trauma (see Pynoos, 1993) and ambiguous loss as a result of parent imprisonment were apparent in the qualitative interviews such as ineffective coping, "recurring nightmares in which children witnessed their incarcerated parent's death, or in which they themselves were murdered" (Bocknek et al., 2009, p. 329), hypervigilance, guilt and a sense of responsibility, and fear of police officers. In these instances of parental incarceration, children's coping can be characterized as avoidant and consistent with self-protective mechanisms used by children to (1) distance themselves from trauma and traumatic reminders, and (2) control physical arousal and anxiety (see, e.g., Pynoos, 1993).

Other clues regarding children's experience of traumatic separation are revealed in developmental psychologist Julie Poehlmann's (2005c) analysis of the impact of maternal incarceration on young children's attachment representations. All children in this study had incarcerated mothers who were primary caregivers, suggesting they were important attachment figures. Indirect evidence of traumatic separation was documented, with the majority of the children's mothers and caregivers reporting the presence of strong emotions and behavioral reactions after the separation, including sadness, worry and confusion, loneliness, anger, fear, depression, crying, developmental regressions, and sleep problems. Ultimately, findings indicated that two-thirds of the children held attachment representations that were characterized by intense ambivalence, disorganization, violence, or detachment. More secure representations were linked with children being older and not reacting to the separation with anger. The study findings give indirect support that separations from incarcerated mothers are traumatic (i.e., characterized by intense emotion and behavioral changes), and that older children may have an advantage in terms of maintaining more positive attachments with their mothers.

Evidence of children's experience of traumatic separation has also been directly observed within the context of visitation, and also based on caregiver reports (Arditti, 2003; Arditti et al., 2003). My jail visitation study (2003) utilizes another purposeful sample, with family demographics consistent with nationally representative samples of those impacted by parental incarceration. More specifically, participants were disproportionately poor and African American, and the majority of children and visitors were at the jail to visit fathers. Field observations and interview notes documented several instances of children having difficulties stemming from traumatic separation due to incarceration. For example, one mother described her daughter's behavioral regression (encopresis, that is, defecating in her pants), which she attributed to the trauma of parental incarceration: "She [the mother] described many of the difficulties that the child was having, particularly that she was defecating in her pants, although she had been potty trained for well over a year. Since her father's incarceration she wants to use diapers" (Arditti, 2003, p. 128).

Another field observation entry recounts the traumatic experience of a child in the jail waiting area during family visitation hours:

A child of about 5 came in the front door and immediately ran to the locked door, crying and jumping up to try to get in. His mother tried to quiet him, talking to him as she pulled him away from the door. She pointed to the deputies inside the glass encasement, "See them? They're gonna come get you," referring to his trying to get into the locked door. He continued to cry over and over "Oh daddy," "I want daddy, I want daddy, I want daddy," pushing against his mother, "daddy, daddy, daddy." After about 10 minutes the mother took him to the bathroom—I could hear him screaming louder and louder, "I want daddy, I want daddy, I want daddy." The child could not be quieted and the mother sounded if she were near tears herself. "Ya gotta' wait," she said. The child was now screaming very loudly "I WANT DADDY, I WANT DADDY, DADDY, DADDY..."

Finally, the mother yelled for him to shut up. He continued to scream for a while longer. Finally, she came out, sat down, and just held him until he fell asleep. The room became very quiet. (Arditti, 2003, p. 129)

Other examples of child trauma were evident while conducting the jail study as families struggled with the no-contact visiting rules, which are common in most jails across the country. The prisoners were not allowed to touch family members during visits, and we listened to caregivers tell us stories about children helplessly banging on the glass separating them from their parent. One participant told us her young son became hysterical because "he thought his father had no legs" based on what the child could see (i.e., torso only) through the glass. Certainly, the children did not comprehend what was happening, and that lack of understanding, compounded with emotions arising from the separation from the parent, contributed to the intensity of the traumatic experience.

Family Effects: Economic Decline, Parenting Quality, and Caregiver Stability

An array of important consequences stem from parental incarceration that have bearing on child and family well-being. Therefore, many negative child outcomes associated with parental incarceration are often indirect and can be classified as secondary effects (Hagan & Dinovitzer, 1999; Parke & Clarke-Stewart, 2003). Indirect effects result in part from contextual changes, such as declines in economic adequacy, and process changes undermining family stability and parenting quality (Arditti et al., 2003; Johnson, 2009; Phillips et al., 2006; Watts & Nightengale, 1996).

Economic Decline

Ron's case points to the economic strains that are associated with single parenthood and his partner's incarceration. Ron struggles to provide for his children as he did prior to Rene's imprisonment. Children's well-being is profoundly impacted due to the loss of family income associated with parental, and in particular paternal, incarceration. A recent analysis of the Panel Study of Income Dynamics (PSID) revealed that the proportion of children growing up in poverty significantly increases in the years during the father's incarceration (from approximately 22% to 31%). Further, this significant increase in child poverty only modestly declines in the first few years following the father's release from prison, and the child's family income does not recover to preincarceration levels. On average, family income declined by an average of $8,726 (from $38,960 to $30,234; Johnson, 2009). The loss of financial resources to children as result of parental incarceration is due to several factors. First, about half of parents in state prison provided the primary financial support for their minor children, with more than 75% of these reporting employment and salary or wages in the month prior to their arrest. Small samples provide additional insight. For example, my own work (Arditti et al., 2003) revealed that not only did caregivers lose economic support, and in some cases child support, from the parent (the majority of whom were fathers) who because incarcerated, but many caregivers *left their jobs* after the incarceration and began receiving social welfare support. Economic declines are also a result of sending money to the inmate (an average of $75 a month in the jail study) and shouldering their legal costs as illustrated by Ron's case.

Parenting Quality and Stability

In addition to the indirect child effects that may result from the intensification of economic inadequacy, effects of parental incarceration on children may also result from *process* changes between parents and children. Examples of these process changes include weakened attachment bonds between the incarcerated parent and child (Poehlmann, 2005b), alterations in the amount of time caregivers spend with their children (Arditti et al., 2003), and heightened family conflict stemming from a parent's release from prison (Aaron & Dallaire, 2010). Per ecological theory, the most proximal relationship influencing children is likely that of the nonincarcerated caregiver and children under his or her care. This relationship is influenced on many levels by a parent's incarceration, and it is not always in an expected manner. For example, a reinspection of the jail data (Arditti et al., 2003) suggests that about half of the 56 caregivers (the majority of whom were the children's mothers) visiting their jailed family member reported that their relationship with their children has been affected by the incarceration—particularly with regard to the amount of time they spent with their children. We had expected caregivers to spend *less* time with children, reasoning that because of role strain and the loss of income, caregivers would be outside the home working more (like Ron's scenario when he took a second job). However, 28% of caregivers reported *more* time spent with children since the incarceration, and only 11% reported *less* time spent with children since the incarceration. The fact that parental incarceration was associated with caregivers' loss of employment and often their child care helps explain why they may be spending more time with their children. What are the implications of a caregiver spending *more* time with their children, particularly in the context of unemployment? This is a question that is not easily answered, for it obviously depends on the quality of parenting the children receive from their caregiver. If care is good, then more time might be beneficial given sufficient resources and parenting competence; if care is inadequate, particularly in conjunction with economic shortfalls, then more time with children can put them at risk for poor adjustment and health outcomes.

The preceding example from the jail study (regarding caregiver time spent with children) highlights the complexity of determining how children may respond to a parent's incarceration. So much of their subsequent experience depends on the nature of the care they receive during the parent's confinement. To a large degree, the diversity of children's response to incarceration involves the extent to which a parent's imprisonment is associated with risks to the caregiver's mental health, and risk experiences in children's interactions with caregivers (Dallaire & Aaron, 2010). While in some instances incarceration might improve children's caregiving scenarios (such as removing an abusive or neglectful parent from the home), the body of evidence suggests that parental incarceration poses specific risks in terms of the nature of the care received by "children left behind." Overall the empirical literature points to a lack of quality parenting and stability on the part of caregivers responsible for children with incarcerated parents (Mackintosh et al., 2006; Poehlmann, 2005b). Children who have a history of parental, and in particular maternal, incarceration are more likely to experience caregiver risks such as caregiver mental health problems, high levels of caregiver stress, substance abuse (Mackintosh et al., 2006; Phillips, Burns, Wagner, & Barth, 2004; Phillips et al., 2006), caregiver health problems (Arditti et al., 2003), harsh punitive discipline and less parental supervision (Phillips et al., 2006), and family victimization (Aaron & Dallaire, 2010; Phillips et al., 2004, 2006).

As we have discussed, with respect to child outcomes, one indirect pathway of influence resulting from parental incarceration, particularly in the case of fathers' incarceration, involves the frequent changes in the nonincarcerated parents' (usually mothers') romantic relationships that are all too often a feature of justice-involved families (Edin et al., 2001). These frequent relationship changes, in turn, connect with maternal distress and negative parenting practices such as harsh discipline and withdrawal (Arditti, Burton, et al., 2010; Beck et al., 2009; Braman, 2004), which in turn link to deleterious child outcomes (Osborne & McClanahan, 2007).

In addition to any family instability triggered by a parent's incarceration, caregivers responsible for the inmate's children are often unprepared physically, emotionally, and financially to care for the children—particularly over extended periods of time (Hanlon et al., 2007; Hungerford, 1996; Mackintosh et al., 2006). We can see these dynamics at play in Ron's case. Because of Rene's absence and the loss of her salary, Ron has to work two jobs. His availability to his children is severely restricted as a result. Ron's children receive some care by their grandmother; however, they often spend lengthy periods alone while Ron is working. Thus Ron's children are experiencing less parental and adult supervision then they had prior to their mother's incarceration. The supervision they do receive comes from an infirm grandmother who is easy to "take advantage of" and from their tired and stressed father. Taken together, Ron's caregiving scenario does not bode well for his sons.

Caregivers' Experiences

As mentioned previously, the incarceration of a parent often creates an involuntary single-parent household, particularly in the case of paternal incarceration. In other contexts of loss, such as death or military deployment, the involuntariness of single parenthood is met with sympathy, supportive rituals, and child assurance, such as social security or other formal supports. Yet there are no casseroles brought to the house for the "prison widow" and her children. There is no government assistance or formal recognition that a significant loss has occurred in the family that will bear heavily on children's welfare. Indeed, in the more common cases of paternal incarceration, the prison widow and her children are denied important forms of social support. This is unfortunate given that more involuntary forms of separation are more profoundly painful and difficult to grieve (Levinger, 1992). Families, particularly partners of the inmate, are not considered blameless by society. Some of the "blame" falls onto the family because of social stigma and a common perception that the inmate's family knew about or contributed to the criminal activity. Megan Comfort (2008) details how a personal allegiance with a prisoner "sullies" a woman with the stigma of the offender—identifying her as "potentially threatening and deserving of recrimination" (p. 63). Thus family members, and in particular female kin, are subject to degradation and deprivations similar to what their incarcerated family member endures, "blurring the distinction between who is an 'inmate' and who is not" (p. 63). This blurring is illustrated by the words of a female caregiver in my jail study who explained: "Officers treat you badly like *you* are in jail" (Arditti, 2003, p. 125, emphasis added). Another caregiver said: "I feel like I am in jail myself" (Arditti et al., 2003, p. 200).

The jail study also provides evidence that a parent's incarceration may affect caregiver health: 48% of visiting participants reported declining health since their family member's incarceration, with those mothers who shared biological children with the inmate reporting the most dramatic declines. The experience of emotional stress and parenting strain was particularly apparent in the qualitative data. Comments such as "I'm struggling all by myself to handle this," "everything is harder," and "it's rough" were common among participants. One mother summed up her parenting experience since her husband's incarceration in this way: "No peace, no break, no patience, and no help" (Arditti et al., 2003, p. 200).

Given the demographics of the penal population (disproportionately younger men of color), most caregivers responsible for offenders' children are women and African American (Christian & Thomas, 2009; Comfort, 2008; Hanlon et al., 2007). Black women's experience warrants our attention given their likely connections to incarcerated black men (relative to whites) and the resultant impacts these relationships create for already resource-poor women (Christian & Thomas, 2009). Consequences of these connections include further marginalization, role strain due to caring for the prisoner and any shared children, and shouldering incarceration-related expenses (Arditti et al., 2003; Braman, 2004). Grandmothers in particular are heavily relied upon to care for children affected by incarceration, especially as a result of maternal incarceration (see, e.g., Hanlon et al., 2007). This is noteworthy because women are the fastest-growing prison population. Additionally, aging parents of the incarcerated are also relied upon to provide support for the reentering offender parent upon release from confinement. And, a question that is virtually unexplored: What are the implications for families as the number of incarcerated women who are grandmothers themselves serve time and are unavailable to their families? For a large number of at-risk youth in this country, particularly those children whose mothers are incarcerated, grandmothers play a crucial role in raising them. This intergenerational connectedness is a visible feature of African American families, and there is evidence suggesting African American mothers are more inclined to have family members care for their children than white mothers during imprisonment (see Enos, 2001).

Despite the importance of grandparents as potential caregivers among families impacted by incarceration, surrogate caregiving on the part of grandparents can be problematic for the child and grandparent given that many elders are poor and infirm (Hanlon et al., 2007). For example, the National Council on Crime and Delinquency (NCCD) study of 66 caregivers of children whose mothers were incarcerated found most were maternal grandmothers over age 50 with low-income levels and on public assistance (Bloom & Steinhart, 1993). Grandmothers in this study were responsible for an average of 2.3 children aged 8.5 years. Grandparents raising grandchildren are faced with multiple challenges and may be unprepared or unable to deal with the demands of child rearing. Further, grandparents responsible for children who have an incarcerated parent are also commonly caring for other family members staying at the same residence (Dressel & Barnhill, 1990). Grandparents who become responsible for children as a result of incarceration identify an array of problems among the offspring under their care, including school and learning difficulties, behavior problems, and health/mental health difficulties (Bloom & Steinhart, 1993; Harm & Thompson, 1995). These problems may lack resolution as those elders raising children as a result of parental incarceration may be reluctant to seek formal help from agencies and social welfare organizations (Dressel & Barnhill, 1994).

Justice-Involved Families and Child Welfare

Perhaps one of the most profound implications of parental incarceration for children concerns the overlap between familial criminal justice involvement, foster care, and child maltreatment. Approximately 11% of incarcerated mothers and 2% of incarcerated fathers have children in foster care (Glaze & Maruschak, 2008). In fact, one in eight children who were subjects of a Child Welfare Services (CWS) maltreatment report had a parent who was recently arrested (Phillips et al., 2004). However, the connection between a parent's arrest and incarceration and the child welfare service involvement of his or her children is not straightforward and may have more to do with indirect or secondary repercussions surrounding the parents' criminal justice involvement. For example, many of the cumulative disadvantage factors associated with arrest and parental incarceration (i.e., substance abuse, mental illness, family violence) are also risk factors for child maltreatment (Phillips, Dettlaff, & Baldwin, 2010).

Unfortunately, there is much we do not know about the extent and implications of the overlap because child welfare agencies do not routinely track information about parents' criminal justice involvement, and criminal justice entities do not track information about offender parents' children (Phillips et al., 2010). Despite the tremendous effect a parent's criminal justice involvement will have on his or her children, there is no requirement that systems serving children take note of parental incarceration (Bernstein, 2005). Systematic review of case records of 452 urban children in Texas suggests four pathways in which the criminal justice system involvement of children's family members intersects with the child welfare system. First, parental arrest and CWS involvement may have coincided, with maltreatment having come to the attention of the authorities as a result of parental arrest for some other matter (more likely), or parental arrest occurring as a result of a CWS investigation (less likely). Second, parents' criminal histories played into CWS workers' decisions to remove children from the home—parental arrest and incarceration histories often were viewed as threatening a child's safety. Third, in about one in four cases of maltreatment requiring removal from the home, relatives who were examined as placement possibilities had criminal histories. These relatives were often denied custody, and thus in most instances the child was put into foster care. Finally, often CWS became involved with children while their mothers and/or fathers were in jail or prison. These were children who were born to incarcerated mothers, children whose living arrangements during parental incarceration were deemed unsafe, or those whose relative caregivers were no longer willing or able to provide care. The findings of this study are important because they suggest that with the expansion of the criminal justice system in recent years, there is a greater possibility that arresting and incarcerating parents can precipitate children's involvement with CWS and enhance the likelihood of foster care placement. A related study confirms this contention: based on nationally representative data, compared with other children who come to the attention of CWS, children whose parents were recently arrested were younger, disproportionately African American, and significantly more likely to be in out-of-home care than those children who did not experience parental arrest (Phillips et al., 2004).

"Up Close and Personal": Proximal Processes Influencing the Effects of Parental Incarceration on Families and Children

The term *modifiers* refers to those factors during incarceration that influence how children and their family members may respond to a parent's incarceration (Parke & Clarke-Stewart, 2001). On some level, all intraindividual and relational processes discussed thus far can be considered "modifiers" in that they influence family and child outcomes. From among these processes, here it is useful to emphasize three important factors that may serve to influence family outcomes associated with parental incarceration: (1) preincarceration relationship between parent and child, (2) family visitation during incarceration, and (3) offender, caregiver, and child resilience.

Parent-Child Relationship Prior to Incarceration

As we have discussed, child outcomes as a result of parental incarceration tend to depend on the extent to which the offending parent contributed to family well-being and was a part of the family system prior to incarceration (Hagan & Dinovitzer, 1999). For example, in assessing the impact of parental incarceration on children, Johnson's 2009 study only included fathers who had resided with their children prior to arrest (or resided with the children's mother prior to their birth). Hence it is unknown whether the extremely negative effects of parental incarceration revealed in the analysis would hold true for children whose parent was incarcerated during their childhood but did not live with them. Conversely, positive family outcomes are possible, although not readily apparent in the empirical research on parental incarceration, to the extent that incarceration removed parents from the picture who engaged in problematic behaviors that were detrimental and extremely harmful to their family (Jaffee, Moffitt, Caspi, & Taylor, 2003; Sano, 2005). For example, the removal of an abusive, neglectful, or violent parent via imprisonment may provide immediate relief to victimized family members (Nesmith & Ruhland, 2008).[5] Similarly, children living with fathers who engaged in high levels of antisocial behavior were far more likely to develop clinically significant behavior problems than their peers whose fathers also were antisocial but did not reside with their children (Jaffee et al., 2003). Positive outcomes are also possible to the extent that a parent gained resources, skills, or psychological assets during incarceration that would prove to be helpful to their families upon release, particularly in terms of enhancing their competence as parents. There is evidence suggesting that prison time, particularly in conjunction with work release or rehabilitative programs (Cullen & Applegate, 1997), may be a much-needed wake-up call for parents to stop destructive behavior (such as drug abuse), take stock, improve their parenting, and "turn their lives around" (Arditti & Few, 2008; Edin et al., 2001).

A parent's physical presence in the household prior to incarceration has been used as one basic indicator of parental involvement in the literature. The Survey of Inmates (Mumola, 2000) provides two basic measures of parents' physical presence prior to incarceration. First, it seems that less than 50% of parent-prisoners lived with their minor children one month prior to arrest, with more mothers (about 59%) than fathers (about 44%) living with their children before arrest. The number of parents living with their children increases when measured later, "at the time of admission," with about 64% of mothers and 44% of fathers living with their children at the time of incarceration. Therefore, it appears that a good many parents were physically present in their children's household at some point prior to their confinement, with mothers primarily responsible for the day-to-day care of their children (Glaze & Maruschak, 2008).

Beyond the fact of physical residence, the full nature of parents' presence in the family prior to their arrest and incarceration is more of an unknown— so it is difficult to say precisely how separation processes may work in justice-involved families. National data on federal and state prisoners suggest that most incarcerated fathers were less likely than incarcerated mothers to be responsible for the day-to-day care of their children and relied heavily on someone else—typically the mother of their child(ren)—to provide childcare (Glaze & Maruschak, 2008). Other studies suggest that some fathers do indeed spend considerable time with their children before incarceration (e.g., Lattimore et al., 2009; reanalysis of data from Day et al., 2001). A recent study of 3,000 low-income urban families found evidence that paternal incarceration significantly increased young children's externalizing and attention problems, and that these effects were stronger if fathers resided with their children prior to incarceration (although they were significant even for children with nonresident fathers; Geller et al., 2010). Based on this evidence, as well as drawing from the divorce literature relative to the question of the impact of separation of children from a parent (Emery, 1994), one can infer that to the extent that incarceration leads to a separation from an important attachment figure in a child's life, regardless of parent gender or residence, then incarceration will be associated with traumatic separation or its behavioral manifestations.

The literature on incarcerated mothers provides important clues that pre-incarceration parenting involvement is an important "moderator" or factor that influences the strength of the relationship between parental incarceration and negative child effects. Maternal incarceration is generally linked to even more profound child adjustment difficulties and intergenerational incarceration (Huebner & Gustafson, 2007; Phillips et al., 2002, 2006; see Geller et al., 2008; and Cho, 2009a, 2009b, for exceptions). As we have discussed, the more intense consequences that are typically a result of maternal incarceration stem from many mothers' roles as primary caregivers prior to their incarceration.

Research is fairly clear that children with incarcerated mothers who were their primary caregivers seem to suffer more intense negative effects than children who were not living with their mothers prior to the incarceration (Hairston, 1991; Hanlon, Blatchley et al., 2005). Thomas Hanlon's work provides the most powerful support of the relationship between the preincarceration involvement of the parent and child well-being. He found that the incarceration of children's drug-addicted mothers had little effect on their well-being, concluding that this was due to the fact that children were already receiving stable, nonmaternal care prior to their mothers' arrest and imprisonment. One may also infer from this study that children in these scenarios (i.e., nonresident mother and receiving stable care) were not subject to the same level of traumatic separation that children residing with their mothers and then losing them to incarceration would be.

The Paradox of Family Visitation

Webster's defines the term *paradox* as "a tenet contrary to received opinion."[6] A developmental paradox implies social ecologies that have seemingly contradictory qualities or developmental outcomes (Bronfenbrenner, 1979). Visitation can be considered a developmental paradox for two primary reasons. First, despite the delineation of visitation as a key moderator facilitating child adjustment (Parke & Clarke-Stewart, 2001), there is also the potential for visitation to serve as a context for proximal traumatic reminders (Pynoos, 1993). That is, visitation may arouse deeply painful emotions among family members, and in particular children, that involve reliving traumatic separation from the parent. Second, visitation may benefit some family members more than others; for example, family visitation may facilitate social reintegration for the offender parent, but it also more firmly entrenches the family in the institutional life of the inmate. Frequent contact extends the reach and intensity of the influence of the "prison apparatus" on the family referred to as *secondary prisonization* (Comfort, 2008). Visitation is both a context for connection and a context for emotional pain—therein lies the "paradox." Visitation may be particularly difficult for children depending on their developmental status and coping resources. To the extent that visitation is beneficial to children and families, it may be considered a protective factor.

Contact and Visitation Trends
There is considerable variation in contact and visitation trends for incarcerated parents and their families. This is due in part to contextual factors such as parent gender and residence (prior to confinement), visitation and communication policies of the corrections facility, the distance between the offender and his or her children, and sentence length. In other words, the answer to the question of "how much contact do prisoner parents have with their children?" is "It depends."

The most comprehensive information regarding incarcerated parents' contact with their children comes from the Bureau of Justice special report *Parents in Prison and Their Minor Children* (Glaze & Maruschak, 2008). This 2007 survey of state and federal inmates reveals that since their admission, the majority of parents (70% state; 84% federal) had mail contact with their children at some point, more than half had spoken by telephone with their children (53% state and 85% federal), and 42% of state prisoner parents and 55% of federal prisoner parents reported having an in-person visit. Mothers (62%) and fathers (49%) who had lived with their children were more likely to report some type of weekly contact with their children. Conversely, a great many parents reported *never* receiving a visit (58.5% state and 44.7% federal). Similar metrics were reported among a sample of 7,000 Florida offenders in that the majority (58%) of inmates did not receive in-person visits one year prior to release (Bales & Mears, 2008).

The national data also indicate that mothers reported more contact with their children, and parents in federal prisons reported more contact than state prisoners. With regard to mothers having more contact, we can speculate that these differences are due to two factors: (1) mothers are more likely to be residential parents prior to incarceration (Glaze & Maruschak, 2008), suggestive of stronger parent-child ties, and (2) women's facilities tend to have less restrictive visitation and communication policies (Hoffmann, Dickenson, & Dunn, 2007). Still other studies highlight that many mothers do not receive visits from their minor children. For example, one analysis based on 158 inmate-mothers released from a maximum-security state prison in the United States found that more than half of the mothers received no visits from their children while in prison (Casey-Acevedo, Bakken, & Karle, 2004). The lack of visits may be a function of the security level of the facility (assuming that higher-security facilities have more restrictive visitation policies). It is also not entirely clear why federal prisoners had more contact with their children than state prisoners. The difference is hard to interpret because "contact" represents aggregate data in the report (letter, phone, visits). One would expect federal prisoners to receive *fewer* visits because federal facilities tend to house offenders farther from home, and on average, inmates receive longer sentences (Mumola, 2000)—factors that tend to discourage visitation. Greater contact on the part of federal prisoners with their children could be due to the fact that more federal prisoners than state prisoners reported living with their children at arrest and at the time of admission (residence being a factor that is linked with more contact). More contact may also be due to differences in state and federal institutional policies and resources pertaining to phone use and mail, as a greater proportion of federal inmates than state inmates are housed in lower-security facilities.

An analysis of Chicago data revealed similar trends in contact and visitation; however, this data set also included individuals who did not have children (LaVigne, Visher, & Castro, 2005). The vast majority of prisoners reported having at least some telephone or mail contact with family members, intimate partners, and children (92%, 81%, and 53%, respectively). However, the likelihood of having any in-person contact was much lower than the national data suggested. Only about 13% of prisoners reported in-person visits with children or family, and 29% reported visits from intimate partners. About two-thirds of participants reported they had difficulties staying in touch with family primarily because the prison was too far away or telephone calls were too expensive. Indeed, 62% of parents in state prison and 84% of federal prisoners were housed more than 100 miles from their place of residence at arrest (Mumola, 2000).

Contact metrics of smaller, less representative samples vary as a result of facility (jail or state prison) and who reports (caregiver or incarcerated parent). For example, jails are locally operated correctional facilities that tend to be closer to the offender's home, and sentence length is generally shorter than for offenders serving time in state or federal facilities.[7] Caregivers in my jail study (2003) reported frequent visits with their family member: 66% of caregivers reported visiting their family member with the children at least once a month; the remaining reported less frequent visits. Most were living with the inmate prior to his confinement (53 out of 56), two-thirds of visiting caregivers shared children with the inmate, and caregivers lived an average of only 18 miles from the jail. Living farther away from the jail and experiencing visitation difficulties (such as difficulty caring for children during visits, lack of privacy) were associated with fewer visits.

Similar to national trends, about half (51%) of 51 fathers in confinement in Utah and Oregon state prisons reported receiving no visits, 31% reported receiving visits at least monthly, and 17.6% received visits less than monthly. More inmates reported at least monthly contact by phone (59%)—although 17 out of the 51 men reported no phone contact at all. As we would expect, most men contacted their children via cards and letters; however, frequency varied, with about 56% sending mail to their children at least monthly, 40% sending mail less frequently, and only 2 men (4%) reporting no contact with their children by mail. Sending and receiving mail from children was positively correlated. Thus involvement begets involvement. The majority resided with at least one of their children prior to confinement (78%), served a little more than 2 years at the time of the interviews and were confined an average of 200 miles from their prior residence (Day et al., 2001).

In sum, many parents in an array of institutional settings report having contact with their children and families—with mail and phone a more frequent and perhaps easier means of communication. In-person visitation is the most proximal form of contact that potentially has the most impact on parent, children, and caregivers (Arditti, 2003, 2005). Visits are "up close and personal" and are the focal point of contact for offenders, family members, and even correctional facilities with respect to any family-oriented programming (Comfort, 2008). Several factors connect with visitation frequency: having less time to serve (Glaze & Maruschak, 2008), living closer to the corrections facility, and having fewer visitation problems (Arditti et al., 2005). These findings mirror research findings pertaining to divorce in terms of the importance of proximity and visitation quality in determining the frequency of contact between nonresidential parents and their children (see, e.g., Arditti, 1992, using these same measures), suggesting that visitation dynamics may have certain similarities across family contexts.

Benefits of Visitation
Beyond indicators of visitation frequency, much less is known about the quality and nature of in-person prison visits between incarcerated parents

and their children.[8] Visitation can potentially benefit the incarcerated parent and provide emotional and psychological continuity for family members. Many imprisoned parents feel that, on balance, visits with their children are worthwhile and serve to strengthen family bonds. Several studies have demonstrated that visits connect to positive outcomes for the offender parent, including lower recidivism (for mothers in a nursery program during confinement; Carlson, 1998), less parental distress and parenting stress (mothers: Houck & Loper, 2002; Tuerk & Loper, 2006; Poehlmann, 2005b; fathers: Landreth & Lobaugh, 1998), and paternal involvement after release (LaVigne, Naser, et al., 2005). More generic research on offenders (who may or may not be parents) also supports that visitation can improve inmates' behavior while incarcerated (see Bales & Mears, 2008, for summary).

While the preponderance of research suggests that visitation benefits the offender (with exceptions as noted in the next section), less clear are the effects of visits on children and their family members. How visitation affects children depends on multiple factors, including the child's prior relationships with parents, the age and gender of the child, visitation policies and environment at the jail or prison, and whether or not an intervention of some sort has been implemented aimed at facilitating visitation (Poehlmann, et al., 2010). There is limited evidence suggesting that negative outcomes for youth with parents in prison may be mitigated via regular contact. For example, adolescents who reported regular contact with their mothers were less likely to drop out of school or be suspended than children whose mothers were incarcerated but did not have consistent contact (Trice & Brewster, 2004). Young children with regular contact with their mothers may have fewer feelings of alienation (Shlafer & Poehlmann, 2010). Further, family-friendly intervention such as prison nursery programs for mothers and infants (Byrne, Goshin, & Joestl, 2010) and enhanced prison visitation for school-age children and their fathers (Landreth & Lobaugh, 1998) appear to enhance attachment and self-esteem, respectively. Indeed, children often look forward to visits with an incarcerated parent, although they may be sad when they have to leave (Sack & Seidler, 1978).

Difficulties Associated with Visitation

As we have discussed, the typically constrained and uninviting environmental characteristics of traditional visitation settings can create difficulties for offender parents and their family members. Parents and children often have to withstand a lack of privacy (with the incarcerated parent submitting to a strip search prior to and after visits), tedious and lengthy waits, humiliation and rude treatment by correctional officers, and visiting in crowded, noisy, and dirty facilities (Arditti, 2003; Comfort, 2008; Hairston, 2001). Poor visitation conditions suggest a lack of *psychological safety* and do not support an enduring bond between children, family members, and parents. For many, going on visits entails major resource expenditures of time, money, and energy with little return (Christian, 2005).

Visits to a parent in prison or jail can be hard for a child. Correctional visiting practices commonly involve restricting the inmate to his or her seat (often bolted to the floor), subsequently limiting visiting children's movement with few or no options in terms of play activities. Visiting at jails may be particularly problematic for children and caregivers due to the widespread use of "no contact" visits, which prohibit any physical contact between the incarcerated parent and visitors. For example, findings from the jail study highlight the prohibitive developmental conditions of the jail visitation setting. On a typical visitation, children and their caregivers can expect to wait for 30 to 60 minutes before getting called for their turn for a 20-minute, no-contact visit with their family member. During the wait in the visiting area, children were bored and restless and had little to do but hang on their mothers or lie down between the bolted plastic seats on the hard linoleum floor. Upon being called by the deputies to line up, the family then passed through a locked door, a metal detector, an elevator, and another locked door that eventually led to a row of small cubicles to visit the incarcerated parent. Children were required to sit on a small stool and use a telephone to talk to their family member, who was separated from them by a Plexiglas wall (Arditti, 2003).

From an ecological standpoint, the extent to which an environment is *promoting* or *inhibiting* has developmental implications for both parents and youth (Garbarino, 1995). Clearly, traditional prison visitation settings can largely be characterized as *inhibiting* in that they are environments that restrict exploration by children and put pressure on parents to monitor children and provide regulation (Lerner, 1998). Shari and Shane's visitation experience clearly illustrates the developmental implications of a prohibitive visitation environment. Shane is an active young boy, yet visits to the prison do not align well with his developmental capabilities and needs. For 3-year-old Shane, sitting quietly in a chair for extended periods is unworkable and leads to his disruptive behavior. His behavior then creates tension and conflict in the family as both parents try to monitor him and keep him out of trouble. There is a great deal of pressure for both Sheri and her incarcerated husband, as Shane's disruptive behavior draws unwanted attention from the guards that can result in having the visit terminated. We can reason that for Shane and other children in similar visitation conditions, essential ecological features (e.g., free exploration, positive parent-child interactions) that promote positive child development are lacking.

Given the difficulties described in the preceding paragraphs, it is no surprise that several studies find that visitation between children and their incarcerated parent can have negative effects on children such as insecure attachment (Dallaire, Wilson, & Ciccone, 2009; Poehlmann, 2005a), traumatic separation (Arditti, 2003, Arditti & Few, 2008), child attention problems (Dallaire et al., 2009), and uncertainty and frustration on the part of children and a sense of children and caregivers "not wanting to visit" (Arditti, 2003; Arditti & Few, 2008; Nesmith & Ruhland, 2008; Poehlmann, 2010).[9] Interviews conducted directly with 34 children whose fathers were incarcerated revealed a great deal of "awkwardness" during in-person visits that seemed to increase "with the length of the incarceration or distance between communications" (Nesmith & Ruhland, 2008, p. 1124). One root of this awkwardness involved the fact that incarcerated fathers "lost time" during their imprisonment and remained stuck in terms of treating their children the same way they did before confinement: According to Nesmith and Ruhland, "We heard stories [from children] in which incarcerated fathers asked older children questions that felt babyish to the youth such as a reference to a cartoon the child enjoyed long ago, leaving the child embarrassed or frustrated" (p. 1124).

Offenders' Reactions to Prison Visitation
Process mechanisms relevant for understanding the implications of in-person visitation for offender parents include timing and relationship type. There is some evidence suggesting that visits close to the offender's date of release were more likely to reduce the odds of recidivating (Bales & Mears, 2008). The effects of in-person visits with intimate partners seem to be more tenuous than other types of family relationships in that visits were only positive if the relationship prior to incarceration was positive and lacked conflict (LaVigne, Naser, et al., 2005; see also Brodsky, 1975, re: "uncertain" relationships). Thus with respect to the offender parent, the implications of in-person visits may hinge on *who* actually visits and the *quality of the relationship* with the family member. In-person visits with family, and in particular intimate partners, can be a negative influence on the offender if there is a history of poor relationships and conflict (Brodsky, 1975; LaVigne, Naser, et al., 2005).

Other evidence suggests that visits from children may be problematic for the inmate. While in-person visits from a spouse may reduce recidivism, in-person visits from children may be connected to enhanced recidivism after release (Bales & Mears, 2008). Similarly, among a sample of 158 mothers who had been released from a maximum-security state facility, mothers who received visits from their children were *more* likely to engage in serious and violent disciplinary infractions during their incarceration than mothers who did not receive visits from their children (Casey-Acevedo et al., 2004). The authors of the study speculate that while most women were happy and relieved to see their children, the pain of separation may lead to depression or anger, making it difficult to tolerate the conditions of their incarceration (and thus more likely to get into trouble). Further, most studies on women tend to utilize samples from medium- and minimum-security prisons or county jails. It may be that this maximum-security sample is somehow different from other studies examining mothers and visitation. For example, only slightly more than half of the mothers had been living with their children (similar to Hanlon's research on drug-addicted mothers), and about 20% had children in foster care. It may be the mothers in the Casey-Acevedo et al. (2004) study had more strained relationships with caregivers or children with greater behavior problems and other difficulties than in other research on the subject.

Visitation may activate painful emotions on the part of the offender parent. These emotional responses, as well as strained relationships between caregivers and inmates during in-person child visits, and any worries offender parents' may have about how visits affect their children, can contribute to negative visitation effects for offenders. Direct support for this interpretation comes from a qualitative study of 34 children with an incarcerated father and their caregivers (usually children's mothers). In-depth and repeated interview data collected from children and caregivers suggest that an incarcerated parent can become quite upset and angry as a result of children's visits. It was not unusual for incarcerated fathers in the study to want a hug or some sign of affection from a reluctant child during visits: "One father stormed away from the visit in anger when his young daughter would not give him a hug on demand" (Nesmith & Ruhland, 2008, p. 1124). Parent offenders displayed strong emotions as a result of in-person child visits in other qualitative studies, raising questions about the benefits of visitation. For example, some fathers felt bad and ashamed relative to child visits and reported they did not want their children to see them in prison (Arditti et al., 2005; Edin et al., 2001). Other incarcerated parents feel intense guilt about seeing their children suffer as a result of visits. "Pam," an incarcerated mother from my case study (Arditti & Few, 2008), began to cry during her interview as she discussed visits with her three children (aged 7, 5, and 2). Pam described her every-other-month visits with them as emotionally overwhelming "because you are not able to hold them...you can tell they get upset" (Arditti & Few, 2008, p. 310).[10] Another mother, on probation at the time of the interview, echoed similar sentiments and began to cry as she discussed visits from her daughter during her two previous incarcerations: "She [her daughter] couldn't take the pressure of leaving me there... this really hurts. I know that I did hurt her. I not only hurt [voice trembles] my daughter but I hurt my son" (Arditti & Few, 2008, p. 310). Fathers, too, report how emotionally difficult it is for them to see their child become upset during in-person visits. One incarcerated father discussed the difficulties of in-person visits with his young son, after a visit was cut short by prison staff to make room for other visitors: "The last time when he came to visit, he was screaming in the hallway for me, and that was...hard" (Arditti et al., 2005, p. 281). At the very least, conflicting findings regarding the benefits and difficulties of in-person visits with children reflect the complexity of how visits affect both offender parents and their family members.

Offender reactions to visitation are important when considering child and family effects. The offender is still part of the family system, and painful or difficult experiences associated with such contact likely influence whether the offender actively tries to engage the family through visits or discourages visits.

Ambiguity and Emotional Pain
Not only do difficulties and offenders' reactions shape the visitation experience, but visiting an incarcerated family member also reflects the ambiguous nature of loss for families affected by incarceration. Incarcerated parents and their family members likely experience both types of ambiguous loss, fluctuating between visiting "behind the fence" and life on the "outside." As we have discussed, in both types of ambiguous loss and their effects, the uncertainty may cause profound difficulty (Boss, 1999). Many aspects of the visitation situation are clearly beyond the family's control and involve outside constraints—factors that block coping and grieving processes and contribute to the reliving of trauma. The emotional energy that is "activated" during visitation can be positive or painful depending on the level of uncertainty surrounding the incarceration and the prognosis in terms of family reunification. For example, in situations where family members have an approaching "out date," that is, the inmate has a confirmed release date, the family sees an end to the visitation or views the visitation as preparation for reentry, and

the experience may be more positive due to the certainty surrounding it. In situations characterized by a great deal of uncertainty (e.g., sentencing has not occurred, appeals are in place, or the sentence is lengthy and the ability to *sustain* visitation and ties seems uncertain), the experience may be more painful. In particular, the absence of accurate information about the incarcerated parent can be especially difficult for children and can contribute to their ambiguous loss (Bocknek et al., 2009).

Visitation and Secondary Prisonization
Here it is worth mentioning that the conditions associated with visitation "reinforce the curious position that visitors occupy in their relations with the prison: neither fully captive nor fully free" (Comfort, 2008, p. 64). Visitation contact serves as a foundation for the institution's long-term alteration of the family's personal, domestic, and social worlds—or *secondary prisonization* (Comfort, 2008). In this manner, indirect effects of parental incarceration on families can also be conceptualized as a result of secondary prisonization. Secondary prisonization involves the transformation of the nonincarcerated family members' lives—particularly female intimate partners of the male inmate—as a result of interacting with the inmate and the correctional system. Changes may affect the family's social life, routine, priorities, and appearance based on their adaptations in response to a parent's incarceration. Most frequently, these adaptations occur within the context of visiting the incarcerated parent. Prison authorities establish a relationship with the family through repeated processing of and temporary containment of them during visitation. This relationship "generates changes in self-images and behaviors through rituals of debasement and the persistent denial of prestige, that is, through the application of the 'pains of imprisonment' (per Sykes, 1958): the deprivation of liberty, deprivation of goods and services, deprivation of heterosexual relationships, deprivation of autonomy, and deprivation of security" (Comfort, 2008, p. 29). Secondary prisonization implies an unsettling parallel between the nonincarcerated visiting family members and the inmate and suggests that the family is subjected to "weakened versions of the elaborate regulations, concentrated surveillance, and corporeal confinement governing the lives of ensnared felons and thus are secondarily prisonized by their interactions with the penal institution" (Comfort, 2008, p. 29). Additionally, through in-depth study of San Quentin women visiting their intimate partners and husbands, Comfort (2008) confirms the visitation difficulties reported by extant research such as long, frustrating waits, degrading treatment by staff, and crowded, noisy conditions.

Resilience Processes Influencing How Parental Imprisonment Impacts Family

With the exception of just a few studies, very little research is available that is strengths-based or documents the resilience of offender parents, their children, and their family members. The term *resilience* refers to "patterns of positive adaptation in the context of significant risk or adversity" (Masten & Powell, 2003, p. 4) and represents two judgments about an individual. The first judgment is an inference that a person is doing "OK"; the second is that there is or has been significant adversity (Masten & Powell, 2003). A family resilience framework extends these judgments from the individual to the family and suggests that even under extreme hardship and duress, positive *family* outcomes are possible (Luthar, 2006; Masten, 2001; Walsh, 2006). A family resilience perspective identifies protective factors and processes within the family system that seem to "buffer" or lessen a family's vulnerability to adversity, as well as enhance their ability to adapt and demonstrate competence under stress (Conger & Conger, 2002). Qualitative research investigating Chicago's urban poor affirmed resilience processes among even the most "hard-luck" families. Within contexts of extreme disadvantage, resilient families were characterized as very resourceful, place a high value on the parenting role (especially motherhood), protect their children from harm and promote their well-being, and are committed to collective responsibility and strength of character (Jarrett, 2010). Further, family boundaries in resilient families are broad and flexible. This means that family members may share breadwinning and nurturing roles as needed (e.g., one family member may take care of the young children of extended family, so that more members may work and pool resources). Given that many families experiencing incarceration do so within contexts of extreme disadvantage, one can infer family resilience can help, and also, to the extent the seeds of family strength are present in a given family, resilience may be cultivated.

African American families may inherently possess the characteristics that enhance the likelihood of producing positive developmental trajectories for children with incarcerated parents (Miller, 2007). Resilience on the part of African American families is believed to be due to adaptation over centuries of disenfranchisement and cumulative disadvantage. Such adaptations have resulted in contemporary kin networks in which children are a shared responsibility. That is, the strongest ties are consanguineal (blood ties) rather than conjugal (marital ties). Extended residence and child fosterage are central features that distinguish African and European family life. At a broad level, the shared raising of children is a way of strengthening, maintaining, and acknowledging extended family ties (McDaniel & Morgan, 1996: Miller, 1998). Geographic closeness, a strong sense of familial obligation, fluid household boundaries exhibited by the willingness to "absorb" relatives, high familial interactions, and strong systems of mutual aid are all characteristics of resilient African American families (Moras, Shehan, & Berardo, 2007). While minority status is a key contextual risk associated with incarceration, it may also be a protective factor to the extent it equates with family resilience. The fact that African American families tend to view children as a *collective responsibility* is a cultural asset for incarcerated parents and their children, who tend to need a great deal of assistance, particularly in instances of maternal incarceration. Unfortunately, the ameliorating affects of family strengths may take a backseat to negative societal expectations for African American children given "the [societal] belief that they too are destined to follow the criminal paths of their parents and others within the community" (Miller, 2007, p. 29).

In addition to the potential of cultural assets to mitigate the harm to children associated with a parent's incarceration, key protective factors that are theorized to be prominent (see, e.g., Parke & Clarke-Stewart, 2003) include social support by kin or other close and caring adults, caregiver stability, and children's positive relationship with a caregiver. These protective factors correspond to core resilience attributes derived from comprehensive reviews of the resilience literature on children who have faced major adversity. Given the limited empirical data that speak to the issue of resilience, as with other primary processes such as coparenting and traumatic separation, we must look to other, comparable literatures to understand the role of resilience in increasing the offender's psychological functioning, improving parenting behaviors for both offender and caregiver, and how it is that children overcome the adversity typically associated with the imprisonment of one or both parents. Research on children and adolescents who experience trauma in risk contexts such as poverty, child abuse, death of a parent, and addiction reveals that even the most extreme circumstances do not always lead to adjustment disorders or behavior problems (Luthar, 2003; Rutter, 1990; Walsh, 2006). The importance of resilience is quite clear when one considers the numerous difficulties experienced by incarcerated parents and their families.

While research on parental incarceration documents a great deal of risk to children, there are in fact indicators that many children also do well at home and in school contexts. Nesmith and Ruhland (2008) set out to examine family strengths of children whose parent was incarcerated. Using purposeful and snowball sampling procedures, they interviewed 34 children aged 8 to 17 and followed up with two subsequent interviews with the majority of the children. By far the most common reason for parental incarceration in this sample was drug charges (29%). It is worth noting that while the majority of the children's caregivers (all female relatives, mothers, aunts, and grandmothers) reported that children knew the reason their parent was incarcerated, when children were interviewed, 43% said they did not know why their parent was incarcerated, and 38% said they were not sure or answered vaguely. Of particular note was the fact that along with evidence of multiple social challenges for children and their family members, most of the children in this study seemed to be doing well or "OK" at school, with several "excelling beyond their peers" (Nesmith & Ruhland, 2008, p. 1127). Other examples of children "beating the odds" include school outcome findings and a series of studies examining the impact of maternal incarceration. For example, school achievement and dropout were unaffected by mothers' incarceration (Cho, 2009a, 2009b). Research by Hanlon, Blatchley, and colleagues (2005) on the vulnerability of 88 urban children (aged 9 to 14) with incarcerated, drug-addicted mothers also confirmed that in spite of adverse circumstances, the majority of children appeared to be well-adjusted and avoided substance abuse and deviant behavior. With regard to what attributes or processes underlie resilience relative to parental incarceration, researchers credit stable caregiving and the fact that most children in the study were *already* in the care of a relative prior to their mother's confinement as key protective factors buffering children from the adverse effects of both maternal imprisonment and maternal substance abuse (Hanlon, Blatchley, et al., 2005).

Indeed, evidence specific to incarcerated populations suggests that social support, particularly kin support, is an asset for children experiencing parental incarceration. Nesmith and Ruhland (2008) note that some of the children in their study had "strong supportive people and resources to help them" (p. 1127). Although children and caregivers in the study were quite aware of the highly stigmatized context of incarceration and thus valued privacy, a minority of children were able to break their silence and isolation and connect with others like themselves, such as peers who also had a parent in prison, or find trustworthy outsiders who would help them. Similarly, children's close relationships with kin seem to buffer trauma in transitioning to grandmother care (Bloom & Steinhart, 1993).

When children are given the opportunity to tell their story, further evidence of their resilience emerges, including opportunities to help the adults in their families by assuming certain caregiving responsibilities such as providing emotional support to their caregiver or incarcerated parent. While falling into caregiver roles may prove detrimental to children, as in other contexts of adultification such as extreme poverty, the taking on of some adult-like roles can have an "up side." Children who assume adultified roles often have a greater sense of social awareness and responsibility than their non-adultified peers (Burton, 2007). Several children in Nesmith and Ruhland's (2008) study were keenly aware of adult needs, serving as a confidante and protector to their caregiver and otherwise "filling in" for the absent father. Such displays of caregiving may empower children by giving them purpose, responsibility, and opportunities to nurture. To the extent that children's care of adults and family members inspires confidence and self-esteem, it can be considered a protective factor (Masten & Powell, 2003).

Two other attributes associated with resilience within the context of parental incarceration include a positive outlook on life and connections to prosocial organizations (Nesmith & Ruhland, 2008). A positive outlook on life encompasses faith, hope, and a belief that "life has meaning" (Masten & Powell, 2003, p. 13). Prosocial organizations might include church, sports facilities, clubs, and so forth. Several children in one study possessed these attributes of resilience: youth described how looking to the future with confidence, prayer, and activities and social connections through sports and church were important ways to get through hard times and deal with strong emotions such as sadness or anger. One boy's narrative reflects how these protective factors work in his life:

> I kind of remember…the story of Job. Where God let Satan take things from Job…but Job never curses God. Job gets everything back tenfold. I'm kind of hoping that will fall through a little bit. I mean my dad being gone is something that's really good. And football is something that is really good. And I have a lot of fun at church and I have friends from there. (Nesmith & Ruhland, 2008, p. 1127)

The engagement in prosocial activities (e.g., sports, extracurricular activities, and church) as a family strength was further confirmed by another qualitative study of 36 children being raised by 20 grandparent families (9 families in which grandparents were primary caregivers due to parental incarceration; Sands, Goldberg-Glen, & Shin, 2009). Children tended to perceive their grandparents and extended kin in positive terms and placed a high value on the help and attention their grandparents gave them. Children were also enthusiastic about social supports from adults outside the family such as social workers, therapists, "big brothers," babysitters, and scouts. These findings, along with research specific to justice-involved families, clearly indicate that family resilience encompasses (1) opportunities for children to have *something positive to do*, (2) adults who *care for them and show them attention* in concrete and meaningful ways, and (3) a *positive outlook and hope for the future*.

Caregiver Resilience

As discussed previously, caregivers are often under a great deal of strain, particularly if the imprisoned parent was an active participant and financial provider in children's lives prior to his or her incarceration. Caregivers may face stigma and isolation from others who may question their involvement with the incarcerated parent, blame them for the incarcerated parent's criminality, or somehow make assumptions about their values based on the incarcerated parent's actions (Nesmith, Ruhland, & Krueger, 2006). Seeing their children (or the children under their care) experience stigma and blame is particularly difficult for caregivers (Phillips & Gates, 2010). One woman participating in a study of children of incarcerated parents (Nesmith et al., 2006) explained:

> Lots of people think that when you have somebody that's in jail, whether it be husband, or boyfriend, or brother, or whatever, that you're bad too. But it's not true, you know? Just because that person did that, doesn't mean that you would. I've…met people and then it comes out after maybe a two month relationship, and then they think that you accepted or condone that and that's not true. And it doesn't mean that the kid is bad too. It just means that that happened. A lot of people assume. (p. 19)

Recent empirical evidence of stigma in children's school environments confirms caregiver perceptions of children's stigmatization. Teachers with awareness that a student's parent is incarcerated are likely to describe the child as having a chaotic home environment and behavior problems at school (Dallaire, Ciccone, & Wilson, 2010). Yet what is the source of these perceptions? Is it the child's behavior or the stigma of parental incarceration? A follow-up study with elementary school teachers suggests perceptions of children impacted by incarceration are largely influenced by the stigma that is unique to having a parent incarcerated. The study was based on an experimental design and randomly assigned public school teachers. Teachers were asked to respond to hypothetical descriptions about why a child, new to their classroom, was being raised by a grandparent. Scenarios included maternal incarceration along with common reasons caregivers give to children in order to "protect" them from the truth about their mothers' absence such as maternal rehabilitation (mom is away at rehab), maternal education (mom is away at school), and, simply, maternal absence with no specific reason (mom is away). Teachers rated the students in the prison condition as less competent than the other students, with girls in particular at the receiving end of lower expectations when teachers believed mothers were absent due to incarceration. The implications of this simulation are intriguing in that the findings suggest not only that teachers unwittingly may stigmatize those children in their classrooms who have a parent incarcerated, but that their lowered expectations could translate into a self-fulfilling prophecy. Children who belong to a vulnerable group are particularly prone to the negative impact such stigma might have on school performance and behavior (Jussim & Harber, 2005).

The Most Resilient Path: Truth Telling or Passing?

After her husband's arrest and incarceration, Andrea told her 3-year-old daughter, Mariana, that her daddy was on a long "road trip" but that we can "talk to him every day" by phone. However, days turned to weeks, and weeks turned to months, and Andrea has yet to bring her young daughter to visit her father after 7 months of confinement. Mariana persists in asking, "When will Daddy come home from his trip?" While Andrea lied only to shield her daughter from the ugliness of incarceration, she feels she has no other choice but to come clean with Mariana. Andrea takes her daughter to a favorite ice cream place and acknowledges: "I know you miss your daddy...." She apologizes to Mariana for lying and explains that her daddy did something bad and was on an "extra-long time-out," but that they could still go see him. Andrea was amazed at how happy her daughter was, even at 3, to hear the truth. They will be going to their first visit together the next weekend. Andrea decides that even with kids, "honesty is the best policy."

Given the intense stigma associated with parental incarceration, we see how caregivers as well as children are faced with either hiding information about a parent's incarceration or risking judgment and possible ostracism by others. As noted by Irving Goffman (1963) in his classic work *Stigma*, the management of damaging information (in this case the criminal justice involvement of the parent) was seen as critical in terms of one's personal and social identity. According to Goffman (1963), the stigmatized person employs an array of strategies to control discrediting and undisclosed information:

"To display or not to display; to tell or not to tell; to let on or not let on; to lie or not to lie; and in each case, to whom, how, when, and where" (p. 42). By intention or default, the stigmatized person is faced with conforming to what is expected by individuals who are prejudiced against those who are, in fact, the very thing he or she represents (in this case, an offender at worst, or someone closely associated with the offender). It is not surprising, particularly given the recent evidence of teachers' stigmatization with elementary school-age children (Dallaire et al., 2010), that many caregivers may choose to "pass," that is, conceal discreditable facts, about their own and their family member's situation. The ability to pass depends on the visibility of stigma; for a caregiver waiting in the prison visiting room, passing is not an option as her status is more obvious, as is the status of the offender, dressed in prison garb and slippers. However, out in the social world, particularly when one is not known personally, passing is likely inevitable and in, some cases, *adaptive*, by protecting the caregiver and children from stigma and the resultant marginalization.

While passing may reduce the potential for stigmatization, uncertainty may be magnified by misinformation that is given to children about a parent's whereabouts (Bocknek et al., 2009). As we have discussed, the theory of ambiguous loss (Boss, 1999) posits that such uncertainty can potentially heighten children's anxiety and emotional pain. As in Andrea's case, lies and half-truths are often told to children in an effort to protect them from the stigma associated with incarceration. Even in "coming clean," Andrea still tries to soften the truth of Mariana's father's imprisonment by labeling his incarceration as a "long time-out." Researcher Cristina Kampfner (1995) notes that lying to children about their parent's whereabouts may underestimate the acuity of children. She recounts the following example: "After visiting her mother, a child said that she had a secret that could not be told to her grandmother. 'This,' she explained, 'is not a hospital, it is a prison. My grandmother thinks my mother is sick, but she's really in prison'" (p. 93). Further, giving children misinformation about the incarcerated parent is connected to less secure attachment representations in young children (Poehlmann, 2010).

In addition to a lack of straightforwardness with children, caregivers may attempt to downplay children's pain, write the experience out of children's lives by ignoring it, or even mandate silence about a parent's crime, arrest, and incarceration because it gives the family a bad image (Kampfner, 1995). Such a "conspiracy of silence" (Kampfner, 1995, p. 92) not only is ambiguous and confusing but also forces children to "go underground" (Sack & Seidler, 1978) and may potentially exacerbate problems and emotional reactions associated with parental incarceration. Perhaps Kim's ability to stay close to her father and her assessment of herself as a "reasonably secure person" can be attributed to her mother's transparency about her father's incarceration.

Based on the existing data, experts recommend that telling children the truth about a parent's incarceration is the best course (Poehlmann, 2010). Being open with children about a parent's incarceration is believed to help children alleviate their ambiguous loss with the knowledge that their parent did not willfully abandon them (Phillips, 2001). Yet the truth may also create its own pain. Consistent with ambiguous loss tenets, children may resist clarifying information for fear of the consequences of knowing the truth about their parent. That is, the truth would require children to accept that their parent is a criminal and therefore a bad person (Bocknek et al., 2009). To avoid stigmatization, families may choose to conceal the truth about a parent's imprisonment. Experts might advise caregivers to be forthcoming with children, yet caregivers are rarely given guidance with regard to helping children cope with learning the truth about a parent's imprisonment (Phillips & Gates, 2010). Here we acknowledge the complexity of truth telling for families given the highly stigmatized nature of imprisonment. Children themselves are aware of being stigmatized, and even if they know the truth may still conceal it from others in an attempt to protect themselves. Due to the extreme stigma of criminal justice involvement, concealing the truth about their parent's whereabouts, while potentially creating long-term problems for the child, may on some level serve to protect the child from internalizing the "spoiled identity" that is equated with incarceration (Goffman, 1963). For example, one study found that children who knew the truth about a parent's imprisonment were more likely to have elevated PTSD symptoms than those who were told a lie (such as that the incarcerated parent was in the hospital or away at school; Fritsch & Burkhead, 1981).

Such avoidance of the truth by caregivers may be an odd form of adaptation that runs counter to moral assumptions about honesty and transparency in our thoughts and deeds. In thinking about the paradox of truth telling for justice-involved families and the use of "passing" as an adaptive strategy, consider the following account of a caregiver and her two young nephews:

> The caretaker…said with a very happy, cheerful voice, that they're here to visit him [the children's father] in the "super-hero school": "He's here to build muscles." She began talking to the kids about when he came out he'd have large muscles. The children began to banter happily about how strong he'd be. (Arditti, 2003, pp. 130–131)

In reflecting on this interaction between the two boys and their aunt, I commented:

> Jail was super-hero school, and the children gladly bought into this fantasy. The caregiver's refusal to give in to the desperation connected with the setting [i.e., she was initially denied visit due to visiting hour restrictions] was a source of resilience, giving these children a much needed "reality shield" as they walked through the locked doors to see their father. (Arditti, 2003, p. 131)

While controversial, in contexts of incarceration and loss, the caregiver's "optimistic bravado," coupled with the misinformation given to her nephews about their parent, reflects the complicated nature of defining resilience in highly stigmatized settings and stressful circumstances.

Ultimately, concealing the truth from children is a unique form of passing that may protect them, confuse them, or make matters worse depending on the age of the child, the content of the "pass," and the extent to which children interface with the correctional institution and the parent. Resilience in the strange and difficult context of parental incarceration may well involve how one deals with issues of telling and the type of support available to families and children coping with stigma and other realities associated with parental incarceration. It seems a certain level of emotional intelligence is necessary on the part of caregivers in making the choice. "Telling" is a delicate enterprise and can be helpful in terms of recognizing children's experience, as Andrea did by finally talking with Mariana over ice cream and acknowledging that Mariana "missed her daddy." Truth telling may also lessen social isolation to the extent that the dispenser of the information can provide much-needed social support. Connecting with those families experiencing a similar situation is a safe bet if one is lucky enough to have the time, resources, or access to venues of support. For example, one caregiver (Nesmith & Ruhland, 2008) was fortunate enough to have computer access and joined an Internet support group that made her feel less alone. Other sources of support are naturally occurring during the course of a common experience such as visiting at prisons and jails. My own fieldwork (Arditti, 2003) documents how families seemed to rely on other visitors at the jail for support and a sense of belonging:

> They know each other in this horrible place....They greet each other by name and [children] play [with the intern] until it is their turn to go

upstairs—they turn and say goodbye and go and visit their dad. They also get supported here by other children who are in a similar situation. These other children know what it is like to have a parent in jail. (p. 130)

Thus resilience involves a capability to locate support and discern who it may be "safe" or beneficial to tell about a parent's incarceration. Resilience may also involve shielding young children from certain harsh realities, yet providing enough truthful information about the parent to quell children's uncertainty and fears.

Offender Resilience
Within the context of parental incarceration, often the notion of "family resilience" fails to emphasize how the resilience of the offender, or lack thereof, can potentially shape family outcomes, particularly in terms of sustaining mental health during incarceration and a successful reentry transition. It stands to reason that the better offenders cope during confinement, the less distressed they will be, which in turn causes less strain and worry on the part of family members. A limited number of studies on incarcerated populations yield insight regarding offender resilience. Findings from a retrospective study on incarcerated adolescents suggest that resilient youth or "succeeders" (those who do not reoffend after release) experience the structure, rehabilitation (particularly drug treatment) opportunities, positive mentoring, and reflection time as positive components of the correctional system (Todis, Bullis, Waintrup, Schultz, & D'Ambrosio, 2001). The same characteristics that describe resilient youth pertain to youthful offenders, suggesting that resilience processes cut across specific groups (i.e., caregivers, nonincarcerated children, offenders): determination, a positive outlook, and a future orientation characterized the succeeder group. A study of 49 female prisoners, the majority of whom were mothers, revealed a similar pattern of resilience among a subgroup of the women labeled "spirited" (Martin & Hesselbrock, 2001). The spirited subgroup, while having many of the same difficulties as the other women such as mental health risks, a chaotic family history, and drug use, were the "hardiest" due to their family support, their strong internal and spiritual strength, determination, and positive outlook.

Indeed, given the kinds of contextual and process risks experienced by offenders during childhood and adulthood, when researchers specifically address the issue, the extent of resiliency that is uncovered among offenders is remarkable. A comparison of the resilience scores of incarcerated women on the Multidimensional Trauma Resilience and Recovery Interview (MTRR-I) to other groups of trauma survivors revealed high levels of resilience among the incarcerated *despite* the extent and severity of trauma reported by study participants (Bradley & Davino, 2007). The profile of resilient women in the study was marked by high functioning in three core areas: integration of traumatic memories into a coherent life story narrative and sense of self, ability to form intimate and healthy relationships with others, and capacity to actively engage in self-care and regulate emotional affect. Although resilient women still had continuous memories of painful and traumatic events, they appeared to have more actively processed the trauma (more so than their less resilient counterparts) and were thus better able to form positive attachments as adults with friends and with intimate partners. They also had "developed strategies and self-care routines for managing painful affect" (Bradley & Davino, 2007, p. 133). Such trauma processing and the resultant adaptations may involve finding meaning in life based on one's past suffering, avoiding situations that are demeaning, humiliating, or unnecessarily painful, and a view of the self that is not dominated by traumatic experiences.

As with other resilience research, one would assume that family support would be a critical protective factor for offenders in terms of enhancing adjustment and lessening incapacitation; however, there is limited evidence that rigorously tests this presumption. At the time of reentry, a body of work does point to family support as a critical factor in successful reintegration (Travis, 2005); however, during confinement the issue is debatable. For example, one study found that family support (defined as contact and communication with friends and family) had no effect on PTSD symptoms and distress among male inmates (Hochstetler, Murphy, & Simons, 2004). It may be that supportive connections with prison staff and mentors are more important during confinement than support from family.

Summary

Shari, Kim, Zoe, Andrea, and Ron are all are directly and indirectly affected by their family member's incarceration. Yet to society at large, their circumstances and concerns may remain invisible, only coming to our attention if one of them or their children interface with the social welfare or criminal justice system. We can see in each of their cases, as well as in the empirical research, that a family member's incarceration often connects with traumatic separation and a disturbing sequela of economic decline, child adjustment and behavior problems, and caregiver duress. While cumulative disadvantage factors account for a portion of these effects, children dealing with separation from a parent due to incarceration experience difficulties that stem from the stigma and circumstances that are unique to prison confinement compared with other types of parental loss. Parental incarceration alters family processes in critical ways. Emotional loss may go unrecognized, lack resolution, and make it difficult for family members to work through trauma and move forward with their lives. If a parent was involved with his or her family prior to incarceration, family members must adapt to his or her departure in dramatic ways to maintain a meaningful connection with that person. Visitation is an important means to keep family ties alive; however, such contact comes with high economic, emotional, and social opportunity costs. It is no wonder that children are often the recipient of half-truths and outright lies regarding a parent's whereabouts. When truth equates with social shame, it is a hard pill to swallow. Maintaining the connection with an imprisoned family member can equate with pain or other burdens. Thus ties between offender parents and their family members are fragile and can easily deteriorate.

While there is little question that for many families, parental incarceration is often a part of an intergenerational cycle of despair and criminality, it is worthwhile to carefully consider under what conditions children and caregivers may thrive in spite of adversity. Clearly, resource adequacy, responsive and stable caregiving, meaningful emotional and social connections, and developmentally enhancing opportunities for children can foster well-being in spite of the problems a parent's incarceration may pose. Innovative solutions are desperately needed to help not only offenders but also their nonincarcerated family members and children to break dysfunctional cycles, foster developmentally promotive family processes, and offer hope to incarcerated parents and their families. In the next chapter we put the pieces of the puzzle together by presenting a conceptual model that incorporates key contextual factors, internal and family processes, and offender and family outcomes as derived from the coverage presented in this book. Using this model as a "road map," we can then explore the policy and practice implications of a parent's incarceration with an eye toward helping, rather than hurting, those most affected by mass incarceration policies.

6

Conclusion

*Practice and Policy Implications of a Family
Perspective on Parental Incarceration*

Selene's Story

Since the age of 11, Selene Diaz[1] was the child of an incarcerated father. She struggled with this fact emotionally but soon gained acceptance in her inner-city neighborhood by joining a gang. One thing led to another, and after fighting in school, Selene was arrested and sent to juvenile hall at the age of 15. Like so many of her friends there, Selene felt her circumstances were "normal." After her release, a series of drug and theft charges kept her in and out of juvenile hall until she graduated to state prison. Selene's mother was occupied with two part-time jobs and caring for three other children, one of whom was Selene's infant son. Selene had little in the way of support or a model for another way of life. One day at the age of 22, after a 15-month incarceration, Selene was contacted by the Women's Center for Empowerment (WCE), a nonprofit organization devoted to helping marginalized young women who are involved in the criminal justice system. Selene was asked to do outreach on the streets of her city for other young mothers like herself. Selene was shocked to learn that she would be paid for her efforts at WCE, despite her criminal record. Shortly thereafter, Selene was picked up and beaten by the police for spray painting graffiti. When Selene went to the WCE the next day and told her colleagues what happened, she was shocked at their reaction—an overwhelming "This is not OK!" No one had ever stood up for Selene before. The group then organized a demonstration in front of the police department protesting their treatment of Selene.

Selene, now 30, lives independently with her son and works at WCE. She explains that the day of the police protest was a turning point in her life. Selene recalls: "I had never had anyone on my side before, someone to believe in me, someone who lived where I lived and knew where I had been. Up to the time

I was contacted by WCE I was invisible. With WCE at my side, I realized my life could matter. I did not want any girl to go through what I had and so from that point on, I worked to make sure that other girls like me would not be forgotten....when everyone else saw me as a hopeless case, WCE saw me as a stakeholder."

Selene's case is a fictional dramatization; however, the organization that reached out to her is real. The "WCE" is in reality the Center for Young Women's Development (CYWD) in San Francisco, one of the first nonprofits in the United States run and led entirely by young women. The CYWD is designed to target the most marginalized young women in the street economies and justice system and delivers intensive wraparound services with multiple components such as reading education, job readiness training, peer-to-peer mentoring, critical thinking, and political education. Why does this organization work? First and foremost, participants in the program are viewed as clients, that is, people there to get a service, rather than the "throwaways" of society. CYWD's guiding principles include social justice, sisterhood, self-determination, and self-value. Part of its success lies in the fact that many participants self-refer, and they *want* to be there. The CYWD program represents evidenced-based intervention that aligns well with ecological theory and developmental contextualism. CYWD lives by the creed "Wherever young women are, that's where we are" (Hester, 2010). As we will soon discuss, this kind of alignment between a program and the lived experience of parent offenders is critical in promoting change. Further, CYWD's activism aimed at fighting oppression and breaking down social and political barriers for ex-offenders demonstrates a sensitivity to context and a holistic understanding of the challenges associated with incarceration that extend beyond the individual. The primary objective of this chapter is to explore in depth the "principles behind the program." Here we advance family-focused policy and practice that align with our developmental, ecological systems framework of examining families in context. By critically examining current policy reforms and programmatic efforts aimed at incarcerated parents and their families, suggestions for innovation based on the themes and patterns derived from the empirical coverage can be offered. First, an integrative model is presented that summarizes these major themes covered in the book derived from the empirical research. Then a pyramid of principles that link to these major themes is advanced as a means to guide policy reform and intervention. These principles encompass the need to implement social justice, reduce harm, and promote human development among incarcerated parents and their family members.

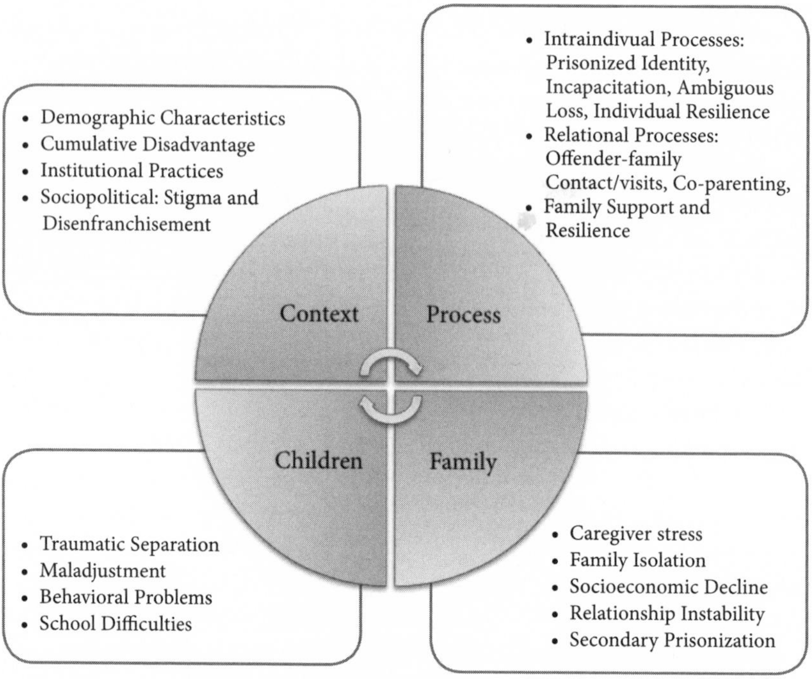
Demographic Characteristics
Cumulative Disadvantage
Institutional Practices
Sociopolitical: Stigma and Disenfranchisement
Intraindivual Processes: Prisonized Identity, Incapacitation, Ambiguous Loss, Individual Resilience
Relational Processes: Offender-family Contact/visits, Co-parenting,
Family Support and Resilience
Context
Process
Children
Family
Traumatic Separation
Maladjustment
Behavioral Problems
School Difficulties
Caregiver stress
Family Isolation
Socioeconomic Decline
Relationship Instability
Secondary Prisonization
A family perspective on parental incarceration

A Family Perspective on Parental Incarceration

Figure 1 illustrates a family perspective of parental incarceration as derived from published empirical findings outlined in earlier chapters. A central feature of the illustration is its wheel-like shape. A wheel suggests dynamic movement, and as we have discussed, parental incarceration is not a discrete event but a process that unfolds over time. Within the wheel, contextual and process changes are represented, as are family and child effects that connect with these changes. All parts of the wheel are interdependent; each section touches (i.e., shares a side or corner) with every other section. This type of interdependence represents the "fused contexts" (Lerner et al., 1999) discussed in chapter 1 that constitute development. The turning arrows in the center of the wheel signify dynamic change and also suggest the possibility of multiple influences—influences that encompass the direct and indirect effects of parental incarceration on children and families. Finally, the wheel representation suggests that child outcomes of parental incarceration cannot be understood apart from family effects (e.g., the quality and stability of the caregiver). Complexity is a feature of the model reflecting the myriad variables and possible configurations that may act at any point in time, influencing child and family well-being.

The integrative model can be translated to inform policy and practice because it points to key areas whereby intervention makes sense and would give the most "bang for the buck." For example, we can see from looking at Figure 1 how important structural changes aimed at alleviating cumulative disadvantage are in terms of shaping parenting processes, as well as enhancing positive outcomes for caregivers and the children in their charge. We can also see how changing institutional practices such as the length of one's sentence or how far from family one is housed can impact contact and communication processes, which in turn, may prove beneficial for the offender and his or her family.

As detailed in previous chapters, a family perspective implies interlocking systems between offender parents, children, and caregivers. A family perspective also implies that family is center stage with regard to policy reform and intervention. A focus on family highlights the importance of child development, offender adjustment, and offender and caregiver parenting competencies. Context, processes, family effects, and child outcomes identified here suggest an array of harms that result from both parental incarceration and the contextual conditions (e.g., cumulative disadvantage, stigma) that are associated with parents' criminal justice involvement. These harms stem primarily from offender incapacitation and the implications parental incarceration has for those responsible for the care of the offender's children. The complexity of the cause-and-effect relationships that contribute or actually cause these harms suggests that intervention and reform strategies must be multipronged and attend to core ecological tenets of development. These central tenets basically involve a social policy agenda that focuses on social justice, risk reduction, and enhancing opportunity with the ultimate goal of promoting human capacity and agency. With this basic developmental and family-focused agenda in mind, we can advance a series of principles to guide efforts to attend to the needs of offender parents and their family members. Figure 2 presents these principles as a hierarchical pyramid such that each "level" of the pyramid depends on the goals of the previous level being met. For example, the provision of evidence-based programs aimed at enhancing family strengths is important but far more effective within a context of sweeping policy reform that addresses social and racial inequities, the

Pyramid of principles

alleviation of cumulative disadvantage, and efforts to reduce our overreliance on incarceration as a first response to social problems. We will discuss these principles from the foundation of the pyramid to its peak.

Principle 1: Advance Social Justice

Marginalization is perhaps the most dangerous form of oppression.[2]

Social justice can be defined as "the elimination of institutionalized domination and oppression" (Young, 1990, p. 15). Such a perspective of social justice moves beyond theories that focus solely on "morally proper" (Young, 1990, p. 15) distributions of benefits (e.g., wealth, income, and material resources) and burdens and considers the institutional context in which distributions are made. This focus on the institutional context is particularly important in thinking about crime and punishment in America as well as their effects on family functioning and structure. As we have discussed, a parent's criminal justice involvement does not occur in a vacuum, but rather in a context characterized by disproportionate impacts on racial and ethnic minorities, cumulative disadvantage, restrictive institutional practices, and social stigma. Social justice involves the degree to which society supports the institutional conditions necessary for the development of one's capacities and self-determination (conditions that, by the way, were met by the CYWD program's empowering methods and political activism). Young argues that this definition of social justice corresponds to two conditions that define injustice: oppression and domination. Clearly incarceration poses severe institutional constraints on self-development (oppression) and participation in determining one's actions (domination) as evidenced in the research coverage concerning incarcerated parents' incapacitation and altered identities.

The increase in the number of incarcerated parents, and subsequently family members connected to the incarcerated, is a social justice issue because it corresponds to deepening racial and ethnic disparities between African Americans and whites, and more recently Hispanics, who have been the fastest-growing group being imprisoned in the past decade. There are 238,000 Hispanics in federal and state prisons and local jails, constituting 15% of the U.S. inmate population. Their numbers have increased from 10.9% of all state and federal inmates in 1985 to 15.6% in 2001. As of 2007, Hispanics were the largest single ethnic group in the federal prison system, fueled in part by changes in immigration law that have multiplied the ways in which undocumented immigrants can be prosecuted and imprisoned (Lopez & Light, 2009). Social inequality is "crystallized" by penal involvement because it is invisible, cumulative, and intergenerational (Western & Pettit, 2010a). As we have seen, prisoners are often drawn from the bottom rungs of society and may not be counted in poverty or unemployment indicators. The harms that result from incarceration are cumulative in the sense that they are experienced by those who already are the least advantaged and have the fewest opportunities. Consistent with a family perspective on parental incarceration, carceral inequalities are intergenerational in that they affect the offender parent, as well as their families and children (Western & Pettit, 2010b). Children who begin life on the bottom rungs are more likely themselves to stay on the bottom rung in adulthood (Ratcliffe & McKernan, 2010; Western & Pettit, 2010b).

Exclusionary Practices

The social injustice perpetuated by our punishment policies stems from the intensification of the activities of the police, courts, and prison that are finely targeted by class, race, and place (i.e., geographically concentrated in the poorest minority neighborhoods; Roberts, 2004; Wacquant, 2010). As noted criminologist Todd Clear (2008) has said, "Incarceration is not equal-opportunity" (p. 100). Ecologically speaking, these broad macro processes serve as the backdrop of family life for those impacted by incarceration. Racial, class, and ethnic disparity in the criminal justice system is widespread and undermines justice and the fairness of the criminal justice system (National Association for the Advancement of Colored People [NAACP], 2011). Disparities in the criminal justice system involve not only treatment within prison but also discrimination at various points within the arrest, prosecution, and adjudication process. Selene's bad treatment by the police is hard to imagine—yet for an invisible young woman with a history of criminal justice involvement, not entirely unprecedented. Social justice disparities impact other areas of life such as employment, income, housing, and access to education (Donzinger, 1996; NAACP, 2011; Sentencing Project, 2008).

With regard to discrimination within the system, one point of disparity that has received recent attention is pretrial detention, which involves the holding of an individual in jail or prison after arrest but prior to his or her trial. Pretrial detention was the subject of a recent global report funded by the Open Society Institute, which demonstrates how the practice disproportionately affects individuals and families living in poverty. Globally, pretrial detainees are more likely to be noncitizens and/or to belong to racial and ethnic groups that are discriminated against because of their descent (Open Society Institute, 2010a). Further, analyses within the United States document that pretrial detainees are disproportionately racial and ethnic minorities (Donzinger, 1996; Schlesinger, 2005). Disparities pertaining to pretrial detention stem from two sources. First, those in poverty are more likely to come into conflict with the criminal justice system in the first place. Second, the poor are more likely to be detained in jail awaiting trial because they are less able to make bail or pay bribes (a widespread issue in developing countries) for their release. It is worth noting that the United States has the world's highest number of pretrial detainees (476,000) and the fourth-highest rate in the world (158 per 100,000; Open Society Institute, 2010a).

Conditions in pretrial detention centers are often worse than in prison and are imposed on individuals who are presumed innocent—a third of whom are ultimately found to be innocent of any charges waged against them (Open Society Institute, 2010b). The consequences of pretrial detention have a ripple effect from the individual to the family, not only in terms of their shared suffering but also because persons awaiting trial cannot work and earn income while detained. Many detainees are employed at the time of arrest and subsequently lose their jobs if detained. In addition to the lost income, families of detainee's must shoulder costs associated with detention such as traveling to visit the detainee, give financial support to the detainee, and, in some countries, provide low-level bribes to corrupt criminal justice officials. Children's lives are disrupted if their parent is detained, and a particular problem in developing countries is that children may be forced out of school and into work to help make up for the lost income of a detained parent (Open Society Institute, 2010a). Perhaps most insidious is the fact that pretrial detention undermines one's ability to mount an adequate legal defense, thus contributing to the likelihood of conviction and further detainment (Donzinger, 1996). Disparities in pretrial detainment highlight how excessive and disparate use of a specific practice at one stage of the criminal justice process can both reflect social inequality and perpetuate it. In the instance of pretrial detention, social justice can be achieved by using pretrial detention only when no other alternative can address flight risks or public safety to the community. Its widespread use for poor, nonviolent drug offenders seems unnecessary and overly harsh. Alternatives to ensure release after arrest and processing could involve the use of personal surety (promise to attend court and stand trial) or other reporting requirements rather than monetary bail. If monetary bail is used, it should be proportionate to a person's income (Open Society Institute, 2010a).

Targeting the issue of pretrial detention is just one example of how one might advance a social justice agenda within criminal justice that ultimately could benefit poor, disadvantaged parents caught up in the system. Reforms aimed at developing alternatives to pretrial detention represent efforts to "level the playing field" within a broad scope of social inequities that impact offender parents and their family members.

Enfranchisement as a Pathway to Social Justice

Social justice demands a reversal of practices that disenfranchise individuals as a result of their incarceration. The implications of disenfranchisement are most evident at the time of the offender parent's reentry into family and community life. As we have discussed, time behind bars likely diminishes, rather enhances, the odds of parents who have been incarcerated living crime-free lives on the outside largely through their unemployability, their weakened or severed ties with family, their incapacitation, and their prisonized identities (Loury, 2010). These problems are exacerbated because incarceration concretely denies citizenship rights to those already on the margins, further perpetuating inequality through felon disenfranchisement laws. Civic exclusion stems largely from the "invisible punishments" (see Travis, 2002, who coined the phrase) that accompany incarceration and extend beyond the offenders' sentences (Roberts, 2004, p. 1291). Invisible punishments are legal barriers that are particularly harmful to the economic, political, and social well-being of African American families given their disproportionate incarceration in the United States (Mauer & Chesney-Lind, 2002). These invisible punishments constitute a civic death that involves denying ex-prisoners access to (1) cultural capital (e.g., ineligibility for educational loans), (2) social redistribution (e.g., ineligibility for federally funded health and welfare benefits), and (3) political participation (e.g., ineligibility to vote; Wacquant, 2001). Many of the invisible punishments experienced by the formerly incarcerated were buried in the welfare reform package passed by Congress in 1996 (the Personal Responsibility and Work Opportunity Reconciliation Act [PRWORA]) and target drug offenders, although states can opt out of the provision. As of 2003, twenty states enforced a ban on welfare benefits in full. We can expect that the denial of welfare benefits disproportionately impacts minorities not only but also the growing number of mothers who are in the criminal justice system due to a drug offense. For example, in 2002, an estimated 92,000 women were ineligible to receive welfare benefits due to exclusionary practices impacting former drug offenders (Mauer, 2003). More recent reviews of state policies suggest that there has been some shift in terms of the number of states implementing the full ban and an increase in states "opting out" of the permanent ban on welfare benefits for ex–drug offenders. As of December 2009, a total of 30 states had altered the ban to allow people who meet certain conditions (such as passing drug tests, participating in treatment) to receive food stamps or welfare assistance. Eleven states continue to adopt the federal restrictions in full, and nine states have lifted the ban entirely (Treadwell & Kingsbury, 2009; Treadwell, personal communication, November 13, 2010).[3] The current increase in the number of states altering the ban or lifting it entirely represents a growing awareness that food stamps and cash assistance are essential to the health and stability of families. Although federal legislation recently introduced to Congress aimed at repealing the Temporary Assistance for Needy Families (TANF) ban for drug offenders has failed to move forward, states increasingly are recognizing the practice may be counterproductive. Critics of existing policy argue that the lifetime ban should be eliminated altogether in the interest of fostering social reintegration and rehabilitation of drug offenders. Ultimately, the federal provision is an example of invisible punishments that harm not only offenders but also their children and family members, who lose the benefits as well.

Invisible punishments stemming from disenfranchisement are a social justice issue because they cause difficulties for those parents and families most in need. For example, ineligibility for student loans is especially problematic for lower-income students who need assistance; denial of food stamps will contribute to hunger only for those families who struggle to put food on the table; political disenfranchisement will impact those communities who are most affected by incarceration and substantially dilutes the voting power of African American communities, where huge numbers of citizens are excluded from the electoral process (Mauer, 2003; Roberts, 2004). As of 2008, under existing felon disenfranchisement laws, an estimated 5 million people were ineligible to vote in the U.S. presidential election. This figure includes nearly 4 million individuals who reside in the 35 states that prohibit voting among persons on probation or parole, and/or people who have completed their sentence. The racial disparities within the criminal justice system translate into relatively high rates of disenfranchisement among African Americans, with one in every eight adult black males ineligible to vote (King, 2008).

Within the criminal justice system, a comprehensive package of reforms aimed at resisting overcriminalization, implementing fairness throughout preconviction and sentencing, providing alternatives to incarceration, and enfranchising offenders is necessary to reduce social inequality and promote social justice (2009 Criminal Justice Transition Coalition, 2008). Glimmers of hope exist in terms of turning the tide of social injustice in broad and specific ways. At the federal level, the passage of the National Criminal Justice Commission Act by the House of Representatives in July 2010 represented an important step in addressing social disparities within the criminal justice system. The bill (S. 306) has been reintroduced in the Senate (February, 2011, 112th Congress) by Senator Jim Webb and is still awaiting action. If passed, it would create a blue-ribbon bipartisan commission of experts charged with reviewing the nation's criminal justice system and offering concrete recommendations for reform ("Webb's National Criminal Justice Commission Act," 2011; Criminal Justice Bill Fact Sheet, 2010). Further, tax credit incentives are now available for small businesses that hire employees in certain targeted groups, *including ex-felons*. The tax credits are part of broader legislation in the Hiring Incentives to Restore Employment (HIRE) Act and in effect for 2010–2011 (Baum, 2010). On the state level, Maryland and Minnesota have both enacted legislation to strengthen employment options for felony offenders (Porter, 2010).

Best practices have also been identified by the Sentencing Project and the Council of State Governments Justice Center, which highlight states that have enacted strategies to reduce racial, social, and economic inequality and ensure family economic well-being. For example, within the past 10 years, 19 states have reformed their disenfranchisement policies to expand voter eligibility, resulting in approximately 760,000 persons regaining their right to vote (King, 2008). Political inclusion may also have indirect "family-friendly" benefits. A recent study conducted in Oregon (where ex-felons can vote) found that those parolees and probationers who exercised their right to vote had lower rates of recidivism than ex-felons who did not vote, suggesting that family stability is enhanced via civic inclusion (Uggen & Inderbitzin, 2009). Enfranchisement also involves continued momentum in states' efforts to expand welfare benefits for those impacted by incarceration, form partnerships with housing authorities in order to assist incarcerated individuals to find housing before or after release, and help parents meet child support obligations after release from jail or prison (Nickel, Garland, & Kane, 2009). Finally, best practices also encompass state and local efforts to reduce racial disparity through respectful policing, race-neutral pretrial risk assessment, prosecutorial monitoring, and judicial research (Sentencing Project, 2008).

In addition to best practices and criminal justice policy reform aimed at supporting families, reducing racial disparities, and enfranchising ex-felons, social justice demands health security. Health is a critical dimension of well-being: physical and mental health is fundamental for parental competency, family functioning, and positive developmental trajectories in children. Bringing about the conditions necessary for people to be healthy, and specifically, parents and children impacted by incarceration, can be considered one of the direct requirements of social justice (Powers & Faden, 2006). Health care is a particularly acute need for prisoners reentering the community who bear a high burden of chronic health conditions (e.g., asthma, depression), infectious diseases (e.g., tuberculosis, hepatitis), and unmet health needs (Davis et al., 2009; Travis, 2005). For example, a recent examination of the state of health care in the California criminal justice system found that the majority of inmates reported not having seen a doctor since their admission and were returning uninsured to neighborhoods and communities with limited access to health care resources (Davis et al., 2009). It is likely the state of health affairs in California mirrors the national picture in the United States given the geographic concentration of incarceration and reentry in the most resource-poor communities (Roberts, 2004; Sampson & Loeffler, 2010). In addition to barriers confronting offenders during and after incarceration, as we have discussed, the health of nonincarcerated family members may also be an issue due to inadequacies prior to a parent's incarceration (Arditti, Burton, et al., 2010), as well as health difficulties that may be exacerbated by the stress and strain instigated by a parent's incarceration (Arditti et al., 2003).

On March 23, 2010, the Patient Protection and Affordable Care Act (PPACA) became law in the United States. What does this reform mean with regard to offender parents and their families? While PPACA does not contain specific provisions for prisoners, it certainly stands to advantage their family members who previously lacked either health insurance or access to health care. Beginning in 2014, the Health Care and Education Affordability Reconciliation Act HCEARA and PPACA will provide funding for expanded Medicaid coverage for all individuals whose incomes are under 133% of the federal poverty level. Further, the PPACA provides promising mechanisms to establish community health centers to provide basic health services in underserved areas (Beddoe, 2010). We can assume, as long as there are no exclusionary provisions in the PPACA, that health care reform represents an important step in advancing social justice for those individuals and families most likely to interface with the criminal justice system, and least likely under the current prereform system to enjoy the benefits of good health.

In sum, just as a holistic, family-centered approach is necessary for understanding the experience and implications of parental incarceration, a holistic and systemic set of reforms and interventions is necessary to resolve social justice issues within and without the criminal justice system. The disparate and widespread use of exclusionary practices aimed at disenfranchising the offender, as well as targeted practices such as pretrial detainment, which immediately disadvantage those at the time of arrest, are key examples of the complexity of the criminal justice system and its embeddedness in larger systems of oppression. Advancing a social justice agenda within criminal justice involves acknowledging the cumulative nature of racial and ethnic disparities at each point of decision making along the criminal justice continuum (i.e., arrest, detainment, sentencing, etc.) and communication and collaboration among key stakeholders (i.e., courts, prisons, probation, social welfare, health systems; Sentencing Project, 2008; Spohn, 2000). Resolution of social inequality outside the criminal justice system involves a targeted focus on expanding educational, work, and health-enhancing benefits and life opportunities. Broad mechanisms for promoting social equality include reducing prison populations (particularly in neighborhoods with significant concentrations of people going to prison; NAACP, 2011), enfranchisement of the offender parent, and support for his or her family. Expansion of social justice in these areas of life will help restrict inequality in the criminal justice system and the need for penal solutions for social problems such as poverty and unemployment (Wacquant, 2010). Social justice serves as a foundation and guiding framework for our next principle for policy and practice: harm reduction.

Principle 2: Do No Harm: Harm Reduction as a Framework for Reform and Intervention

> A nation's value system and treatment of persons who violate the norms are closely intertwined.[4]

> Our responses to crime often exacerbate the problem.[5]

A paradigm shift from criminal sanction policy to harm reduction is an important step in curbing the nation's appetite for punishment and lessening the negative consequences for offenders, family, and society that stem from mass incarceration. Such reform and related programming are a promising element of creating a context for social justice and a means to offset the harms associated with incarceration on multiple systemic levels. The continuum of harm reduction may range from sweeping legislation aimed at decriminalizing risky behaviors and diverting certain groups of people from the criminal justice system altogether, to midlevel solutions within criminal justice providing alternatives to incarceration for criminal offenders, to specific interventions focused on reducing harms to incarcerated offenders and their families such as special arrest procedures when children are present or improved visitation in prison.

Harm reduction is a fundamental strategy to reduce risk for offender parents and their families and is based on a public health philosophy that seeks to lessen the consequences of risky behavior. A core tenet of public health is that people should have the knowledge, facilities, and freedom to maintain and improve their own health; within prisons social justice demands that prisoners should have the health resources and care that is available to those not in prison (World Health Organization [WHO], 2005). Harm reduction pursues a social justice response that encompasses (1) a fundamental respect for civil liberties, tolerance, and human rights (Hathaway, 2001); (2) an alternative to prohibition of high-risk lifestyle choices instead of criminalizing such behaviors and choices; and (3) a focus on reducing public health harms (such as HIV and hepatitis C resulting from injecting drugs in prisons) to those who are already in prison (Kerr, 2006; Nodine, 2006; WHO, 2005). A harm reduction framework supports the idea that people should not be dis-enfranchised because they take risks (Marlatt, 2002).

With respect to the criminal justice system, harm reduction is most often applied to drug use and thus has great bearing on those offenders who are incarcerated for drug-related activities (Arditti & McClintock, 2001; Stover, Weilandt, Zurhold, Hartwig, & Thane, 2008). Harm reduction has gained widespread acceptance as a drug control strategy in Britain, the Netherlands, and other developed countries (Open Society Institute, 2007; Van Wormer, 1999) and shifts the definition of drug use from one that emphasizes criminal sanctions to one of public health, education, and the net well-being of soci-ety (Arditti & McClintock, 2001). From a harm reduction framework, the net well-being of society will always be a function of the total harm to society that may result from a particular problem *and* any collective action taken to "solve" the problem.

In calculating total harm from a family perspective, we must consider not only the social consequences of parents' risky behaviors but also the conse-quences of their incarceration. We have discussed in previous chapters (and summarized in Figure 1) some of the more salient consequences of paren-tal incarceration. Recent attention aimed at the effects of incarceration on children and prisoner reentry signifies social concern regarding the costs of incarceration. This attention to the direct and indirect costs associated with incarceration can be interpreted as an emerging awareness of the potential harms of criminal sanction policy—particularly for nonviolent drug offend-ers who constitute a hefty portion of prisoners in the United States. Until recently, the invisibility of these harms to parents, families, and society has been due to a lack of systematic data collection, the lag between punitive intervention and the longer time period it takes for harms to become salient, and the fact that the negative individual and family consequences that may result from mass imprisonment policy are borne disproportionately by eth-nic minorities and the poor, who lack the political power to make themselves heard.

In applying a "do no harm" principle for intervention and reform, the crux of the issue is determining the extent to which incarceration creates more harm than good with respect to public safety and the reduction of certain kinds of crime committed by parent offenders. It would seem, given the cov-erage provided in this book with respect to the impact of parental incarcera-tion, that alternatives to criminal sanction policy are desperately needed if we are to take seriously the problems of prisoner reentry, the creation of sin-gle-parent households, and the undesirable and unique effects that parental incarceration has on children. While certain aspects of harm reduction may not be appropriate for violent or career criminals (Western & Pettit, 2010a), the promise of a "do no harm" framework is that it provides an alternative set of responses to certain kinds of social problems and risky behaviors that contribute to and constitute lawbreaking.

At its broadest and most politicized, harm reduction as a strategy involves legislative changes that would dismantle legal restrictions against the use and sale of drugs (DuPont & Voth, 1995; Roe, 2005). More widely accepted is the notion of harm reduction as an alternative to incarceration with the explicit aim of containing the corrections population and reducing not only the costs associated with incarceration but also the impact of incarceration on the offender's economic mobility (Western & Pettit, 2010a). Emphasis is placed on diverting lower-risk offenders (typically defined as nonviolent) to community supervision with sanctions and services designed to reduce recidivism. Support for diversion is driven by a value-neutral, cost-benefit rationale focused on dollars and cents such that "a day in prison costs nearly $80.00 compared with a day on probation supervision, which costs $3.50" (Western & Pettit, 2010b, p. 25). Community supervision is seen as preferable because it is cheaper than incarceration and also affords the offender the opportunity to work, build human and social capital, care for his or her children, and pay restitution and other fines rather than drain resources.

Barriers to Harm Reduction

They're trying to build a prison, (for you and me to live in).[6]

Despite critique that points to the inefficacy of criminal sanctions to deter certain types of crime, particularly the use of illicit drugs (e.g., Csete, 2010; Drucker, 1999; Nadelman, 1998), not everyone believes harm reduction is the answer. The evidence with respect to drug use and addiction is generally supportive of such an approach in Western Europe (Csete, 2010) and within prisons (Stover et al., 2008; WHO, 2005). Yet advocates of criminal sanction policy cite the purported failures of harm reduction as reason enough to intensify prohibition (Csete, 2010). For example, the Drug Enforcement Administration used Britain's attempts to reduce the harms to drug users over the past 20 years as the fodder for its argument for continued efforts aimed at reducing the supply of drugs and harsh penalties for drug offenders. It insists that harm reduction drug policy leads to an "explosion of addiction" and is not the right model for the United States (Drug Enforcement Administration, 2003). Closer inspection of the scientific evidence pertaining to the efficacy of harm reduction in the United Kingdom reveals a mixed picture whereby drug use persisted despite the fact that certain health outcomes (HIV/AIDS, hepatitis C) did not worsen under harm reduction efforts (McKeganey, 2006). However, there is no scientific link in the UK evidence that harm reduction caused drug use and crime, or that criminal sanctions would have prevented it. Rather, it is concluded that too much focus has been put on the individual drug user rather than the families and communities in which drug use occurs, and that future harm reduction efforts must be broader, invested in drug prevention, and resolve shortfalls in drug treatment (McKeganey, 2006).

What are the roots of the predominantly punitive approach taken by the United States for dealing with those individuals who violate social norms and legal codes of conduct? Historical scholars trace the nation's propensity toward punishment, sometimes labeled "harm induction," as influenced by Puritanism and the doctrines of predestination:

> The Puritans believed that persons were either to be saved or condemned— this was their destiny. Sooner or later persons would give evidence of the category to which they belonged. Those who had reason to fear the worst would inevitably sink to the lowest echelons of society. In accordance with the will of God, punishment of offenders was harsh. (Van Wormer, 1999, p. 38, online version)

The ethos of Puritanism arguably still manifests itself in American society today and is considered by some scholars to be a "species of political... absolutism" (Zafirovski, 2007, p. 3, online version) that permeates a criminal justice policy based on social control strategies, coercion, and draconian sanctions. For example, critics of the drug war have argued that punishment under mandatory minimums is overly harsh, rigid, and restrictive (Austin & Irwin, 2001; Mauer, 2006). Puritan-inspired "tough on crime" institutions and policies are seen as rendering and perpetuating America as the world leader in mass incarceration for "sins and/or minor crimes" (Zafirovski, 2007, p. 7, online version). The manifestation of puritanical doctrine via the criminal justice system, that is, how American society defines crime and responses to criminal transgression, has been described as an anomaly insofar as the United States might be considered a modern political democracy

(Pager, 2003). The influence of a Puritan ethos of predestination, of "doing the time if you do the crime," has resulted in considerable economic, social, and family harms.

Consistent with American society's Puritan beginnings, resistance to a paradigm shift in criminal justice policy involves the intense moral judgments associated with crime and risky behaviors such as drug use. These judgments make it politically difficult to move from an emphasis on criminal sanction to harm reduction (MacCoun, 1998). Despite harm reduction's underlying concern with human rights, these values are downplayed and rarely articulated in favor of the illusion of neutrality (Hathaway, 2001). Advocates of harm reduction policy believe that perhaps the greatest challenge involved in a paradigm shift lies in more articulately and visibly promoting harm reduction ideals. Harm reduction may well be supported via empirical analysis, hence its widespread acceptance within academic public health circles. However, social change may only be achieved by boldly challenging criminal sanction policy on moral grounds and articulating current criminal sanctions (and in particular drug policy) as inhumane and irrational (Hathaway, 2001).

Indeed, agenda setting, legislation, and policy formulation are shaped not only by moral judgments about social problems but also by social constructions about the shared characteristics of a particular group of people. Social constructions are value-laden stereotypes about certain groups of people created by history, religion, socialization, the media, and so on. Examples of positive constructions are "deserving" and "honest," while negative constructions include images such as "selfish," "dishonest," and "undeserving" (Schneider & Ingram, 1993). The theory of target populations helps explain American society's widespread use of incarceration and the draconian policy developments of the last 20-plus years. According to this theory, groups can be understood by examining the convergence of both power and social constructions. Four types of target groups represent this convergence: the *advantaged* who have both political power and positive constructions (e.g., the elderly, veterans), the *contenders* who have political power but may be perceived negatively (e.g., big unions, minorities), the *dependents* who lack power but have positive social construction (e.g., children, the disabled), and, finally, the *deviants* who lack both political power and positive constructions (e.g., criminals, drug addicts, illegal immigrants). Policy and resources directed toward advantaged groups will be overprescribed because powerful segments of the populations have considerable influence in getting their issues on legislative agendas. Political actions directed at advantaged groups also address the easiest problems for policy makers to solve. Similarly, policies directed toward deviant groups are also high on the legislative agenda; however, negatively constructed powerless groups will usually be the targets of punishment policy, and the extent of their burdens will often be greater than needed to achieve the desired results. The continued popularity of tough-on-crime legislation, over which deviants have no control, vividly illustrates the attractiveness of punishment directed at powerless and negatively viewed people (Schneider & Ingram, 1993).

Harm reduction emphasizes actions that reduce total harm to society, a plan that would require altered social constructions about who is deserving of such efforts. Social constructions regarding criminals as undeserving are persistent and deeply ingrained in American culture. American punishment policies reveal these social constructions:

> Many Americans have concluded…that those languishing at the margins of our society are simply reaping what they have sown. Their suffering has nothing to do with us. As a consequence, there is no broadly based demand for reform—no moral outrage…in the face of what is a massive collective failure. American political culture…accepts as credible…the conclusion that the offending individual is *unworthy*. (Loury, 2010, p. 138, emphasis added)

A paradigm shift will involve constructing positive images about deviant populations that disproportionately end up in prison (drug users, unauthorized immigrants, etc.), a decidedly difficult task given long-standing beliefs about who is in prison and why. Moving away from incarceration and associated legal policies such as mandatory minimum sentences, especially for nonviolent offenders, would be consistent with a harm reduction strategy. Ultimately a harm reduction framework implies that incarceration should be a last resort rather than a first response. It also implies utilizing strategies within more specific contexts to reduce harm, such as special arrest procedures when children are present, humane treatment in prison, rehabilitation programs for offenders, and so forth.

One thing is for sure: we cannot keep doing what we have done in the past. A paradigm shift from "harm induction to harm reduction" (Van Wormer, 1999) certainly seems to be a necessary element of policy reform. One would think that due to the flagging economy such a shift may be more likely than in previous years. For example, 2009 is the first year we have seen a decrease in prison population in 26 states, although the population of federal prisoners still grew (Pew Center on States, 2010). Yet in addition to ideological barriers, institutional barriers still exist that thwart widespread use of alternatives to incarceration. Given the substantial increase in funding for the penal system and law enforcement bureaucracy, there is likely to be institutional resistance to harm reduction policy that might threaten this budgetary and agency growth (Hagedorn, 1995). Sociologist Loïc Wacquant (2010) documents the "astonishing growth" of prison and jail expenditures over the last three decades: "Prison and jail expenditures in America jumped from $7 billion in 1980 to $57 billion in 2000 and exceeded $70 billion in 2007, even as crime…stagnated and then declined…after 1993" (p. 76). Meanwhile, criminal justice expenditures grew almost sevenfold, from $33 billion to $216 billion.

Expenditures on corrections are concurrent not only with declines in crime but also with fundamental declines in the investment of children and families: the upsizing of the government's carceral role has been proportionate to its downsizing of its welfare and educational role (NAACP, 2011; Wacquant, 2010). For example, from 1980 to 2006, on average, state spending on prisons consumed a larger share of general fund dollars (second only to health) and is concurrent not only with decreases in crime but also with declines in spending on education at all levels as well as welfare and social services (NAACP, 2011). The result of prison spending was a budgetary boom of 660%, in sharp contrast to multiple administrations proclaiming to limit public spending and big government (see, e.g., Drug Enforcement Administration, 2003). Rather than reining in government, penal and criminal justice spending financed an additional 1 million staff, making corrections the third-largest employer in the nation (with Manpower Inc. and Wal-Mart as numbers one and two, respectively) with a monthly payroll of $2.4 billion (Wacquant, 2010).

The expansion of the "penal state" concurrent with declines in crime (particularly violent crime) provides evidence of a "prison industrial complex," whereby crime control as an industry is dependent on having a sufficient number of prisoners to sustain the industry regardless of whether crime is rising or incarceration is necessary (Donzinger, 1996). Such bureaucracies "seek to live" (Hagedorn, 1995), hence drug reform aimed at harm reduction will not completely solve our nation's overreliance on incarceration. For example, any advances made in drug policy reform to divert drug offenders from incarceration or change the way we handle drug use may be canceled out by the "war on illegal immigration." A recent investigation by National Public Radio (NPR) reveals that prison economics helped drive Arizona immigration law. It shows a behind-the-scenes effort to help draft and pass Arizona Senate Bill 1070 by the private prison industry—an industry that had no doubt that it could fill up its prisons for years to come with men, women, and children caught without proof of legal entry. The law is currently being challenged in the courts, but if is it upheld, police are required to lock up anyone they stop who cannot show proof of legal entry into the United States. When the bill was passed in April 2010, critics protested on the grounds of racial profiling, while supporters saw the bill's passage as a "positive step to curb illegal immigration" (Sullivan, 2010, para. 1). According to the NPR report, "The law could send hundreds of thousands of illegal immigrants to prison in a way never done before. And it could mean hundreds of millions of dollars in profits to private prison companies responsible for housing them" (Sullivan, 2010, p. 2). The NPR report and the prospect of imprisoning even more Hispanics than we currently do provide a frightening example of an industry that seeks to sustain itself and even grow in a time of economic downturn. Unauthorized immigrants are the new "deviants," and both their powerlessness and their negative social constructions foretell they will likely experience burdens that are both punitive and overprescribed.

While the issue of illegal immigration suggests that prison growth continues to be a possibility in some sectors of corrections such as the federal system, spending on corrections has been driven to the breaking point in several states. Costs have skyrocketed not only due to sheer numbers but also because of the rising health care and geriatric costs of inmates. Whereas in the past politicians have been afraid of appearing "soft on crime" and thus wary of promoting diverse alternatives to incarceration, today's financial crisis has created new pressures to rethink how we fight crime in America (Warren, 2008). While the pyramid of principles (Figure 2) advanced here is based on the premise that attending to social inequality will lessen the need for and possibility of incarceration, harm reduction encompasses efforts to create alternatives to incarceration and respond to those already in the criminal justice system. Given shrinking budgets, many states are exploring two principal levers to "tame" prison growth (Warren, 2008). The first involves sentencing reform aimed at shortening sentences, departing from or eliminating determinant sentencing, and ensuring parole. The second lever involves reducing prison admissions via diversion programs such as drug courts and community supervision for nonviolent offenders. Here we examine both elements of reform from a harm-reduction lens.

Sentencing Reform as Harm Reduction

We have discussed how mandatory minimum sentencing has fueled prison growth, largely through its impact on the drug offenders filling our nation's prisons. Indeed, the prison population has swelled despite declines in violent and property crime since 1992 (Schmitt, Warner, & Gupta, 2010). Nonviolent drug offenders constitute a huge proportion of the prison population and serve lengthy sentences that many consider unduly harsh (Tonry, 1996). The origins of mandatory minimum or "determinant" sentencing that has so impacted families today can be traced by to the 1970s and 1980s, when the U.S. Sentencing Commission was charged with sentencing reform. By the 1980s, crime and punishment had become a hot political issue, and "law and order" was galvanized as a way for Republicans, seeking the white southern working-class vote, to undermine "soft on crime" Democrats. The call for reform came within a political climate where people believed that incapacitation and punishment would deter crime (Tonry, 2005).

The original aims of the Sentencing Commission were to ensure procedural fairness and reduce racial disparities in sentencing. Contrary to these purposes, the Sentencing Reform Act contained numerous provisions calling for harsher sentencing, creating a paradox with respect to inequities pertaining to race: "The cruelest irony of the...sentencing reform movement is that diminution of racial discrimination in sentencing was a primary aim and exacerbation of racial disparities is a major result" (Tonry & Hatlestad, 1997, p. 217). In addition to the racial disparities that were believed to stem from mandatory minimum sentencing, the indiscriminate use of incapacitative crime control strategies has been viewed as ineffective with regard to deterring crime (Bewley-Taylor, Hallam, & Allen, 2009; Justice Policy Institute, 2009; Tonry, 2005). Congress's enactment in 1986 of mandatory minimum sentences for drug crimes was the ultimate "bait and switch" in that it capitalized on the public's growing fear of crime and superpredators (the bait), but rather than incarcerating violent offenders, a "switch" of sorts occurred (Donzinger, 1996): nonviolent drug offenders were sent to prison without the possibility of parole, sometimes receiving sentences that were more severe than punishments for violent offenders (Bewley-Taylor et al., 2009). Further, sentencing was often at odds with what judges and legal practitioners closest to a case believed to be fair, creating difficult tensions within the courtroom and between the judiciary and the legislature (Tonry, 2005). The use of mandatories gave prosecutors, not judges, discretion over whether to reduce a charge, accept or deny a plea bargain, or reward or deny a defendant's substantial assistance (i.e., informant testimony), and ultimately granting them undue influence in determining the final sentence (Donzinger, 1996; Miller, 1996; Wright & Lewin, 1998). With regard to families, mandatory minimums limited the possibility that the court would consider an offender's extenuating circumstances. Such circumstances often included whether or not an individual had children or other dependents for which he or she was responsible (Arditti & McClintock, 2001).

Mandatory minimums contributed to and perpetuated social inequality and were responsible for subjecting so many nonviolent offenders to the incapacitating and stigmatizing effects of the prison system. In this manner, sentencing reform is a critical social justice issue, and mandatory minimum policies are in a state of reexamination. The momentum for sentencing reform may stem from the prohibitive costs of incarcerating so many people (e.g., Porter, 2010) and the collateral costs associated with carceral sentencing for the offender such as prison overcrowding and recidivism (Mauer, 2010). Regardless of the underlying motivation behind sentencing reform, rethinking sentencing policies may enhance public safety, advance social justice, reduce racial disparity, and help incarcerated parents and their families. Sentencing reform is pivotal to harm reduction by limiting or deterring incarceration, thus reducing the harms associated with a parent's incarceration. Sentencing reform stands to benefit mothers, given their widespread conviction for nonviolent drug crimes, as well as families of color, who are disproportionately impacted by severe determinant sentencing guidelines.

A recent report from the Sentencing Project (Porter, 2010) highlights initiatives in sentencing reform along with changes in probation and parole practices. As some examples of reform at the state level (1) Minnesota established a "safety valve" provision that allows the court to sentence without regard to the mandatory minimum for low-level felony offenses for possession or sale of a controlled substance; (2) New York enacted significant reforms to the Rockefeller drug laws, some of the harshest mandatories in the country, by eliminating mandatory sentences for certain first- and second-time drug offenses; and (3) Rhode Island eliminated mandatory sentences for drug possession charges and granted judges discretion in certain drug cases.

In addition to scaling back the scope of determinant sentencing, many states are taking steps to reduce the length of prison stays. With 46 states facing budget deficits, early release of prisoners, particularly nonviolent offenders who have already served their minimum sentence, is being considered by states such as California, Michigan, Kentucky, South Carolina, and at least six other states (Moore, 2009; Ramirez, 2009) and implemented in Nevada (Pew Center on States, 2010). Mechanisms to shorten the length of time served include "good time" incentives, removing caps on how much time off one can earn from time served, and parole strategies (Pew Center on States, 2010; Porter, 2010).

Alternatives to Incarceration

A second lever to reduce harm involves diversion. A number of states have taken the lead in diversifying their criminal sanctions in ways that save money and still protect public safety. A recent report identified Texas and Kansas as "well on their way" in terms of implementing alternatives to incarceration. Both states have adopted a two-pronged strategy that provides incentives to reduce recidivism with greater use of community supervision for lower-risk offenders. In an increasing number of states, drug courts are utilized that offer treatment as well as penalties for missing treatment or failing a drug test (Warren, 2008). Community-based drug treatment provides a strong case for the efficacy of diversion as a means for states to save money and avoid the indirect costs associated with the incapacitating effects of incarceration for offenders with substance addiction. New York's Drug Treatment Alternative to Prison (DTAP) program is an example of one such diversion effort. Participation in DTAP significantly reduced recidivism and was highly cost-effective compared with incarcerating nonviolent drug felons and providing treatment in prison (National Center on Addiction and Substance Abuse, 2003). From a family perspective, we know too well that the "costs" of parental imprisonment run deep and extend beyond the dollars it takes to house an inmate. Keeping parents in the community can reduce the need for public assistance by enabling them to meet their financial and familial obligations and prevent ruptured parent-child bonds.

In sum, a family perspective suggests that harm reduction must be multisystemic and attend to social inequality, limit the extent to which we criminalize and incarcerate broad classes of people, and make concerted efforts to reduce the harms associated not only with certain kinds of risky behavior (such as drug use) but also with imprisonment. Containing prison populations is a necessary aspect of harm reduction, but it is incomplete because it does not attend to the conditions and laws that bring people into the criminal justice system in the first place. For example, probation may be an attractive cost-saving alternative for low-risk offenders; however, they are still part of a system that marginalizes and targets certain individuals and groups. Fundamental issues regarding social inequality must be addressed before diversion strategies, alternative law enforcement practices, drug use interventions, and prison programs are meaningful. Harm reduction is a strategy, not a safety net, and should not obscure the social, legal, and economic sources of harms stemming from behaviors deemed risky or criminal sanctions aimed at stopping unlawful activity (Roe, 2005).

Principle 3: Promote Human Development

Civil society rests upon contributions by all sectors and institutions of a nation in support of social justice. Such contributions to civil society would assure that there is a "level playing field" for individuals to pursue lives marked by positive and healthy contributions to self, family, and community.[7]

Resilience rests, fundamentally, on relationships.[8]

Principles of social justice and harm reduction serve to broadly influence the social, economic, and legal systems in which human development occurs. The promotion of human development among offender parents and their families acknowledges these multiple spheres of influence that bear on offender parents, their children, and their family members. With respect to parental incarceration, here we more specifically consider what it means to promote human development by examining programs and policies that are focused on contexts and processes that directly impact the developing person (broadly defined as the offender parent or the child/family). Thus our concern moves from the macro (political and economic systems, social inequality, broad institutional paradigms of punishment) to the micro as we focus on "evidence-based" programs that hold promise in promoting family well-being, competent parenting, and positive developmental outcomes for those parent offenders who are incarcerated as well as their kin. We use the term *micro* here in the sense that it is through the promotion of human development that intervention and specific policies might bear on the proximal family processes (such as parent-child interaction, maternal distress, and coparenting) that we have demonstrated as critical in understanding the trajectory of parental incarceration.

First and foremost, promoting human development involves applying principles of developmental science in order to enhance the well-being of parents, children, and communities impacted by incarceration (Lerner, Fisher, & Weinberg, 2000). As we have discussed, these principles focus on the dynamics of person-context interactions, proximal processes, and an ecological approach to human development (Bronfenbrenner, 1979; Lerner, 1998; Lerner et al., 1999). In the language of applied developmental science, the basis for change involves systemic reorganization, defined as alterations in multiple levels of organization (i.e., individual, family, community, society) with the recognition that variables are linked, and change in one part will produce change in another (Farmer & Farmer, 2001; Lerner & Castellino, 2002). Practically speaking, promoting human development also involves outreach research through which scholars and scholarly institutions can integrate the "voices and concerns of children, youth, and families...and join with communities in the maintenance and perpetuation of civil society" (Lerner et al., 2000, pp. 11–12). Supporting positive development enhances the life chances of vulnerable families and children and is an essential cornerstone for improving the odds for those caught up in the net of the criminal justice system.

We have discussed how context and process intertwine and create problematic outcomes for both offender parents and their families; applying principles of developmental science is a means for prevention and enhancing interventions that (1) are sensitive to individual and cultural differences; (2) occur in naturalistic settings where participants live their lives; (3) reduce risk *and* promote reorganization on multiple levels (i.e., acknowledge change in one area will produce change in another); (4) are responsive to developmental status and the timing of interventions (Farmer & Farmer, 2001; Lerner & Castellino, 2002; Lerner et al., 2000); and (5) focus on relationships (Luthar, Cicchetti, & Becker, 2000). Indeed, perhaps the most critical principle of the application of a developmental orientation involves the central focus on family relationships. Such an emphasis gives rise to programs and policies that aim to empower parents, establish parent-professional partnerships, and acknowledge the significance of dynamic family interactions for individual and family well-being (Guralnick, 2005). We have discussed in depth the significance of context for shaping processes pertinent to understanding parental incarceration, and how internal (such as parental identity, the extent of the offender's incapacitation) and relational processes (such as family contact and coparenting) are of profound importance in determining the quality of care children receive, as well as various aspects of child adjustment. Indeed, a central feature of promoting human development is the notion that healthy relationships play a crucial role in fostering well-being. Committed and loving relationships have a "high protective potential" (Luthar & Brown, 2007, p. 943); our identification of key relational processes impacted by parental incarceration provides fertile ground for developmentally enhancing interventions for children, adults, and families. Here we will consider specific interventions and program models with the principles of developmental science in mind.

Intervention and "Goodness of Fit"

Carla is dedicated to helping others and oversees service delivery at her church. She was enthusiastic about receiving a Mentoring Children of Prisoners (MCP) grant to set up a youth mentoring program to help children with a parent in prison. She expresses frustration regarding the progress of the program. At a group meeting for human services professionals working with families impacted by incarceration, she announces: "We need children for our program. I have over 20 volunteers to mentor these children, but I cannot find children with an incarcerated parent to be in our program!"

Community Corrections District 45 was excited about the preliminary evidence demonstrating the efficacy of its intensive drug treatment program for preventing recidivism. It decided to extend the program to include all offenders, regardless of whether addiction was an issue. A group of low-risk offenders (minimal or no drug use, positive ties with family) were placed in an intensive drug treatment–oriented halfway house that had been shown to be effective with high-risk offenders with serious drug addiction. The halfway house program involved one-on-one counseling, group therapy, and close monitoring. Upon follow-up, the low-risk offenders who were placed in the intensive halfway house program showed an increase in recidivism compared with a group or low-risk offenders who lived with their families and received community supervision, whose chance of recidivism decreased.

Lisa is a lone mother not by choice but by default. Her husband has been incarcerated for 3 years, and she is overwhelmed not only by work and family responsibilities but by the changes in her children's behavior. It seems her 14-year-old son, Joey, is starting to "run wild," and she is getting reports that he is cutting school. Lisa learns about a local mentoring program where the agency will assign her son a volunteer friend to spend time with him every week. She thinks this might be a good idea as Joey needs a role model and some supervision. Things started out well, and Joey really liked his new match, Brian. Joey's school attendance improved, and he seemed to benefit from the special times he spent with Brian. However, after 10 weeks Brian stopped calling and coming around. It turns out Brian had switched jobs, and his long commute prohibited his further involvement in the mentoring program. Joey has returned to his "old ways" and not only is skipping school but also was recently caught shoplifting with some friends. Lisa thinks the experience with Brian and the abrupt termination of his calls and visits with Joey has just made things worse.

The CYWD program discussed earlier, which essentially helped turn Selene's life around, meets many of the criteria discussed in terms of promoting human development, most notably the view of clients as active agents in their own lives and the naturalistic delivery of services within clients' communities. Unfortunately, many programs and practices aimed at offenders and their families lack the theoretical foundation necessary to promote human development in its fullest sense. Furthermore, programs and interventions may not specifically address the contextual challenges (e.g., cumulative disadvantage, mental health problems) and process mechanisms identified in this book. The examples given here are based on real programs aimed at incarcerated parents and/or their family members. What all these examples have in common is a lack of fit between program and offender or family needs. The concept of "goodness of fit" is a useful lens through which to consider intervention and policy aimed at incarcerated parents and their families. Both ecological theory and developmental contextualism suggest that healthy development and family functioning depend on the match between the needs and resources of the developing individual or family and the resources, supports, and capacities of the multiple environments within which the person or family is located. With regard to children, the match between a child's proximal environments (e.g., home, school, community) determines to a large extent whether one is able to meet basic needs, form supportive relationships, and develop social competence, all of which greatly influence the child's life trajectory (Lerner, 1993). By extension, the issue of fit will have bearing on the offender parent's life pathway as well as the family's developmental trajectory. The bottom line is that involvement in the criminal justice system tends not to "fit" developmental needs for parents or children. Prison environments and the corresponding marginalization and incapacitation of the offender are antithetical to human development, as are the corresponding burdens for families.

A recognition of this fundamental "mismatch" between prison and human development is warranted before discussing the benefits or inadequacies of any specific program. Nell Bernstein's account of his visit to a Girl Scouts Behind Bars (GSBB)[9] program in a women's facility in Oregon illustrates the paradox of corrections programming aimed at enhancing mother-daughter bonds. The program involved several dozen women and children who used the visiting room for a biweekly, three-hour gathering. On alternate weeks, the women meet inside the prison and the girls convened on the outside. When the program session ended and it was time for the children to leave, Bernstein observed the following:

> As the women lined up to leave through one door and the girls through another, an eight-year-old...leaned heavily into the shoulder of a ponytailed volunteer, tears streaming down her cheeks as she waved good-bye to her mother across the room. "Say goodbye to your mom," the volunteer instructed. The girl complied, nearly inaudibly. She couldn't stop crying. "Say it louder," the volunteer coached her weeping charge. "Be nice. She's not going to see you for a while" (Bernstein, 2005, pp. 246–247)

As we have discussed, visitation can be painful for both parents and child, even in a program offering positive opportunities for interaction and bonding. Yet, GSBB rests precariously on a fundamental lack of fit between what the girls and mothers might need, the nature of correctional environments, and the broader policies that may have sent the women to prison in the first place:

> There was little question that the Girl Scouts and other programs...are excellent examples of their kind; the women went out of their way to tell me so. But as the girls filed out in a glum line—I couldn't help but hear

the trumpeting of the elephant in the living room: *the fact of incarceration itself.* (Bernstein, 2005, p. 247, emphasis added)

Indeed, as correctional institutions develop their family focus, perhaps implementing parenting programs or enhanced visitation, the population under their control has grown at an astonishing rate. Strengthening family bonds behind bars is an inescapable paradox because, as Bernstein astutely points out, "We have separated so very many children from the parents who now sit in prison classrooms, nodding solemnly as they are told how much their children need them" (p. 248).

Beyond the fundamental paradox that is parental incarceration, a goodness-of-fit lens draws our attention to a basic mismatch between parenting interventions for prisoners and the parenting realities of prisoners. While a rich body of work focuses on parent training, with few exceptions, it has not been translated into parenting programs for prisoners. Most commonly, in-prison parenting interventions have been drawn from universal parenting programs aimed at providing broad psychoeducational support (Loper & Novero, 2010). Typical skills included in these programs may not be applicable to parents on the inside (e.g., how to handle child misbehavior), who have little opportunity for practice. Further, generic parenting skills do not address the unique needs or offender parents such as prison-specific communication strategies, visitation, legal rights, and dealing with intense emotions related to separation from children (Loper & Novero, 2010). In this manner, many parenting programs implemented in prison can be seen as lacking ecological fit.

Mentoring Programs
In addition to parenting programs within prison walls, goodness of fit is also questionable with respect to widely popular mentoring programs aimed at children with an incarcerated parent. Mentoring programs typically involve time-limited one-on-one interaction between an eligible, "at-risk" youth and an adult volunteer. These programs have become increasingly common in recent years, with an estimated 5 million American youth involved in school- or community-based volunteer mentoring programs (Grossman & Rhodes, 2002). It is believed that mentorship will help troubled youth through the provision of social support and role modeling (Keating, Tomishima, Foster, & Alessandri, 2002). Additionally, the helping relationship is thought to help improve parent-child relationships and correct any negative perceptions

that children may hold about themselves or their relationships with adults by demonstrating that positive caring relationships are possible (Grossman & Rhodes, 2002). Big Brothers/Big Sisters is perhaps the most widely recognized mentoring programs. Overall, the mentoring literature has demonstrated that youth in relationships that have lasted at least a year report the largest number of benefits, with fewer effects noted for shorter relationships, and decrements to youth, such as increased alcohol use, for those in mentoring relationships that terminated in less than 3 months (Grossman & Rhodes, 2002). When benefits to participation in mentoring programs do emerge, they tend to be modest in terms of their practical significance (Zwiebach, Rhodes, & Rappaport, 2010).

In 2003, President George W. Bush stated the need to direct more attention to children of incarcerated parents. In response, the Department of Health and Human Services (DHSS) created the Mentoring Children of Prisoners (MCP) program, a faith-based and community initiative. In 2003, the Administration of Children and Families (ACF) granted $8.9 million to 52 programs; as of July 2008, the program celebrated its 100,000th match (U.S. DHHS, 2008). This specific expansion of mentoring programs to the population of children experiencing the incarceration of a parent is an example of "fervor without infrastructure" (Freedman, 1993, p. 93), or utilizing simple solutions to solve complex problems.[10] Voluntaristic programs are an idealized panacea, often proposed as quick, cheap, and easy solutions for problems no matter how exceptional: "As such, mentoring serves to distract attention from deep-seated problems that cannot be simply marketed away" (Freedman, 1993, p. 93). Indeed, the proliferation of volunteer mentor programs aimed at vulnerable children impacted by incarceration likely includes efforts that are neither as intensive nor as lasting as more mature and solidified programs such as Big Brothers/Big Sisters (Grossman & Rhodes, 2002). An overinvestment in mentoring to solve the damage to parent-child relationships created by incarceration, or to respond to the needs of overburdened caregivers, can result in a cycle of disappointment for children, their families, and the mentors themselves (Freedman, 1993).

The example of the program coordinator who had attracted volunteer mentors yet had no children enrolled in the program also represents "fervor without infrastructure." Well-meaning volunteers are available, but where are the children? A goodness-of-fit lens suggests the dearth of children is the result of a mismatch between what families impacted by incarceration need and what the program has to offer. Further, the failure to find children for the program may suggest that the volunteer mentors do not come from the same communities in which families impacted by incarceration are likely to be located. Such mismatches are bound to repeat the cycle of disappointment that undermines such programs—a cycle that involves high expectations and "difficulties in forging relationships across great social distance, and worsening economic circumstances" (Freedman, 1993, p. 93). Like Joey, who lost his match shortly after entering a mentoring program, the big losers of such a cycle will be the children.

Thus it is unclear if mentoring programs transfer well to children with a parent in prison given the unique risks that connect with the experience of parental incarceration. Evidence supporting the use of these programs with children from incarcerated homes comes from studies demonstrating that mentoring has the greatest positive effects among youth from backgrounds of high environmental risk (Zwiebach et al., 2010). Given the typically disadvantaged backgrounds among justice-involved families, goodness of fit is evident on this particular parameter of risk. With regard to other elements of children's experience, mentoring programs tend to ignore children's diverse response to parental incarceration (Zwiebach et al., 2010) and generally are not specifically sensitive to children's ambiguous loss and the impact the mentoring relationship may have on the incarcerated parent. The incarcerated parent is all but invisible to the mentoring program process, and it is unknown how a mentoring relationship may influence the fragile parent-child relationship. While mentoring staff or volunteers may not see themselves as replacements for the incarcerated parent, given prisonized parenting identities, the involuntariness of incarceration could contribute to a parent's sense of being replaced and further compromise a healthy connection with children.

Mentoring programs for children with a parent in prison hold promise to the extent they can be sustained and designed to specifically address the needs of families impacted by incarceration. Admittedly, program success may be a challenge given high rates of residential mobility for enrolled families and wavering commitment on the part of mentors (Jucovy, 2003). An evaluation of the Philadelphia Amachi program noted some benefits to children who participated in the program related to school success and the reduced risk of drug use. However, consistent with the mentoring research, benefits to children only become evident after 12 months (Jucovy, 2003). Out of 556 Amachi matches in Philadelphia, a substantial number terminated—44% within 18 months, and 25% in less than 12 months. A similar evaluation of a different program (Mentoring Connections) found even higher rates of termination: of the 57 matches enrolled in its sample, more than one-third of the matches were not meeting 6 months after the start of the program (Shlafer, Poehlmann, Coffino, & Hanneman, 2009). The high rate of early termination is a cause for concern given children's histories of relationship disruption and disappointment. Clearly this type of scenario is especially contraindicated with children who have experienced traumatic separation or multiple disruptions in their family relationships and who have unresolved issues pertaining to loss. Rigorous program evaluation is needed, as well as remaining mindful of the potential negative consequences and complexities of introducing a mentoring relationship to children who may have discontinuities in their care or individual risk factors that require more intensive intervention (Zwiebach et al., 2010). Nonstigmatizing intervention aimed at empowering and supporting naturally occurring relationships within a child's school or community may hold more promise in terms of promoting human development. When a presenting problem is highly stigmatized (as in the case of parental incarceration), efforts to mobilize support from *within* the natural network, as opposed to *outside* intervention, tend to be quite effective (Gottlieb, 2000).

Mental Health and Drug Treatment

Finally, as it is for parenting and mentoring programs, goodness of fit is an important criterion for mental health and drug treatment programs aimed specifically at the offender. As we have discussed, unmet mental health and drug treatment needs can seriously undermine parenting competence. Project Greenlight, a short-term, prison-based reentry program in New York, is a case in point. Based on empirical and anecdotal evidence about what prisoners need to succeed at reentry, the program included cognitive-behavioral and practical skills training, employment and housing assistance, family counseling, and drug education and awareness during incarceration. Despite the fact that corrections personnel, community advocates, and policy makers had viewed Project Greenlight positively, when the program was evaluated, several findings were in sharp contrast to expectations. Most notably, Project Greenlight participants fared much worse in rearrest and parole revocation rates than did the two control groups at the 1-year follow-up mark (Wilson & Davis, 2006). Why didn't the program work? Wilson, in commenting on the lessons learned from Project Greenlight, notes the problems that arise when there is a lack of understanding regarding the complexity of human behavior and the processes by which a program might work (Wilson, 2007). Applying a "good idea" to a complex problem, similar to what we discussed with regard to mentoring programs, can actually do more harm than good. Further, in attempting to offer a multitude of services in prison, program developers failed to offer much needed structured follow-up *in the community*, unwittingly perpetuating a lack of fit. Per human developmental principles, timing and context of intervention might have made all the difference for participants.

We see a similar lack of fit in the case of District 45 and the placement of low-risk offenders in halfway house programs that involve intensive services. In a study examining 7,000 Ohio offenders who were placed in either halfway houses or community supervision, once again certain findings were at odds with expectations. Placing low-risk offenders in halfway house program actually increased the chances of reoffending by an average of 5%; several of the least effective halfway house programs produced a 30% or higher increase in recidivism. However, among high-risk offenders, several of the more successful halfway house programs resulted in a 30% or higher reduction in recidivism (Latessa, 2008). The halfway house investigation, which demonstrates how programs may produce discrepant and often unexpected outcomes among different groups, offers a striking example of how one size "doesn't fit all." The examples provided here regarding mentoring programs and offender interventions emphasize the danger of implementing programs designed for a specific purpose to another population that may have substantially different needs, as well as the importance of fully understanding the mechanisms of developmental change.

Multisystemic Parenting Programs

Despite the fundamental paradox that is "parenting in prison," as well as evidence that programs aimed at offender parents and their family members may not necessarily demonstrate "goodness of fit," the number of parenting programs within prisons is on the rise. Such programs vary in content but tend to focus on enhancing inmate knowledge and skills that are believed to improve parenting and general family functioning (Pollock, 2002). The typical prison-based parenting program is short-term and classroom-based (Eddy, Kjellstrand, Martinez, & Newton, 2010). Parents in jails are typically not the recipients of such programs, and even within state and federal facilities, programs may extend to only a minority of inmates (Loper & Tuerk, 2006). A recent review of parenting programs offered within correctional institutions notes that there is no obvious consistency among programs in terms of content and delivery and very little in the way of systematic evaluation, and that most classes tend to be taught by volunteers with varying levels of expertise in parenting training and human development (Loper & Tuerk, 2006). Programs may show modest short-term gains in targeting parenting outcomes; however, these conclusions are often drawn from pretest/posttest evaluation designs with no comparison group, creating questions regarding their validity (Loper & Novero, 2010).[11]

As discussed earlier in the case of Girl Scouts Behind Bars, in-prison parenting programs generally involve limited opportunities for parents in prison to apply new parenting knowledge within the context of their relationships with their children. As we have discussed, contact between incarcerated parents and their children is highly variable and, for some parents, nonexistent. In some cases, contact between parent and child may be contraindicated, and offender participation in the program may prove detrimental to the family. Because of these complexities and the limited opportunities to parent, it is not surprising that many programs within correctional settings lack ecological fit. Further, outcome evaluations tend to focus on concepts *related* to parenting such as offender adjustment or attitudes toward parenting, rather than more direct parenting behaviors and child adjustment outcomes (Loper & Tuerk, 2006). Additionally, many programs focus only on the individual parent and lack the relational component that is so critical in the promotion of human development. From a child's perspective, programming cannot substitute for the daily presence of a parent (Bernstein, 2005).

Given the caveats discussed here, there is clearly a need for innovation with regard to programs aimed incarcerated parents that more closely align with developmental principles, illustrate goodness of fit, and offer interactive opportunities to apply new knowledge and skills. Given the complexity that is human development, the most promising programs aimed at incarcerated parents and their families are multimodal and target contextual challenges that disrupt parenting and involve family and community outside of the prison. Effective programming also is sensitive to timing and may offer family support during the reentry period. A central purpose of multimodal intervention is to provide incarcerated parents, caregivers, and children with enough support over time to ensure positive change (Eddy et al., 2010). Parenting Inside Out (PIO), a program designed specifically for justice-involved parents, is one such example of a multipronged program that focuses on enhancing positive family interaction and supporting parenting within and outside of prison (Eddy et al., 2008). PIO encompasses parent education and therapeutic visitation during incarceration, as well as collaboration with community agencies to support both the offender parent and the caregiver. The program meets criteria for the promotion of human development given its potential to reduce contextual risk and promote systemic reorganization (i.e., change) over time among multiple systemic levels (i.e. the individual, the family, and the community).

The 4-H Living Interaction Family Education (LIFE) Program is another example of a multimodal program with several levels of intervention. This family-strengthening program for incarcerated parents or grandparents, the children affected by their incarceration, and the target child's caregiver is a holistic intervention involving separate programmatic elements for offenders, target children, and caregivers, as well as components that bring all participants together at one time. The program seeks to promote strong, healthy, and nurturing family environments for the children, while helping the offenders become positive role models and mentors for their child. This goal is accomplished through the three central aspects of the 4-H LIFE Program: offender parenting skills classes; offender planning and leadership meetings; 4-H Family Club meetings that include the offender, target child, and caregiver, and 4-H participation for children and families in their home communities. Parenting and planning and leadership meetings occur weekly. The parenting classes provide offenders with opportunities to develop and improve parenting skills. During the planning/leadership meetings, offenders work with a 4-H LIFE program leader to plan the upcoming Family Club meeting. 4-H Family Club meetings occur monthly inside the correctional institution and can be classified as enhanced visits. Enhanced visits have less stringent visiting room rules, which helps create a more relaxed and child-focused atmosphere. The programmatic elements of 4-H LIFE reflect recent calls for holistic, multimodal programs (Cecil et al., 2008; Eddy et al., 2010; Nickel et al., 2009) and address limitations identified in other programs (Kennon, Mackintosh, & Meyers, 2009). Since its start in 2000, 4-H LIFE has been implemented in four correctional centers across Missouri and is in the process of being replicated nationwide. To date, evaluation results of the program are preliminary but promising. Baseline and follow-up data collected from 79 prisoners enrolled as participants in 4-H LIFE or in a control group (parents not in the program who receive traditional visitation from their families) revealed that 4-H Life participants reported significantly fewer visitation problems and greater communication with their children over a period of 6 months than those offenders in the control group (Gillespie, Beckmeyer, & Arditti, 2010).

Empowering Incarcerated Parents through Postmodern Interventions

We have discussed the implications of helpless prisonized parenting identities for the offender parent and the implications for the family. Further, we have documented the stigma associated with incarceration and how it spreads to the family. On the broadest level, we have discussed earlier in this chapter how felon status puts one in a deviant population category that targets offender parents, and by way of association their family members, with disproportionate burdens. These facts point to the importance of therapeutic intervention aimed at helping offenders reconstruct damaged identities. Identity work is an important step in empowering offender parents and could make the difference between successful reentry and returning to prison.

Postmodern therapies hold particular promise in working with offender parents. These modalities tend to focus on helping people recognize their inner resources and strengths and strategize solutions to problems. This is done in a nonjudgmental, supportive forum that subscribes to narrative therapy pioneer Michael White's words: "The person is not the problem, the problem is the problem." Locating a problem outside of the person is a technique called externalizing the problem and creates space for the offender parent to envision a new self—a critical issue given the weightiness of felon status and social judgment toward those involved in the criminal justice system. Such an approach is particularly apt with marginalized individuals and groups in that it is nonintrusive and nonstigmatizing and encourages self-reflection.

While such intervention, often defined as postmodern therapy (Ungar, 2008) or narrative therapy (White, 1995), can take multiple forms, it is based on the idea that clients are experts in defining their problems and are thus the best equipped to locate solutions. Further, postmodern therapies let clients define their experience of oppression (Ungar, 2008). Articulating these experiences allows one to discuss perceived family or social injustice and receive validation from the practitioner or "audience" for the story. Bottling up perceived injustice may result in internalizing or externalizing anger—symptoms that are prevalent for children with an incarcerated parent. Pent-up rage is also a critical issue for offenders, who are often angered over injustice and unfairness (Suter, Byrne, Byrne, Howells, & Day, 2002) and might easily perceive others as "disrespecting" them, prompting retaliation or aggression (Butler & Maruna, 2009; Terry, 2003). Indeed, postmodern therapeutic applications are specifically designed to shift power imbalances—by telling one's story, and working together to create a new story, the offender can go from "helpless dad" or "guilty mom" to responsible parent and, by doing so, begins to define those actions that characterize responsible parenting. Further, the new story can move one from entrenched identities as a victim or a "criminal" to a redefinition of self whereby one loses the "convict mystique" and embraces more human, prosocial identities.

We can see ecological principles at work in an innovative prison program involving "outsider witnessing" known as the Inside/Outside program. An outsider witness is an invited audience to a therapy conversation who listens to and acknowledges stories and identity claims of the person consulting with the therapist (Smith & Gibson, 2006). In the case of this specific program, outsiders specially recruited from the community witnessed the stories of men incarcerated in a prison in Victoria, Australia. The premise of the program stems from precepts of narrative therapy whereby identities are believed to be formed through one's relationships with others: "If you only see yourself in relation to a 'prisoner' identity, if your only relationships are with other 'inmates' or those who are your 'guards' then there are very limited options available to redefine who you are and what you stand for in life" (Smith & Gibson, 2006, p. 47). We can see how theoretically appropriate such a program would be given the alterations incarceration brings to how parents view themselves and the incapacitation that is often synonymous with imprisonment. The program was quite meaningful to the offender participants:

> It was empowering for the men to understand that there were people in the community who did not prejudge them....the sessions provided a rare opportunity to leave their prisoner identities behind, albeit for a short time. The outsiders often asked "the insiders" about their future plans and goals beyond their time in prison. The men found this reconnection with hopes and goals very helpful; it strengthened their sense of themselves as being "not only a prisoner." (Smith & Gibson, 2006, p. 50)

Inside/Outside is a unique example of a program that is predicated on empowerment and identity work. It demonstrates the potential of a postmodern approach for strengthening positive parenting identities and preparing prisoners to reconnect with family.

Postmodern work tends to be short-term and highly focused—thus it is appealing to insurance companies and clients alike. In addition to in-person therapeutic programs such as Inside/Outside, it can also be conducted at a distance via letter writing. Maybin's (2000) examination of letter writing between death row prisoners and their "pen friends" in the United Kingdom provides a rare glimpse into how the process of writing and receiving letters shapes identity. For some parents who are prisoners, written correspondence may be the only type of reflective dialogue, the meat of postmodern therapies, available to them. We have discussed the significance of letter writing as a means of communication between the offender and family members; however, its use in a therapeutic relationship is untested. The distance afforded by letter writing (as opposed to in-person or verbal contact) allowed for a freer presentation of self that was less entrenched in certain positions or scripts (e.g., hustler identity), fostering self-reflection and identity reconstruction. Thus distance is a strength of the intervention:

> The lack of an immediate physical or social context for the encounter [between prisoner and pen friend]…create[s] a space within which the letter writers have the opportunity to represent or reconstruct themselves as people, and to rewrite their own histories in new ways. This is particularly crucial for the prisoners. (Maybin, 2000, p. 168)

Giving prisoners the opportunity during confinement to take part in identity work focused on reconstructing parenthood, moving them from helpless to capable, makes particular sense in the months prior to release as parents prepare for reentry and any attempts to establish or renew relationships with children (Arditti et al., 2005). Whether in person or through letters, postmodern modalities offer intriguing possibilities for identity reconstruction and empowerment for parent offenders.

Building Strengths and Fostering Resilience

Within the context of corrections, by far the predominant approach to managing offenders during incarceration and after release has been "deficit-based." Deficit-based approaches focus largely on controlling behavior through coercion and punishment, strategies that are the least likely to promote internalization and long-term change (Burnett & Maruna, 2006; Maruna & Lebel, 2003). In light of the increasing attention given to issues of ex-prisoner rehabilitation and reentry, an alternative paradigm is emerging that is strengths-based. A strengths-based approach focuses not on a person's deficits but on the positive contribution the person can make (Maruna & Lebel, 2003). A starting point is the assumption that parents and children are "active agents" who, even in the most developmentally prohibitive contexts, have the capability to set in motion "enhancing processes of interaction" (Bronfenbrenner, 1995, p. 634). Strength-based interventions are particularly efficacious with the underserved and disenfranchised in that they are "nonblaming" and characterized by nonthreatening therapeutic approaches (Kagan, Reid, Roberts, & Silverman-Pollow, 1987; Snell-Johns, Mendez, & Smith, 2004). Strength-based practices are widely used in social work and characterized by several criteria, including systematic assessment of strengths, client-set goal attainment, emphasis on one's natural community and resources, giving clients the authority to make meaningful choices, and hope-inducing relationships (Rapp, Saleebey, & Sullivan, 2005).

Given its focus on naturally occurring assets and resources, a strengths-based approach clearly holds promise in the promotion of human development for offender parents and their families. Within criminal justice, strengths-based programs have been largely focused on the individual offender and involve efforts to transform reentering offenders from receivers of help to dispensers of help (Burnett & Maruna, 2006). In a strengths-based framework, such efforts could involve prison labor during confinement or community service after release so long as it is voluntarily agreed upon and involves challenging and interesting tasks that utilize the talents of the offender in useful, visible roles (Burnett & Maruna, 2006). While implementation of such programs is limited, existing evidence suggests that offenders would likely benefit from rewarding opportunities to "give back" to family and/or community (e.g., Arditti & Parkman, 2011). Such efforts are potentially empowering and help counter the sense of hopelessness and alienation that characterizes the experience of many offenders.

Beyond the benefits a strengths-based approach may hold for the offender during confinement or at reentry, a focus on strengths can be extended to the offender's family. As we have discussed, an essential feature of the promotion of human development involves healthy family relationships. In this manner we can think of family relationships as a source of resilience (Walsh, 2006). Family strengths can be defined as relationship qualities that contribute to the emotional health and well-being of the family (Family Strengths Perspective, 2011). They can be seen as a protective factor on multiple levels, helping to counter the adversities associated with incarceration for the offender, his or her children, and the family as a whole. Examples of these strengths include family togetherness, loyalty, support, protection, communication, and importance (DeFrain, Asay, & Geggie, 2010; Hillis et al., 2010).

The promotion of human development equates with a family-centered approach to practice and policy. Such an approach encompasses services that strengthen the ability of the family to offer support to an individual member, as well as services and policies that work with the family as a unit (DeFrain et al., 2010). At the core of a family-centered approach is a focus on maximizing family choices, sharing power, and honoring self-determination—especially important given the sense of helplessness, invisibility, and mistrust that defines many families' experience with corrections and the broader criminal justice system (Arditti, Joest, et al., 2010). At the core of this approach is the belief that by considering strengths, resilience will be fostered in terms of family members' ability to withstand and rebound from adversity.

Family-centered, strengths-based approaches are fundamentally *relational* and align with ecological principles of human development highlighting proximal family processes impacting offenders and their children. We have discussed how quality caregiving and cooperative family ties promote positive child outcomes and engage incarcerated and previously incarcerated parents in their families. We have also highlighted the importance of family support throughout incarceration and particularly at reentry in facilitating the offender parent's successful reintegration. The La Bodega model demonstrates family-centered practice that strengthens family bonds in order to enhance their ability to support the offender at reentry. It also demonstrates *plasticity*, that is, intervention targeted at particularly stressful transitions when families and their members may need additional support. The explicit goal of La Bodega is to prevent offender recidivism and relapse for ex-offenders with a history of drug abuse. The La Bodega model, implemented by Family Justice, utilizes supportive inquiry techniques to identify family strengths, ex-offender strengths, and naturally occurring sources of support to aid the ex-offender and his or her family through the reentry process (Meyerson & Otteson, 2009; Shapiro, 1998). Participants and their families are generally socioeconomically disadvantaged and located in urban areas. An evaluation of the program revealed that illicit drug use among ex-offenders dropped from 80% to 42%, and this decline was significantly more pronounced than in a comparison group of ex-offenders. Further, families themselves seemed to benefit: La Bodega families obtained needed social and medical services at higher rates than the comparison group and reported a significantly stronger sense of being supported emotionally and materially in their relationships (Sullivan, Mino, Nelson, & Pope, 2002).

Whether applied to offenders or families, strengths-based approaches hold great promise in promoting human development. They are particularly attractive given their sensitivity to stigma and are inherently empowering by helping to heal damaged parental identities, offering opportunities to "give back," or by supporting families to facilitate their well-being as well as their ability to help the offender get back on his or her feet after release. Perhaps the greatest advantage of strengths-based intervention and policies is their alignment with ecological principles of development and process components (e.g., identity, family support) of parental incarceration.

Summary and Conclusions

> The journey of a thousand miles starts with a single step.
> Tao Te Ching [12]

Much has been written about policy reform and best practices aimed at helping incarcerated parents and their families. Yet often the realities of program implementation, budget shortfalls, political biases, and the highly challenged lives of parent offenders and their families all serve to hinder progress in solving the problems associated with parental incarceration. In this book we used theory and the available empirical literature to specify key contextual factors and individual and family processes to get a handle on the "big picture." Without a good idea of the big picture, it is difficult to develop sound interventions and policy reforms aimed at incarcerated parents and their families that will make a difference. Consistent with the theoretical foundation of the book, which entails a focus on ecological systems and developmental science, change in one part will inevitably produce change somewhere else in the system. It is on this basis that the pyramid of principles was built. But society must embrace these principles in order to turn the tide of mass and targeted incarceration and the destruction of countless families. We must ask ourselves, can the extensive damage that comes with criminalizing so many in our society be undone? Engaging in the advancement of social justice, harm reduction, and the promotion of human development is the "journey of a thousand miles"—a journey that will result in fewer parents being incarcerated, and less risk for those offenders and their families who do ultimately interface with corrections.

Harm reduction and the promotion of human development need not wait until social justice is achieved. While it is foundational to change the lives of vulnerable and often troubled parents and their families, social justice may be the hardest principle to achieve. The journey *can* begin with a "single step," a single life, a single family, although we must take care not to mistake superficial efforts for the real change that is needed. As Jeremy Travis (2005) observes, although there may be ample reason to be pessimistic about the state of justice, recent indications of reform and interest in parent offenders and their children discussed here offer hope. For example, within corrections and human services, there is a tremendous and worthwhile movement toward replicating evidence-based practices and program models (Joplin et al., 2004). Such models are deemed to be proven based on scientific results, although this does not necessarily mean that it is clear *why* a particular program might work and under what circumstances (Wilson, 2007). The context, process, and outcome framework that served as a road map to integrate the empirical literature helps us to understand the "how" and "why" of parental incarceration and points to policy and intervention that targets not only the socioeconomic, political landscape but also factors that impact parenting (e.g., identity), family functioning (e.g., coparenting, contact processes), and child outcomes (e.g., PTSD). We can prevent many of the difficulties children and their families face by not incarcerating broad classes of nonviolent offenders and by seeking to strengthen families. Criminal justice involvement is a red flag that parents and their children are in trouble given typical patterns of problematic family-of-origin histories, intergenerational cycles of substance use and criminality, and cumulative disadvantage.

As in the case of the halfway house experiment and Project Greenlight, an overemphasis on determining "what works" in terms of rehabilitating offenders or reintegration back to the community can actually reduce opportunities for innovation and may even be detrimental to the population being served if programming is inappropriately applied (Burnett & Maruna, 2006; Meyerson & Otteson, 2009)—hence the importance of applying policy and programs that are research-based, theoretically informed, and effective across a broad range of specific interventions. There is plenty of room for innovation with regard to intervention that capitalizes on family strengths and natural contexts of support and that utilizes postmodern and multimodal approaches. Further, in thinking about policy and intervention, it is important to recognize the value of "practical theory." Practical theory is based on the experiences, hunches, and views of those on the "front line"—professionals who engage closely with the incarcerated and their families. By extension, practical theory should also include the voices of the incarcerated and their family members. Practical theory helps fill in the gaps where the empirical research is not definitive or nonexistent or provides little in the way of answers (Burton & Chapman, 2004). Practical theory is based on what many practitioners, researchers, and reformers interested in parental incarceration know only too well: there are messy and contradictory realities to a given problem or set of issues (clearly evidenced, e.g., by the "paradox of visitation" or MCP programs, as we have discussed). Research will always leave gaps—particularly given the challenges inherent in studying incarcerated and marginalized populations and the absence of in-depth family-relevant information that attends to processes influencing parental incarceration outcomes.

Evidence that does not engage fully with practical theory is likely to have little impact on practice, and ultimately intervention or reform will fall short of achieving the desired outcome (Burton & Chapman, 2004). The delineation of context and process factors and their impact on offender parents and their family members is largely informed by published empirical research and summarizes the relationships among key variables, as we have discussed in previous chapters. We can think of the published research as formal sources of evidence. The holistic coverage provided here is a critical first step in laying the groundwork for comprehensive policy and practice recommendations aimed at families interfacing with the criminal justice system. However, we might also benefit from other more practical sources of knowledge that are not covered here. These sources include local knowledge and semiformal sources of information that may not be published (Burton & Chapman, 2004). These less formal sources of knowing embrace dilemmas that are connected to service delivery, particularly at the community level, and mismatches that might occur between dominant research-based strategies of intervention and the realities of the field. Lisa's experience with the mentoring program is an example of such a "mismatch." Formal theory and research suggest that children can benefit from spending time with a positive adult role model; however, real life can prove to be messy, and its messiness can contribute to counterproductive programs and policies. For example, science cannot predict that Brian will stop seeing Joey, yet Lisa's observations of how the mentoring program has negatively affected Joey may prove crucial for informing service delivery and dealing with unexpected developments. Similarly, Carla's inability to make progress with her volunteer program suggests a lack of fit between what she has to offer in the way of services and what the families impacted by incarceration in her community might need. It is only by attending to these discrepancies and contradictions that we might develop innovative practice and policy recommendations that build on both past successes and past failures.

Appendix

Evidence map of selected empirical studies sampling incarcerated parents and their families

Study	Quan	Qual	Mothers	Fathers	Family	Sample Size/ Type	Comparison Group	Longitudinal
Aaron & Dallaire, 2010	X				C, CG	874 C, 150 of which had parent incarcerated and their parents	X	follow-up
Arditti & Few, 2008		X	X			10 Jail & Prison		follow-up
Arditti & Few, 2006	X	X	X			28 Jail		follow-up
Arditti et al., 2003	X	X			CG/W/ IP[1]	56 Jail		
Arditti, 2003	X	X			CG/W/ IP	56 Jail		
Arditti, et al., 2005		X		X		51 Prison		
Arditti et al., 2010		X	X			14 Jail & Prison		X[2]

1. Caregivers/Wives/Intimate partners of male inmates
2. Data from a longitudinal ethnographic study: Three-City Study

Theory	Major Findings	Methodological Comments
Cumulative Risk model	Recent parental incarceration predicted family conflict, victimization, and parent reports of child delinquency	Multiple informants, data triangulation; adequate reliability; control variables in analyses; 22% attrition of parent response at follow-up
Grounded Theory	Manifestations of maternal distress were the backbone of women's reentry stories; mothers' distress was intensified by the punitive & traumatic context of prison thus undermining their reentry trajectories and relationships with children	Case study method described; in-depth interviews yielding thick description; member checking; data and investigator triangulation
Feminism, Ecological	Mothers' release for the prison is associated with shifts in family configuration. Their mental health risks connect between resource adequacy and parental stress.	Methods and investigator triangulation
Theory of loss	Families were at risk economically before incarceration, and the most vulnerable became even more financially strained afterward. Problems are created by incarceration included parenting strain, emotional stress, and concerns about children's loss of involvement with their incarcerated parent.	Methods, data, and investigator triangulation; study participants represented larger population
Ecological, Ambiguous Loss	Issues that emerged within the context of family visiting at the jail included concerns of the lack of physical contact affecting inmate's children, and various obstacles and barriers connected to the setting and harsh, disrespectful treatment by jail staff.	Methods and data triangulation
Identity	Many fathers perceived mothers' gatekeeping, or efforts to prevent contact, as evidence of their powerlessness.	Investigator triangulation; intercoder reliability check
Cumulative disadvantage theory; Grounded theory	In response to high levels of maternal distress and accumulated disadvantage, most mothers exhibited harsh discipline of their children, whereas some mothers transformed their distress by advocating for their children under difficult circumstances.	Exemplar case study approach; investigator triangulation

Study	Quan	Qual	Mothers	Fathers	Family	Sample Size/ Type	Com-parison Group	Longitudinal
Baker et al., 2010		X	X		CG	40 Jail		follow-up
Berry & Eigen-berg, 2003	X		X			109 Prison		
Bocknek et al., 2008	X	X			CM & F[3]	35 Prison		
Braman, 2004		X			couples	10[4] Prison		follow-up
Brown & Bloom, 2009		X	X			25 Parole (from prison)		follow-up with case note
Carl-son & Cervera, 1991	X	X		X	W	63,39 Prison	X[5]	
Casey-Acevedo et al., 2004	X		X			158,222 Prison	X	
Cho, 2009a	X				CM	4135; 9346 Jail	X	tested twice

3. Majority of children in study had an incarcerated father
4. Over two hundred interviews conducted with 10 couples over 3 years
5. Compared inmates and their wives in the Family Reunion Program (FRP) with non-FRP inmates

Theory	Major Findings	Methodological Comments
Co-parenting theory	Findings suggest that the mother-grand-mother co-parenting relationships were tied to children's functioning.	Multiple informants; observational data system with good inter-rater reliability; excellent alphas reported for assessment measures
Role Strain (social exclusion implicit to study)	Women in prison who are White, had served longer sentences, had not lived with their children prior to incarceration, and did not approve of their children's custody arrangements were found to have signifi-cantly high levels of role strain. They will experience less role strain if they are allowed to engage in mothering activities.	Purposive sample generally representative of the population at the prison site; reliability alphas for contact items very good
Ambiguous loss theory	Finding showed that children's post-traumatic stress mediate the relationship between trauma and decreased mental health functioning. Internalizing, rather than externalizing, was a common reaction to emotional stress from the ambiguous loss.	Descriptive study with methods triangulation; excellent alpha reported for posttraumatic stress assessment; however, alphas for other child outcomes fair to poor.
Anthropologi-cal interpretation of Social Capital Theory	Families revealed that the burden of stigma persists and that it often falls more heavily on non-offending family members than on the offenders themselves. The result is that relationships at the individual and commu-nity level diminished and distorted to guard information about incarceration.	In-depth repeated interviews
Identity theory, Desistance theory, Gender	Prison damages fragile maternal identi-ties making the role of motherhood less influential in successful reentry; evidence of cumulative disadvantage and troubled motherhood prior to incarceration; most women do not have the resources to set up their own households after prison; caregiv-ers often had unresolved issues with mother upon reentry	In depth life-history interview; data triangulation; multiple infor-mants; sample consistent with state prison population
	To assess the impact of incarceration on the family by measuring family function-ing, results showed that both families with or without participating the Family Reunion Program (FRP) were cohesive but not adaptable. FRP inmates reported feeling closer to their families than non-FRP inmates.	Methods triangulation; fair to good alphas reported for measures
Not specified, social control theory implicit	The inmates who do receive visits from their minor children have more difficulty adjust-ing to institutionalization and are more likely to engage in both serious and violent infractions.	Purposive sample noted; detailed description of what constitutes disciplinary infractions and formu-lation of visitation rate; controls in logistic regression
Psych, Soc, Eco-nomic Costs	The results of this study suggest that separa-tion between an imprisoned mother and her elementary school-aged children does not cause children to suffer in terms of increased retention rates.	3 separate longitudinal data bases; Statistical model specified; exact block matching for comparison group; conditional DID regression estimator used[6]

6. Conditional difference-in-difference (DID) regression estimator technique helps avoid bias which would occur if children selected into "prison" group due to unobserved characteristics that are not controlled for via matching.

Study	Quan	Qual	Mothers	Fathers	Family	Sample Size/ Type	Comparison Group	Longitudinal
Cho, 2009b	X				CM	2173; 4689 Prison	X	X
Christian, 2005		X			CG/W/ IP	19 Prison		
Clark et al., 2005	X	X		X	IP	43, 21 Prison (England)		
Comfort, 2008		X			W/IP	50 Prison		
Dallaire, 2007b	X		X	X		690/324[7] 4029/1103[8] Jail & Prison	Compare mothers/ fathers	
Dallaire & Wilson, 2010	X	X	X	X	C, CM	46/49/32/32 Jail	Within group with some children witnessing arrest & sentencing	
DeHart & Altshuler, 2009		X	X		C	60 Prison		

7. Mothers of minor/adult children
8. Fathers of minor/adult children

Theory	Major Findings	Methodological Comments
Cost Benefit Analysis	Although children with imprisoned mothers have lower test scores than the average child attending public elementary school, they do not appear to perform worse because of their mother's imprisonment.	Panel Data; statistical model specified; bias accounted for statistically via fixed effects
Intersectionality, grounded theory	This study highlighted the collateral consequences of incarceration, especially what is required for families to maintain contact with prisoners. Relationships before incarceration, prisoners' efforts to improve himself, the economic resources, and the social support system may influence how families stay connected to prisoners over time.	Data triangulation; extensive time in the field; participants representative of population of family members using transportation provided by NY prison system for visitation
Ecological	The prison context overwhelms "responsible" or "active" fathering for prisoners; fathering identity fragmented; couple relationships fragile and relationship quality associated with how often fathers saw their children.	Detailed description of purposive sampling strategy across 3 British prisons; findings contextualized with U.S research using same survey (Arditti et al., 2005)
Prisonization	Female intimate partners of male inmates showed evidence of "secondary prisonization"—that is, adopting the mores, customs and norms of the prison environment. Women created psychological presence of partner outside of prison walls.	Immersion in the field over an extended period of time; thick description regarding setting and methods
Risk Factor Model	Maternal incarceration over paternal incarceration represents a risk for children to be incarcerated themselves. Accumulated risks increases intergenerational incarceration; children with both parent's incarcerated may be at especially high risk for problem behavior.	Nationally representative data; z-approximation tests used t compensate for comparing groups of different size
Mechanisms of Risk	Children who witnessed their parent's criminal activity, arrest, and sentencing had more maladjustment re: emotional regulation, performed worse on a receptive vocabulary test, and exhibited more anxiety and depression than children who had an incarcerated parent but did not witness these events.	Small sample with limited power by use of multiple informants re: children's maladjustment including child reports. Standardized measures with good internal consistency
Grounded theory	Children experience violence in their lives with incarcerated mother, including child witnessing of violence, emotional sequelae, bodily harm from abuse and neglect, sexual abuse, and birth defects from prenatal violence.	Random selection of participants; in-depth interviews and debriefing; reflexive field notes; data triangulation

Study	Quan	Qual	Mothers	Fathers	Family	Sample Size/ Type	Com- parison Group	Longitudinal
Edin et al., 2004		X		X		300 Jail, Prison, & Court Ordered Drug Rehab		Repeated interview
Enos, 1997		X	X			13 Prison		
Enos, 2001		X	X			31 Prison		
Fair- child, 2009	X	X		X		38 Prison (minimum security)		
Fritsch & Birk- head, 1981	X		X	X		91 Prison (minimum security)		
Geller et al., 2008	X		X	X		8,728 Jail or Prison	X	Repeated interview[9]
Golden, 2005		X	X		C	1,511 Jail or Deten- tion Center		

9. A longitudinal family survey

Theory	Major Findings	Methodological Comments
Life course, Desistence	Incarcerated fathers who believe incarceration has profound effects on their relationships both with their children and their children's mothers may manage to avoid incarceration again. For male inmates with continued ties with children and the mothers of these children, their journey in renegotiating a fathering role was certainly easier.	Large N for an underrepresented group; life history interviews conducted over 5 years; sample stratified by age and ethnicity in two cities
Feminist	The options available for incarcerated mother in placing their children, maintaining contact, and maintaining place in families vary widely and are related to race, ethnicity, and other variables.	Purposive case study; Immersion in the field; reflexivity; in-depth interviews yielding thick description; brief profiles provided of participants
Feminist, Identity, grounded theory	Women in prison identify concern for their children as their primary priority. The impact of race, ethnicity, and marginality on women in prison could be traced through how inmate mothers find places for their children, and negotiate rights to their children under challenging circumstances.	Detailed description of research setting; immersion in the field; data triangulation; repeated readings of the interview transcripts; reflexivity; constant comparison; profiles provided of participants
Attachment Theory	Largest category of respondents was classified as having unresolved/disorganized/disoriented attachment representations; their childhood was characterized by unresolved loss, trauma, and abuse.	For qual data, 2 independent coders with 75% inter-rater reliability; use of established measure of adult attachment
Not specified, however coverage focused on unique nature of loss of parent due to incarceration.	Parental absence is a multi-dimensional variable that takes on added meaning depending on whether the child believes the parent is absent for socially acceptable reasons or for reasons that carry a stigma. In this study, sex of the absent parent was shown to be correlated with the type behavior exhibited, absence of the father with acting-out and absence of the mother with acting-in behavior.	Exploratory study; randomly selected sample with detailed good description of participants
Assortive mating	Children of incarcerated parents face more economic and residential instability than their counterparts. Children of incarcerated fathers also display more behavior problems, though other developmental differences are insignificant. Several family differences are magnified when both parents have been incarcerated.	Fragile Families Data Set comprised of multiple informants; data triangulation; most alphas reported good, although one subscale retained with low alpha. Inclusion of confounding covariates in analyses; bias accounted for statistically via fixed effects modeling
Feminist	The author argued that persistent poverty, family disruption, lack of health care, poor quality schools, unsafe neighborhoods, abuse, violence, and fragmented community networks all characterize the lives of many incarcerated minority mothers and their children; yet, these societal problems remain invisible to the public eye. That is, the key factor at the center of women's criminality is structural inequality, which restricts these women's life choices.	Reflexivity, field immersion, multiple informants

Study	Quan	Qual	Mothers	Fathers	Family	Sample Size/ Type	Com- parison Group	Longitudinal
Greene et al., 2008	X	X	X			102 Jail		
Hanlon, Blatch- ley, et al., 2005	X				CM	88 Prison		
Hanlon, O'Grady, et al., 2005	X	X	X			167 Prison		
Houck & Loper, 2002	X		X			362 Prison		
Hun- gerford, 1996	X	X	X		CG/C	150,107/398 Pre-Release Center for Women		follow-up[10]
Kampf- ner, 1995		X			CM, CC	36, 36		
Kinner et al., 2007	X				CF	2399 (Australia)		X

10. Structured interviews with mothers were followed by questionnaires

Theory	Major Findings	Methodological Comments
Risk factor model; criminogenic conditions	This study shows that the majority of the incarcerated mothers come from families where criminogenic risk factors, such as poverty, physical abuse, sexual abuse, and witnessing violence. Short- and long-term attempts to cope with these traumatic childhood experiences, however, led the majority of them to jail.	Purposeful sample with methods triangulation
Social learning	The majority of children in this study with incarcerated mothers were neither especially deviant nor maladjusted, all but a small percentage having successfully avoided substance abuse and the adoption of a deviant lifestyle at this point in their development. Primary caregivers of the children may have attenuated the negative impact ordinarily associated with a mother's absence from the home.	Methods triangulation; multiple informants; good to excellent alphas on most measures used in study; widely used assessment tools
Risk factor model	For the incarcerated drug-abuse mothers, results revealed significant relationships between higher risk levels and less favorable current adjustment. Despite the potential disruption stemming from their mothers' drug use and incarceration, their children were protected from the negative consequences of these circumstances by a kinship phenomenon prevalent among African American families.	Good response rate; widely used assessment tools
Not specified, although coverage pertaining to the stress of incarceration provided	This study demonstrated a clear relationship between incarcerated mothers' feelings of parenting stress and emotional and behavioral maladjustment. Incarcerated mothers who report high levels of anxiety and depression and who exhibit behavioral difficulties tend to experience feelings of inadequacy and loss as a parent.	Racially diverse sample; well established measures utilized although subscale alphas varied from poor to excellent; some data triangulation to check accuracy of mother reports
	The majority of the inmate mothers reported that their children's caregivers were the best possible choices they could have arranged. However, the caregivers expressed what they accepted the children's care usually being made voluntarily, so they unprepared for the tasks.	Sequential mixed methods design; multiple informants
Posttraumatic Stress Theory	Children of incarcerated mothers displayed evidence of PTSD symptoms, even several years after separation. Children with incarcerated mothers had less social support than a control group of children whose mothers were at home.	Thick description although used convenience sample
Not specified, some discussion of risk and parental modeling	Poor child outcomes in adolescence largely accounted for by social and familial risk factors; for boys only paternal arrest linked to substance use.	Good alpha reported for one assessment; weighted analysis used to account for those lost to follow-up; sensitivity analyses conducted to account for changes over time

Study	Quan	Qual	Mothers	Fathers	Family	Sample Size/ Type	Com- parison Group	Longitudinal
Johnson, 2009	X				CF	3540 Prison		X[11]
Johnson & Wald- fogel, 2004	X		X	X		2047,6870 Prison		
Lanier, 1993	X			X		302 Prison		
LaVigne, Naser, et al., 2005	X			X		233 Prison		X
Lowen- stein, 1986	X				W	118 Prison		
Mackin- tosh et al., 2006	X	X			CG/ CM	25/69 Jail		
Meek, 2007		X		X		39 Prison (England)		
Modecki & Wilson, 2009	X			X		50 Jail		

11. Panel Survey of Income Dynamics

Theory	Major Findings	Methodological Comments
Cumulative Risk Model	Parental imprisonment was connected to poor mental health in children, and a trend toward antisocial outcomes for children after parental imprisonment. Incarceration magnified economic, educational, and social disadvantage for the offender and his or her family.	Nationally representative sample of adults and children; control variables included; model tests for unobserved bias included
Risk Factor Model	Offender parents' mental health needs remain unmet and return to their families with drug and mental health vulnerabilities may lead to nonparental care arrangements for children.	Population based data set; subjects with missing data dropped; extensive set of control variables included in multinomial regression
System theory	The findings showed that some male inmates with poor father-child relationships were more likely to be depressed and to experience an elevated level of concern about the father-child relationship.	Random sample from large state prison with 80% response rate; sample demographics similar to prison population at site and in New York State; good reliability alphas reported for measures; control variables included; conservative test[12]
Not specified, but coverage on family dynamics and recidivism provided	Findings indicate that level and type of family contact typically mediate the effect of pre-prison relationship quality on both post-prison family relationship quality and support, but that in-prison contact can be a negative influence if intimate partner relationships are already poor.	Five facility sample from one state; 2 in-depth repeated interviews; excellent reliability alphas reported for all measures; use of control variables, interaction terms, and testing of multiple models to confirm hypotheses.
Family Systems	Findings indicated that the ability of the children to adjust successfully to father's imprisonment was related to familial and personal resources of the mother and to the stigmatizing effects of the criminal event.	Widely used measures with acceptable reliability; factor structure of children's adjustment measure explored
Protective factors, parental warmth/ acceptance	Children who felt lower levels of warmth and acceptance from their caregivers self-reported greater internalizing and externalizing behaviors. Caregivers' warmth and acceptance toward the children was lower when they assessed the children's behavior as difficult and the caregivers' parenting stress was high.	Methods triangulation; widely use measures for quant portion with very good reliability alphas
The social psychological concept of possible selves	Findings present a constructive picture of the parenting aspirations and concerns of young fathers in prison. Hoped-for and feared possible selves are the most frequently referred by participants in this study.	High inter-rater reliability of coding (90%). Content analysis linked to established conceptual categories
Systems model; responsive and restrictive parenting	Study showed that incarcerated fathers with less education, lengthier incarceration, more likely to report using restrictive parenting practices. Having children with fewer intimate partners associated with responsive parenting.	Description of purposeful recruitment strategies; use of established measure of parenting practices; methods triangulation; debriefing after interview

12. Adjusted R² used as coefficient to explain variance

Study	Quan	Qual	Mothers	Fathers	Family	Sample Size/Type	Comparison Group	Longitudinal
Murray & Farrington, 2008	X				CM[13]	411 Prison	X	X
Naser & Visher, 2006	X	limited			family[14]	247 Released from Prison		X
Nesmith & Ruhland, 2008		X			C/CG[15]	34[16] Prison		X
Nurse, 2002		X		X		258[17] Youth Detention		
Phillips et al., 2002	X				C	258 Jail or Prison		follow-up
Phillips et al., 2006	X				C[18]	1420 CJS involvement	X	X[19]

13. Prospective study of UK males aged 8-48 separated from parents due to incarceration, death, or divorce

14. Comprised primarily of female family members who resided at some point with reentering male prisoners; 90% of sample African American

15. Although authors interviewed both children and their caregivers, in this article, they discussed only the child portion of the study; the caregiver perspective will be presented in a forthcoming article

16. 32 with incarcerated fathers, 2 with incarcerated mothers

17. Also 20 randomly selected in depth interviews (drawn from the 258)

18. By age 16, 47% of children had parent involved in CJS: of these 41.6% had father in CJS, 10.4% had mother in CJS

19. Data were from a longitudinal epidemiologic study of youth from 11 rural counties in North Carolina.

Theory	Major Findings	Methodological Comments
Trauma theory, life course perspective, selection perspective	Parental imprisonment predicted worse internalizing outcomes than other forms of parent-child separation. Prisoners' children were more likely than their peers to show both internalizing and antisocial problems throughout their lives.	Fair to excellent alphas reported for most measures; control variables included in analyses
Not specified, but coverage pertaining to family and reentry success provided	Findings indicated that these family members are highly supportive of their formerly incarcerated relative, providing financial and emotional support. But family members also experience significant hardships during the reentry period, including financial strain and increased anxiety.	Repeated in-depth interviews (1 at pre-release; 2 post-release); comparative test to determine sample bias. Very good alphas on measures of spirituality and religious support
Not specified, however, risk and resilience perspective evident	This study explored the impact of parental incarceration from the children's own perspectives. Findings showed that children revealed a variety stresses around social isolation and worrying about their caregivers, but also demonstrated resilience in locating venues for support and self-sufficiency.	Multiple informants; engagement with participants over repeated interviews; random transcription checks; three independent coders and collaborative coding of content
Not specified, focus on fatherhood	The stigma bleeds onto family members via their association with the offender; families may in turn avoid visitation or contact with the offender, thus severely limiting opportunities for offender-child interaction during confinement. Incarceration changes how parents see themselves. Young fathers held "meaning standards" of parenting which centered around their vision of a "good father" as a "person who provides guidance, love and financial support to his children."	Racially and ethnically diverse sample; extensive immersion in the field; data and method triangulation; sequential design (8 month observation period informed survey development); pretesting of survey instrument; detailed description of recruitment strategy; response rate of 64% adequate; in-depth interviews yielding thick description; strategies to minimize bias include attention to survey content, interviewer matching, and observational work in different context
Risk Factor Model	Subjects who experienced parental incarceration had been exposed to significantly more risk factors during their lifetimes including parental substance abuse, extreme poverty, and abuse or neglect. They were more likely than other youth to present with attention- deficit/hyperactivity and conduct disorders.	Fair to good reliability alphas reported
Risk Factor Model	Findings showed that children whose parents become involved in the criminal justice system are at the risk of parental substance abuse and parental mental health problems. Incarceration and other outcomes of arrest linked with the increased likelihood of children developing serious emotional and behavioral problems, and of becoming involved with criminal authorities.	80% response rate for families in the sample; multiple informants (parent and child); data weighted to represent general population from which sample recruited; statistical modeling accounts for error stemming from within subjects and design effects

Study	Quan	Qual	Mothers	Fathers	Family	Sample Size/Type	Comparison Group	Longitudinal
Phillips & Zhao, 2010	X				Children who were the subject of mal-treat-ment reports	1869, 122 of whom witnessed a parent's arrest	X	X
Poehl-mann, 2005a	X				CM	60 Prison		
Poehl-mann, 2005b	X	X	X			94 Prison		
Poehl-mann, 2005c	X	X	X		CG/C	60,60/60 Prison		
Richie, 2001		X	X			42 Jail or Prison		
Roy & Dyson, 2005		X		X		40 Prison Work-Release Program		

Theory	Major Findings	Methodological Comments
	Witnessing of parental arrest significantly predicted heightened Posttraumatic Stress Symptoms. Children who witnessed their parents' arrests were also more likely to be exposed to violence, victims of violence, witness nonviolent crime, and live in families that had trouble meeting their basic needs.	Population based study with reliable measures; well executed multivariate analyses with controls. However, study limited to children who are the subject of maltreatment reports.
Attachment	Most children of imprisoned mothers in this study held representations of insecure relationships with mothers and caregivers. However, secure relationships were more likely when children lived in a stable caregiving situation, when children reacted to separation from the mother with sadness rather than anger, and when children were older.	Characteristics of participants mirrored national surveys of incarcerated women; method triangulation; multiple informants; very good reliability alphas for measures used. Codes with inadequate inter-rater reliability dropped.
Relational developmental theory	Mother–child relationships were more positive when mothers had more frequent telephone contact with older children. Moreover, conflicted relationships with caregivers related to less contact between mothers and their children.	Methods triangulation; excellent reliability alphas reported; control variables included in analyses
Attachment	Children of incarcerated mothers experienced risks at multiple contextual levels. With the high risk status, children's intellectual outcomes were compromised. Caregiver risks were also associated with children's intellectual outcomes. The relation between caregiver risks and children's intellectual outcomes was mediated by quality of the current family environment.	Characteristics of participants mirrored national surveys of incarcerated women, method triangulation; multiple informants; adequate or excellent reliability alphas reported
Gender, Feminist, Grounded theory	Gender, ethnic identity, and economic status converge to make the situation incarcerated women face very complicated. Women of color returning from jail do not feel embraced by their communities, and they are not identified as having the right to demand services from it.	In-depth interviews; study participants' represented larger population of incarcerated women
Identity theory	Partnering relationships for incarcerated fathers were marked by confusion and conflict. However, in this study, half of incarcerated fathers referred to be encouraged in parenting involvement through the maternal efforts. That is, both incarcerated fathers and their children's mothers could develop a sense of empathy with each others' challenges, and that this empathy could be vital to the encouragement of men's involvement.	In-depth interviews; sources of data triangulation and member checks

Study	Quan	Qual	Mothers	Fathers	Family	Sample Size/ Type	Com- parison Group	Longitudinal
Sack & Seidler, 1978		X			CF	22 Prison		
Snyder et al., 2001	X	X	X			58 Prison	X[20]	
Swisher & Waller, 2008	X			X	W/IP	1002 Jail		Follow-up survey
Thomp- son & Harm, 2000	X		X			104 Prison		
Todis et al., 2001		X			C[21]	15 Youth correc- tional facilities		X
Trice & Brewster, 2004	X		X		CG/C	41,47/58 Prison	X[22]	
Tripp, 2001		X		X		16 Jail		

20. Compared mother-child visitation program (MCVP) participants with convenience sample of non-MCVP participants.
21. 15 youth in a correctional facility
22. 41 parents of friends known by the children in the study

Theory	Major Findings	Methodological Comments
Not specified	Findings indicated that the children placed a high value on prison visits but also experienced inner conflict over fathers' imprisonment. Children in the study seemed isolated from peers and showed evidence of depression and anxiety.	Clinical interviews
Feminist	Research indicated that incarcerated mothers in the mother-child visitation program (MCVP) maintained more frequent contact with their children and were more focused on the needs of the children than non-MCVP participants.	Methods triangulation; reflexivity
Race and ethnicity; life course theory, responsible fatherhood	Fathers' current incarceration presented serious obstacles to maintaining contact with children and interfered with the establishment of informal financial support agreements with mothers. Findings also revealed significant differences across White, African American, and Latino fathers.	Population based study using Fragile Families database; good reliability alphas reported; probability adjusted standard errors; multiple models with interaction terms and controls
Not specified	This study found that the PFP (Parenting from Prison) program in conjunction with frequent visits, had a positive effect on mothers in spite of a history of substance or child abuse. Child visitation had positive influence on their self-esteems, empathy, and parent-child roles.	Fair to good reliability alphas for measures used; qualitative exemplars used to highlight quant data
Resilience	About half the youth were successful; responded well to structure and rehabilitation; positive outlook and determination.	In depth life history interviews over five years; inclusion of observational field notes
Not specified	This study found that children of incarcerated mothers were at high risk for school, community, and home problems. Although these children initially experienced difficulty adapting to structured placements, those how were living in homes with rules and with family members had better educational outcomes, as did children who communicated frequently with their mothers.	Stratified sample to enhance representativeness of women in prison; very high response rate; multiple informants
Grounded theory, symbolic interactionism, social constructionism, and narrative theory	The experience of incarceration and the management of identities are processes that vary within each individual. Many of the samples displayed strong commitment to their pre-incarceration identities. Moreover, incarcerated fathers held high expectations for their personal and family lives upon the completion of their sentence.	Life history interviews directed by interviewees to avoid researcher bias.

Study	Quan	Qual	Mothers	Fathers	Family	Sample Size/ Type	Com-parison Group	Longitudinal
Tripp, 2009		X		X		25 Jail		
Tuerk & Loper, 2006	X		X			357 Prison		
van Olphen et al., 2009		X	X			17 Released after jail		
Western et al., 2004	X			X		3867 Prison	X	X
Wilbur et al., 2007	X				CM	102 Jail		

Theory	Major Findings	Methodological Comments
Symbolic interactionism, social constructionism, narrative analysis	Some distinct notions can be gleaned from this study. First, visits are difficult for inmates in a variety of manners. Second, while incarceration causes many men to become "prisonized," many men in this study displayed strong commitment to their pre-incarceration identities. Third, incarcerated fathers hold high expectations for their personal and family lives upon the completion of their sentence.	Life history interviews directed by interviewees to avoid researcher bias.
Attachment	Results indicated that higher levels of contact between mothers and their children were associated with reduced levels of parenting stress. In particular, letter writing during incarceration was associated with increased attachment and improved sense of parental competence.	Widely used measure of parenting stress used with adequate to good reliability; response consistency assessed among participants and conflicting reports deleted
Gender and stigma	Incarcerated mothers faced multiple, interrelated problems after release from jail, including drug use and mental health problems, family problems, lack of safe housing or a job that pays a living wage, challenges finding needed services, and social isolation, all stemming at least in part from stigma and discrimination related to their drug use and history of incarceration.	Methods triangulation
Selection, Collateral Consequences	Paying attention to the confinement of incarcerated fathers, linked to growing numbers of single mother households. Authors indicated offenders are at much greater risk for divorce or separation than non-offenders during their imprisonment.	Population based sample; multiple control variables
Risk Factor Model	Authors indicated the largely negative influences of incarceration on offender parents, children, and spouses/intimate partners such that family health declines, child adjustment and academic success is compromised, poverty intensifies, and family relationships deteriorate or cease altogether.	Well-known instruments utilized although alphas not reported. Status of child (i.e., father incarcerated or not) masked to enhance validity; outcome data derived from multiple informants

Notes

1. Reconstructed from researcher field notes; see Arditti, Joest, et al., 2010.

2. Jails and prisons are similar in that they both incarcerate men and women. However, they are very distinct in terms of purpose, oversight, and environment. Jails are typically run by local government, often the sheriff's office, and have a rapid turnover in population. Offenders tend to be confined at jails for much shorter periods, and jail sentences tend not to exceed 18 months. Prisons tend to have longer-term populations, are known for the availability of drugs, and are at a much farther distance from the offender's home (Center for Therapeutic Justice, 2000). Jails may also have more restrictive visitation policies than prisons (Arditti, 2003). The majority of research here draws from studies of parents in prison, with exceptions noted in the appendix.

3. See, e.g., economist Steven Levitt's (2004) challenge of widely held explanations regarding the reasons behind declining crime. His conclusions, that imprisonment and legal abortion are largely responsible for drops in crime during the 1990s, are in sharp contrast to those of King, Mauer, and Young (2005), who conclude that incarceration is responsible for only a small portion of decreases in crime and attribute declines in crime to community responses and a strong economy, among other factors.

4. Although references to national data alone may obscure important differences among states. For example, states with the highest rates of incarceration had diminished returns in terms of any decrease in crime rates. See Gainsborough & Mauer, 2000.

5. Adler (1870–1937) has been considered a founding influence on modern psychology. His contributions include the importance of childhood for adult mental health, the need to treat the whole person, and egalitarian power relations between therapist and client.

6. See, for example, the application of integrative frameworks for understanding (a) theories and techniques of marital and family therapy (Kaslow, Kaslow, & Farber, 1999) and (b) diverse empirical studies on family stress (Helms, Walls, & Demo, 2010).

7. Per Nurse (2002), the "deep break" encompasses policies characterized by social isolation of the prisoner from the outside world.

8. With the exception of population-based studies with broad indicators of criminal justice involvement that include parental arrest as well as incarceration (see, e.g., Phillips et al., 2006).

NOTES TO CHAPTER 2

1. Mary is a pseudonym and represents a composite of real prisoners' experience. Her story was constructed based on the narratives and autobiographies posted on "Prison Talk," an online inmate support community (http://www.prisontalk.com/).

2. Although some argue that minority overrepresentation in prisons is the result of people of color committing more crime (see, e.g., Manhattan Institute senior fellow Heather MacDonald's 2008 argument), one scholarly analysis suggests that this is not the case because blacks and Latinos are more likely to be incarcerated for the same crimes and receive longer sentences (Spohn, 2000).

3. Mumola (2000) notes that for state prisoners, parents report slightly lower levels of *mental illness* than do nonparents. It is difficult to make comparisons between reports because different outcomes are often reported (i.e., mental problems, disorders, illness).

4. In 2005, federal prisons operated at 134% capacity and state prison operated at 107% above capacity (Harrison & Beck, 2006).

NOTES TO CHAPTER 3

1. Allison is a pseudonym for a real person who participated in two research projects examining mothers' reentry into family life after incarceration. Allison had been released and then reincarcerated at the time of this interview (see Arditti & Few, 2006, 2008).

2. Both probation and parole are periods of correctional supervision in which an offender must meet certain conditions (e.g., employment, good character, drug-free lifestyle). Probation is given by a judge and may be a portion of one's sentence or the actual sentence itself. Parole is given by a parole board to a prisoner before the completion of a particular sentence based on good behavior during confinement. The state of Maine and the federal government no longer offer parole (Mays & Winfree, 2009).

3. These numbers may add to more than 100% because some parents have multiple children.

4. Except in instances whereby the removal of mothers from a household provided children relief from abuse or other forms of victimization.

5. Hanlon Blatchley et al., 2005, note that the disruptive effects of maternal incarceration on children are mitigated to the extent that mothers were not primary caregivers prior to their incarceration.

6. Arditti & Few, 2008.

NOTES TO CHAPTER 4

1. Both Charlie and Merle are composites based on material from the website "Prison Talk" and interview material from Arditti et al., 2005.

2. See Blankenhorn, 1995.

3. Jerome's story is quoted from the following source: Green, 2008, pp. 8–9.

1. The exemplar stories presented here were inspired by posts on the "Prison Talk" public forum "For Family and Friends." The exemplars are composites constructed from numerous anonymous posts; pseudonyms are used, and any quoted material has been paraphrased or revised.

2. The prison commissary is a store within the prison at which inmates can shop. Commissary is a privilege that can be taken away in the event of getting written up for a "shot" (i.e., prison violation). Prices for goods have a markup of about 30% (except for stamps), and inmates need to have funds in their account in order to make purchases. Nonincarcerated family members are the main providers of such funds. Examples of commissary items include toiletries, stationery, plastic bowls and spoons, clothing, and food items such as ramen noodles, snacks, dips, drinks, soups, breads, and ice cream. In some cases, frozen meat and wellness items are available. Because prison meals are often considered to be bland or unhealthful, it is common for offenders to purchase commissary food in order to taste something different or attempt a more nutritious diet. Proceeds from commissaries are used to fund prison operations. Some critics believe that commissaries exploit inmates and their families due to the costs to inmates and high profits for the prison industry (see, e.g., Ross & Richards, 2002; Stiles, 2010).

3. Phillips et al. (2006) argue that children whose mothers have a history of arrest, not just incarceration, are exposed to a greater number of risk factors and have more serious problems than children in the general population and in other risk situations (e.g., mental health, child welfare). Mothers' protracted arrest histories were particularly problematic and suggest multiple separations between parent and children.

4. Purposeful samples suggest: "If it can happen here, it can happen anywhere," and in that sense the existing research on children and families experiencing the incarceration of a parent provides more answers than one might initially expect.

5. Although Hagan and Dinovitzer (1999) theorize that even in these cases incarceration will likely compound rather than mitigate preexisting problems in the family.

6. From *Merriam-Webster's Online Dictionary*, http://www.merriam-webster.com/netdict/paradox.

7. Although it should be noted that jails also hold state and federal prisoners during adjudication, appeals, etc.

8. See, for example, Arditti & Keith, 1993.

9. Both the Dallaire and Arditti studies were conducted at local jails, which tend to have the most prohibitive visitation policies.

10. At the medium-security state facility where Pam was held, children were prohibited from sitting on their mother's lap.

NOTES TO CHAPTER 6

1. Selene Diaz is a pseudonym, as is the Center for Women's Empowerment. Selene's case was loosely inspired by the true story of Marlene Sanchez, executive director of San Francisco's Center for Young Women's Development. See http://fcnetwork.org/spotlight.php#more-188 for Marlene's story.

2. Young, 1990, p. 53.

3. The issue of state bans on welfare assistance is a moving target. Sources tend to be inconsistent with regard to the number of states implementing alterations of the federal legislation and the number of states implementing the full ban. While the 2003 figures from Mauer are widely cited, more recent figures suggest an increasing number of states altering the full ban. For example, 2008 figures suggest that 14 states implemented the full ban and 22 states imposed the ban in part (2009 Criminal Justice Transition Coalition, 2008). The Treadwell and Kingsbury (2009) figures represent the most up-to-date review of state policies.

4. van Wormer, 1999, p. 35.

5. I. Matthew Campbell, former assistant state's attorney of Maryland, quoted in the Sentencing Project, 2008, retrieved from http://www.sentencingproject.org.

6. System of a Down, "Prison Song," on *Toxicity*, Sony, 2001.

7. Lerner, Fisher, & Weinberg, 2000, pp. 11–20.

8. Luthar, 2006, p. 780.

9. Girl Scouts Behind Bars (GSBB) was created more than 15 years ago in partnership with the Girl Scout Council of central Maryland and the National Institute of Justice. With more than 40 GSBB programs across the country, the organization aims to strengthen mother-daughter bonds, self-awareness, and leadership (Meyerson & Otteson, 2009).

10. Although for the 2012 budget, the federal government has cut MCP funding in half (from $49 million to $25 million), suggesting that the popularity of mentoring programs specific to children with an incarcerated parent is waning in favor of more evidence-based programs. See *Fiscal Year 2012: Terminations, Reductions, and Savings* at: http://www.whitehouse.gov/sites/default/files/omb/budget/fy2012/assets/trs.pdf.

11. See, for example, *InsideOut Dad Program in Maryland and Ohio Prisons Evaluation requested by the National Fatherhood Initiative*. Report available at www.fatherhood.org/Document.Doc?id=57.

12. From Dreher, 2000, p. 171.

Bibliography

Aaron, L., & Dallaire, D. (2010). Parental incarceration and multiple risk experiences: Effects on family processes and children's delinquency. *Journal of Youth and Adolescence, 39,* 1471–1484.

Abram, K. M., & Teplin, L. A. (1991). Co-occurring disorders among mentally ill jail detainees. *American Psychologist, 46,* 1036–1045.

Adalist-Estrin, A. (1994). Family support and criminal justice. In S. L. Kagan & B. Weissbound (Eds.), *Putting families first: America's family support movement and the challenge of change* (pp. 161–185). San Francisco, CA: Jossey-Bass.

Ahrons, C. (1981). The continuing coparental relationship between divorced spouses. *American Journal of Orthopsychiatry, 51,* 415–428.

Allen, S., & Hawkins, A. (1999). Maternal gatekeeping: Mothers' beliefs and behaviors that inhibit greater father involvement in family work. *Journal of Marriage and Family, 61,* 199–212.

Arditti, J. A. (1992). Factors related to custody, visitation, and child support for divorced fathers: An exploratory analysis. *Journal of Divorce and Remarriage, 17,* 107–119.

Arditti, J. A. (2002, December). Doing family research at the jail: Reflections of a prison widow. *The Qualitative Report, 7.* Retrieved from http://www.nova.edu/ssss/QR/QR7-4/arditti.html

Arditti, J. A. (2003). Locked doors and glass walls: Family visiting at a local jail. *Journal of Loss & Trauma, 8,* 115–138.

Arditti, J. A. (2005). Families and incarceration: An ecological approach. *Families in Society, 86,* 251–258.

Arditti, J. A., & Allen, K. R. (1993). Understanding distressed fathers' perceptions of legal and relational inequities postdivorce. *Family & Conciliation Courts Review, 31,* 461–476.

Arditti, J. A., Burton, L. M., & Neeves-Botelho, S. (2010). Maternal distress and parenting in the context of cumulative disadvantage. *Family Process, 49,* 142–164.

Arditti, J. A., & Few, A. L. (2006). Mothers' reentry into family life after incarceration. *Criminal Justice Policy Review, 17,* 103–123.

Arditti, J. A., & Few, A. L. (2008). Maternal distress and women's reentry into family and community life. *Family Process, 47,* 303–321.

Arditti, J. A., & Grzywacz, J. (2011). *A demedicalized view of maternal distress: Conceptualization and instrument development.* Manuscript submitted for publication.

Arditti, J. A., Joest, K. S., Lambert-Shute, J., & Walker, L. (2010). The role of emotions in fieldwork: A self-study of family research in a corrections setting. *Qualitative Report, 15,* 1387–1414.

Arditti, J. A., & Keith, T. Z. (1993). Visitation frequency, child support payment, and the father-child relationship postdivorce. *Journal of Marriage and the Family, 55,* 699–712.

Arditti, J. A., Lambert-Shute, J., & Joest, K. (2003). Saturday morning at the jail: Implications of incarceration for families and children. *Family Relations, 52,* 195–204.

Arditti, J. A., & McClintock, C. (2001). Drug policy and families: Casualties of the war. *Marriage and Family Review, 32,* 11–32.

Arditti, J. A., & Parkman, T. (2011). Young men's reentry after incarceration: A developmental paradox, *Family Relations, 60,* 205–220.

Arditti, J. A., Smock, S., & Parkman, T. (2005). "It's been hard to be a father": A qualitative exploration of incarcerated fatherhood. *Fathering, 3,* 267–288.

Arendell, T. (1995). *Fathers and divorce.* Thousand Oaks, CA: Sage.

Arendell, T. (2000). Conceiving and investigating motherhood: The decade's scholarship. *Journal of Marriage and Family, 62,* 1192–1207.

Austin, J., Bruce, M., Carroll, L., McCall, P., & Richards, S. (2000, November). The use of incarceration in the United States [National Policy White Paper, American Society of Criminology]. Retrieved from http://www.ssc.wisc.edu/~oliver/RACIAL/Reports/ascincarcerationdraft.pdf

Austin, J., & Irwin, J. (2001). *It's about time: America's imprisonment binge.* Belmont, CA: Wadsworth.

Austin, W., & Bates, F. (1974). Ethological indicators of dominance and territory in a human captive population. *Social Forces, 52,* 447–455.

Bahr, S. J., Armstrong, A., Gibbs, B., Harris, P., & Fisher, J. (2005). The reentry process: How parolees adjust to release from prison. *Fathering, 3,* 243–265.

Baker, J., McHale, J., Strozier, A., & Cecil, D. (2010). Mother-grandmother coparenting relationships in families with incarcerated mothers: A pilot investigation. *Family Process, 49,* 165–184.

Bales, W. D., & Mears, D. P. (2008). Inmate social ties and the transition to society: Does visitation reduce recidivism? *Journal of Research in Crime and Delinquency, 45,* 287–321.

Barak, G., Flavin, J., & Leighton, P. (2001). *Class, race, gender, and crime: Social realities of justice in America.* Los Angeles, CA: Roxbury.

Barclay, L. M., & Lloyd, B. (1996). The misery of motherhood: Alternative approaches to maternal distress. *Midwifery, 12,* 136–139.

Baum, S. D. (2010, June 4). Employment/Tax-IRS reminds us that recent legislation offers special tax incentives for small businesses to provide health care and hire new workers [Erisa Lawyer blog post]. Retrieved from http://www.irs.gov/irs/article/0,,id=223909,00.html

Beck, A., Cooper, C., McLanahan, S., & Brooks-Gunn, J. (2009). *Relationship transitions and maternal parenting* (Working paper 1131). Retrieved from Princeton University, Center for Research on Child Wellbeing website: http://crcw.princeton.edu/workingpapers/WP08-12-FF.pdf

Beddoes, P. V. (2010, Apr 9). How did NACo priorities fair in the final health care reform law? *The Courthouse Journal, 11.* Retrieved from http://www.wacounties.org/CHJ/2010/CHJ-1110.pdf

Belsky, J. (1984). The determinants of parenting: A process model. *Child Development, 55,* 83–96.

Bernstein, N. (2005). *All alone in the world: Children of the incarcerated*. New York, NY: New Press.

Berry, P., & Eigenberg, H. (2003). Role strain and incarcerated mothers: Understanding the process of mothering. *Women & Criminal Justice, 15*, 101–119.

Bewley-Taylor, D., Hallam, C., & Allen, R. (2009). *The incarceration of drug offenders: An overview* (Report 16). Retrieved from University of London, International Centre for Prison Studies website: http://www.idpc.net/php-bin/documents/Beckley_Report_16_2_FINAL_EN.pdf

Block, K., & Potthast, M. (1998). Girl Scouts Beyond Bars: Facilitating parent-child contact in correctional settings. *Child Welfare, 77*, 561–578.

Bloom, B., Owen, B., Covington, S. (2003, June). Gender-responsive strategies: Research practice, and guiding principles for women offenders. *National Institute of Corrections* (NIC Accession Number 018017). Washington, DC: U.S. Department of Justice, National Institute of Corrections.

Bloom, B., & Steinhart, D. (1993).*Why punish the children: A reappraisal of the children of incarcerated mothers in America*. Atlanta, GA: Carter Center.

Blumstein, A., & Beck, A. (1999). Population growth in U.S. prisons, 1980–1996. In M. Tonry & J. Petersilia (Eds.), *Prisons: Crime and justice* (Vol. 26, pp. 17–61). Chicago, IL: University of Chicago Press.

Bocknek, E. L., Sanderson, J., & Britner, P. A. (2009). Ambiguous loss and posttraumatic stress of school-aged children of prisoners. *Journal of Child and Family Studies, 18*, 323–333.

Bogenschneider, K. (2002). *Family policy matters: How policymaking affects families*. Mahwah, NJ: LEA.

Bornstein, M. (2002). Preface. In M. Bornstein (Ed.) *Handbook of parenting: Vol. 3. Being and becoming a parent* (pp. xi–xiv). Mahwah, NJ: LEA.

Bornstein, M., & Bradley, R. (2003). Socioeconomic status, parenting, and child development: An introduction. In M. Bornstein & R. Bradley (Eds.), *Socioeconomic status, parenting, and child development* (pp. 1–10). Mahwah, NJ: LEA.

Boss, P. (1999). *Ambiguous loss: Learning to live with unresolved grief*. Cambridge, MA: Harvard University Press.

Boss, P. (2004). Ambiguous loss. In F. Walsh & M. McGoldrick (Eds.), *Living beyond Loss* (pp. 237–246). New York, NY: W. W. Norton & Company.

Bourdieu, P. (1999). *The weight of the world: Social suffering in contemporary society*. Stanford, CA: Stanford University Press.

Boyd, S. C. (1999). *Mothers and illicit drug use: Transcending the myths*. Toronto, Canada: Toronto University Press.

Boyd, S. C. (2004). *From witches to crack moms: Women, drug law, and policy*. Durham, NC: Carolina Academic Press.

Bradley, R., & Davino, K. (2007). Interpersonal violence, recovery, and resilience in incarcerated women. *Journal of Aggression, Maltreatment & Trauma, 14*, 123–146.

Braithwaite, R. L., Treadwell, H. M., & Arriola, K. R. J. (2005). Health disparities and incarcerated women: A population ignored. *American Journal of Public Health, 95*, 1679–1681.

Braman, D. (2004). *Doing time on the outside: Incarceration and family life in urban America*. Ann Arbor, MI: University of Michigan Press.

Braman, D., & Wood, J. (2003). From one generation to the next: How criminal sanctions are reshaping family life in urban America. In J. Travis & M. Waul (Eds.), *Prisoners once removed* (pp. 157–188). Washington, DC: Urban Institute Press.

Brandstaedter, J., & Lerner, R. (1999). Development, action, and intentionality: A view of the issues. In J. Brandsaedter and R. M. Lerner (Eds.), *Action and self-development: Theory and research through the life-span* (pp. ix–xx). Thousand Oaks, CA: Sage.

Broderick, C., & Smith, J. (1979). The general systems approach to the family. In W. Burr, R. Hill, F. I. Nye, & I. Reiss (Eds.), *Contemporary theories about the family* (Vol. 2, pp. 112–129). New York, NY: Free Press.

Brodsky, S. (1975). *Families and friends of men in prison.* Lexington, MA: Lexington Books.

Bronfenbrenner, U. (1977). Toward an experimental ecology of human development. *American Psychologist, 32,* 582–590.

Bronfenbrenner, U. (1979). *The ecology of human development.* Cambridge, MA: Harvard University Press.

Bronfenbrenner, U. (1995). Developmental ecology through space and time: A future perspective. In P. Moen, G. Elder, & K. Luscher (Eds.), *Examining lives in context: Perspectives on the ecology of human development* (pp. 619–646). Washington, DC: American Psychological Association.

Brooks-Gunn, J., & Duncan, G. J. (1997). The effects of poverty on children. *Future of Children, 7,* 55–71.

Brown, M., & Bloom, B. (2009). Reentry and renegotiating motherhood: Maternal identity and success on parole. *Crime and Delinquency, 55,* 313–336.

Burke, P. J. (1991). Identity processes and social stress. *American Sociological Review, 56,* 836–849.

Burke, P. J. (1996). Social identities and psychological stress. In H. B. Kaplan (Ed.), *Psychosocial stress: Perspectives on structure, theory, life-course, and methods* (pp. 141–174). San Diego, CA: Academic Press.

Burnett, R., & Maruna, S. (2006). The kindness of prisoners: Strengths-based resettlement in theory and in action. *Criminology & Criminal Justice, 6,* 83–106.

Burton, L. M. (2007). Childhood adultification in economically disadvantaged families: A conceptual model. *Family Relations, 56,* 329–345.

Burton, M., & Chapman, M. (2004). Problems of evidence based practice in community based services. *Journal of Learning Disabilities, 8,* 56–70.

Butler, M., & Maruna, S. (2009). The impact of disrespect on prisoners' aggression: Outcomes of experimentally inducing violence-supportive cognitions. *Psychology, Crime, & Law, 15,* 235–250.

Byrne, M., Goshin, L., & Joestl, S. (2010). Intergenerational transmission of attachment for infants raised in a prison nursery. *Attachment & Human Development, 12,* 375–393.

Campbell, N. (2000). *Using women: Gender, drug policy, and social justice.* London, UK: Routledge.

Carlson, B. E., & Cervera, N. (1991). Inmates and their families: Conjugal visits, family contact and family functioning. *Criminal Justice and Behavior, 18,* 318–331.

Carlson, J. R. (1998). Evaluating the effectiveness of a live-in nursery within a women's prison. *Journal of Offender Rehabilitation, 34,* 67–83.

Carlson, M. J., & Furstenberg, F. F. (2006). The prevalence and correlates of multipart-nered fertility among urban U.S. parents. *Journal of Marriage and the Family, 68,* 718–732.

Carlson, M. J., & McLanahan, S. S. (2002). Fragile families, father involvement, and public policy. In C. S. Tamis-LeMonda & N. Cabrera (Eds.), *Handbook of father involvement, multidisciplinary perspectives* (pp. 461–488). Mahwah, NJ: Erlbaum.

Carlson, M. J., McLanahan, S. S., & Brooks-Gunn, J. (2008). Co-parenting and nonresi-dent fathers' involvement with young children after a nonmarital birth. *Demography, 45,* 461–488.

Casey-Acevedo, K., Bakken, T., & Karle, A. (2004). Children visiting mothers in prison: The effects on mothers' behavior and disciplinary adjustment. *The Australian and New Zealand Journal of Criminology, 37,* 418–430.

Cecil, D. K., McHale, J., Strozier, A., & Pietsch, J. (2008). Female inmates, family caregiv-ers, and young children's adjustment: A research agenda and implications for correc-tions programming. *Journal of Criminal Justice, 36,* 513–521.

Center for Therapeutic Justice. (2000). *American jails: There is a difference between prisons and jails.* Retrieved from http://www.therapeuticjustice.com/programPDFs/JAILS%20are%20not%20prisons.pdf

Chesney-Lind, M. (1986).Women and crime: The female offender. *Signs, 12,* 78–96.

Chesney-Lind, M. (1997). *The female offender: Girls, women, and crime.* Thousand Oaks, CA: Sage.

Chipman, S., Olsen, S., Klein, S., Hart, C., & Robinson, C.. (2000). Differences in retro-spective perceptions of parenting of male and female inmates and non-inmates. *Family Relations, 49,* 5–11.

Cho, R. (2009a). Impact of maternal imprisonment on children's probability of grade retention. *Journal of Urban Economics, 65,* 11–23.

Cho, R. (2009b). The impact of maternal imprisonment on children's educational achieve-ment: Results from children in Chicago public schools. *Journal of Human Resources, 44,* 772–797.

Christian, J. (2005). Riding the bus: Barriers to prison visitation and family management strategies. *Journal of Contemporary Criminal Justice, 21,* 31–48.

Christian, J., & Thomas, S. (2009). Examining the intersections of race, gender, and mass imprisonment. *Journal of Ethnicity in Criminal Justice, 7,* 69–84.

Cicchetti, D. (2006). Development and psychopathology. In D. Cicchetti & D. Cohen (Eds.), *Developmental psychopathology: Vol. 1. Theory and method* (pp. 1–23). Hoboken, NJ: John Wiley & Sons.

Clarke, L., O'Brien, M., Day, R., Godwin, H., Connolly, J., Hemmings, J., van Leeson, T. (2005). Fathering behind bars in English prisons: Imprisoned fathers' identity and contact with their children. *Fathering, 3,* 221–241.

Clear, T. R. (2007). *Imprisoning communities: How mass incarceration makes disadvan-taged neighborhoods worse.* New York, NY: Oxford University Press.

Clear. T. R. (2008). The effects of high imprisonment rates on communities. In M. Tonry (Ed.)., *Crime and justice: A review of research 37* (pp. 97–132). Chicago, IL: University of Chicago Press.

Clear, T. R., Rose, D. R., & Ryder, J. (2001). Incarceration and the community: The prob-lem of removing and returning offenders. *Crime and Delinquency, 47,* 335–351.

Clemmer, D. (1940). *The prison community*. New York, NY: Holt, Rinehart, and Winston.

Comfort, M. (2008). *Doing time together: Love and family in the shadow of prison*. Chicago, IL: University of Chicago Press.

Conger, R. D., & Conger, K. J. (2002). Resilience in Midwestern families: Selected findings from the first decade of a prospective, longitudinal study. *Journal of Marriage and Family, 64*, 361–373.

Conrad, P. (1992). Medicalization and social control. *Annual Review of Sociology, 18*, 209–232.

Cook, D., Mulrow, C., & Haynes, R. (1997). Systematic reviews: Synthesis of best evidence for clinical decisions. *Annals of Internal Medicine, 126*, 376–380.

Correctional Association of New York. (2009). *Women in prison: Fact sheet 2009*. Retrieved from http://www.correctionalassociation.org/publications/download/wipp/factsheets/Wome_in_Prison_Fact_Sheet_2009_FINAL.pdf

Costa, R. D. (2003). Now I lay me down to sleep: A look at overnight visitation rights available to incarcerated mothers. *New England Journal of Criminal and Criminal Confinement, 29*, 67–97.

Covington, P. (1995). *Breaking the cycle of despair: Children of incarcerated mothers*. New York: Women's Prison Association and Home.

Crenshaw, K. (1991). Mapping the margins: Intersectionality, identity, politics and violence against women of color. *Stanford Law Review, 43*, 1241–1299.

Criminal Justice Bill Fact Sheet. (2010, July). *Sen. Webb's National Criminal Justice Commission Act of 2010*. Retrieved from http://www.scribd.com/doc/35005432/Criminal-Justice-Bill-Factsheet-July-20105

Csete, J. (2010). *From the mountaintops: What the world can learn from drug policy change in Switzerland*. Open Society Foundation Drug Policy Program. Retrieved from http://www.soros.org/initiatives/drugpolicy/articles_publications/publications/csete-mountaintops-20101021

Cullen, F. T., & Applegate, B. K. (Eds.). (1997). *Offender rehabilitation: Effective correctional intervention*. Aldershot, UK: Ashgate Dartmouth.

Cummings, E. M., Davies, P. T., & Campbell, S. B. (2000). *Developmental psychopathology and family process: Theory, research, and clinical implications*. New York, NY: Guilford Press.

Dallaire, D. (2007a). Children with incarcerated mothers: Developmental outcomes, special challenges and recommendations. *Journal of Applied Developmental Psychology, 28*, 15–24.

Dallaire, D. (2007b). Incarcerated mothers and fathers: A comparison of risks for children and families. *Family Relations, 56*, 440–453.

Dallaire, D., & Aaron, L. (2010). Middle childhood: Family, school, and peer contexts for children affected by parental incarceration. In J. Poehlmann & M. Eddy (Eds.), *Children of incarcerated parents: A handbook for researchers and practitioners* (pp. 101–119). Washington, DC: Urban Institute Press.

Dallaire, D., Ciccone, A., & Wilson, L. (2010). Teachers' expectations of and their experiences with children with incarcerated mothers. *Journal of Applied Developmental Psychology, 31*, 281–290.

Dallaire, D., & Wilson, L. C. (2010). The relation of exposure to parental criminal activity, arrest, and sentencing to children's maladjustment. *Journal of Child and Family Studies, 19*, 404-418.

Dallaire, D., Wilson, L. C., & Ciccone, A. (2009, April). *Representations of attachment relationships in family drawings of children with incarcerated parents.* Paper presented at the biennial meeting of the Society for Research in Child Development, Denver, CO.

Das, V., & Kleinman, A. (2001). Introduction. In V. Das (Ed.), *Remaking a world: Violence, social suffering, and recovery* (pp. 1–30). Berkeley and Los Angeles, CA: University of California Press.

Davies, R. P. (1980). Stigmatization of prisoners' families. *Prison Service Journal, 40,* 12–14.

Davis, L. M., Nicosia, N., Overton, A., Miyashiro, L., Derose, K., Fain, T., …Williams, E. (2009). *Understanding the public health implications of prisoner reentry in California: Phase I report.* Santa Monica, CA: RAND Corporation. Retrieved from http://www.rand.org/pubs/technical_reports/TR687

Dawn, D. (2002). *Health emergency 2003: The spread of drug-related AIDS and other deadly diseases among African Americans and Latinos.* New York, NY: Harm Reduction Coalition. Retrieved from: http://www. harmreduction.org

Day, R., Acock, A., Arditti, J., & Bahr, S. (2001). *From prison to home: Men's reentry into family and community life* [Data file]. Rexburg, ID: Brigham Young University.

Day, R., Acock, A., Bahr, S., & Arditti, J. (2005). Incarcerated fathers returning home to children and families: Introduction to the special issue and a primer on doing research with men in prison. *Fathering, 3,* 183–200.

Day, R. D., Lewis, C., O'Brien, M., & Lamb, M. E. (2005). Fatherhood and father involvement: Emerging constructs and theoretical orientations. In V. L. Bengston, A. C. Acock, K. R. Allen, P. Dillworth-Anderson, & D. M. Klein (Eds.), *Sourcebook of family theory and research* (pp. 341–366). Thousand Oaks, CA: Sage.

Deater-Deckard, K., & Dodge, K. A. (1997). Externalizing behavior problems and discipline revisited: Nonlinear effects and variation by culture, context, and gender. *Psychological Inquiry, 8,* 161–175.

DeFrain, J., Asay, S., & Geggie, J. (2010). Family strengths: An international perspective. In F. Arney & D. Scott (Eds.), *Working with vulnerable families: A partnership approach* (p. 29–47). New York, NY: Cambridge University Press.

DeGarmo, D. S., & Forgatch, M. S. (1997). Confidant support and maternal distress: Predictors of parenting practices for divorced mothers. *Personal Relationships, 4,* 305–317.

DeHart, D. D., & Altshuler, S. J. (2009). Violence exposure among children of incarcerated mothers. *Child and Adolescent Social Work Journal, 26,* 467–479.

Deschenes, E., Owen, B., & Crow, J. (2006). *Recidivism among female prisoners: Secondary analysis of the 1994 BJS recidivism data set* (final report submitted to the U.S. Department of Justice). Retrieved from www.ncjrs.gov/pdffiles1/nij/grants/216950.pdf

Doherty, W., Kouneski, E., & Erickson, M. (1998). Responsible fathering: An overview and conceptual framework. *Journal of Marriage and the Family, 60,* 277–292.

Doka, K. (1989). *Disenfranchised grief: Recognizing hidden sorrow.* Lexington, MA: Lexington Books.

Donzinger, S. R. (Ed.). (1996). *The real war on crime: The report of the national criminal justice commission.* New York, NY: Harper Perennial.

Dreher, D. (2000). *The Tao of inner peace.* New York, NY: Plume.

Dressel, P. (1994). And we keep on building prisons: Racism, poverty, and challenges to the welfare state. *Journal of Society and Social Welfare, 21,* 7–30.

Dressel, P., & Barnhill, S. (1990). *Three generations at risk*. Atlanta, GA: Aid to Imprisoned Mothers.

Dressel, P., & Barnhill, S. (1994). Reframing gerontological thought practice: The cases of grandmothers with daughters in prison. *Gerontologist, 34*, 685–691.

Drucker, E. (1999). Drug prohibition and public health: 25 years of evidence. *Public Health Reports, 114*, 14–29.

Drug Enforcement Administration, U.S. Department of Justice. (2003). *Speaking out against drug legalization*. Retrieved from http://www.usdoj.gov/dea/demand/speakout/speaking_out-may03.pdf

Dunn, E., & Arbuckle, J. G., Jr. (2002). *Impact of the LIFE program: An enhanced visitation program for the children of incarcerated parents*. Columbia, MO: University of Missouri-Columbia. Retrieved from http://outreach.missouri.edu/fcrp/lifeevaluation/

DuPont, R. L., & Voth, E. A. (1995). Drug legalization, harm reduction, and drug policy. *Annals of Internal Medicine, 123*, 461–469.

Dyer, J. (2007, November*). Imprisoned fathers and their families: A view from multiple theories*. Paper presented at the Theory Construction and Research Methodology Pre-Conference (TCRM), National Council on Family Relations, Pittsburgh, PA.

Dyer, W. J., Wardle, B., & Day, R. D. (2004, April). *Effects of incarceration on successful prisoner reentry: A symbolic interaction perspective*. Paper presented at the meeting of the Pacific Sociological Association. San Francisco, CA.

Eddy, J. M., Kjellstrand, J., Martinez, C., & Newton, R. (2010). Theory-based multimodal parenting intervention for incarcerated parents and their children. In J. M. Eddy & Poehlmann (Eds.), *Children of incarcerated parents: A handbook for researchers and practitioners* (pp. 237–261). Washington, DC: Urban Institute Press.

Eddy, J. M., Martinez, C., Schiffman, T., Newton, R., Olin, L., Leve, L., … Shortt, J. W. (2008). Development of a multisystemic parent management training intervention for incarcerated parents, their children and families. *Clinical Psychologist, 12*, 86–98.

Edin, K., Nelson, T., & Paranal, R. (2001). *Fatherhood and incarceration as potential turning points in the criminal careers of unskilled men* (pp. 1–33). Evanston, IL: Northwestern University Institute for Policy Research. Retrieved from http://www.northwestern.edu/ipr/publications/papers/2001/fatherhood.pdf

Emery, R. (1994). *Renegotiating family relationships: Divorce, child custody, and mediation*. New York, NY: Guilford Press.

Enos, S. (1997). Managing motherhood in prison: The impact of race and ethnicity on child placements. *Women & Therapy, 20*, 57–73.

Enos, S. (2001). *Mothering from the inside: Parenting in a women's prison*. Albany, NY: SUNY Press.

Fairchild, S. R. (2009). Attachment representations and parental memories of incarcerated fathers. *Journal of Child and Adolescent Social Work, 26*, 361–377.

Family Strengths Perspective: The Quality of Strong Families. (2011). *JRank marriage and family encyclopedia* [Family Strengths and Universal Values]. Net Industries. Retrieved from http://family.jrank.org/pages/596/Family-Strengths.html

Farmer, T., & Farmer, E. (2001). Developmental science, systems of care, and prevention of emotional and behavioral problems in youth. *American Journal of Orthopsychiatry, 71*, 171–181.

Federal Bureau of Investigation (FBI). (2009). *Crime in the United States (Uniform Crime Report)*. Retrieved from U.S. Department of Justice, Criminal Justice Information Services Division website: http://www2.fbi.gov/ucr/cius2009/data/table_01.html

Federal Bureau of Investigation (FBI). (2010). *Preliminary semiannual uniform crime report (Uniform Crime Report)*. Retrieved from U.S. Department of Justice, Criminal Justice Information Services Division website: http://www.fbi.gov/about-us/cjis/ucr/crime-in-the-u.s/2010/preliminary-crime-in-the-us-2009

Feldman, R. (2007). Maternal versus child risk and the development of parent-child and family relationships in five high-risk populations. *Development and Psychopathology, 19*, 293–312.

Feshbach, N. D. (1986). Chronic maternal stress and its assessment. In J. N. Butcher & C. D. Spielberger (Eds.), *Advances in personality assessment* (Vol. 5., pp. 41–70). Hillsdale, NJ: Erlbaum.

Foster, H., & Hagan, J. (2007). Incarceration and intergenerational social exclusion. *Social Problems, 54*, 399–433.

Freedman, M. (1993). *The kindness of strangers: Adult mentors, urban youth, and the new volunteerism*. San Francisco, CA: Jossey-Bass.

Fritsch, T. A., & Burkhead., J. D. (1981). Behavioral reactions of children to parental absence due to imprisonment. *Family Relations, 30*, 83–88.

Furstenberg, F. F., & Cherlin, A. (1991). *Divided families: What happens to children when parents part*. Cambridge, MA: Harvard University Press.

Gainsborough, J., & Mauer, M. (2000). *Diminishing returns: Crime and incarceration in the 1990's*. Washington, DC: Sentencing Project.

Garbarino, J. (1995). *Raising children in a social toxic environment*. San Francisco, CA: Jossey-Bass.

Gaskins, S. (2004). "Women of circumstance"—The effects of mandatory minimum sentencing on women minimally involved in drug crimes. *American Criminal Law Review, 41*, 1533–2004.

Geller, A., Cooper, C., Garfinkel, I., & Mincy, R. (2010). *Beyond absenteeism: Father incarceration and its effects on children's development*. Retrieved from http://crcw.princeton.edu/workingpapers/WP09-20-FF.pdf

Geller, A., Garfinkel, I., Cooper, C., & Mincy, R. (2008). Parental incarceration and child wellbeing: Implications for urban families (Working paper 1080). Retrieved from http://crcw.princeton.edu/workingpapers/WP08-10-FF.pdf

Gibbons, J. J., & de B. Katzenbach, N. (2006). *Confronting confinement: A report of the commission on safety and abuse in America's prison*. New York, NY: Vera Institute of Justice.

Gillespie, T., Beckmeyer, J., & Arditti, J. (2010, November). *The 4-H Life program: Facilitating family relationships during incarceration*. Paper presented at the annual meeting of the National Council on Family Relations, Minneapolis, MN.

Glaze, L., & Maruschak, L. (2008, August). *Parents in prison and their minor children*. Bureau of Justice Statistics Special Report (NCJ222984). Washington, DC: U.S. Department of Justice, Office of Justice Programs.

Goetting, A. (1985). Racism, sexism, and ageism in the prison community. *Federal Probation, 44*, 10–22.

Goffman, E. (1961). *Asylums: Essays on the social situation of mental patients and other inmates*. New York, NY: Random House.

Goffman, E. (1963). *Stigma: Notes on the management of spoiled identity*. Upper Saddle River, NJ: Prentice-Hall.

Golden, R. (2005). *War on the family: Mothers in prison and the families they leave behind*. New York, NY: Routledge.

Goodman, C., & Silverstein, M. (2002). Grandmothers raising grandchildren: Family structure and well-being in culturally diverse families. *Gerontologist, 42*, 676–689.

Gottlieb, B. H. (2000). Selecting and planning support interventions. In S. Cohen, L. Underwood, & B. H. Gottlieb (Eds.), *Social support measurement and intervention: A guide for health and social scientists* (pp. 195–211). New York, NY: Oxford University Press.

Grall, T. (2006). *Custodial mothers and fathers and their child support: 2003* (Current Population Reports pp. 60–230). Retrieved from http://www.census.gov/prod/2006pubs/p60-230.pdf

Green, J. (2008, Summer). Full time for 40 hours: Weekend visits and picnics make it easier to be a father. *Rise, 10*, pp. 8–9.

Greene, S., Haney, C., & Hurtado, A. (2000). Cycles of pain: Risk factors in the lives of incarcerated mothers and their children. *Prison Journal, 80*, 3–23.

Greenfield, L. A., & Snell, T. L. (1999). *Women offenders*. Washington, DC: U.S. Department of Justice, Bureau of Justice Statistics.

Grossman, J., & Rhodes, J. (2002). The test of time: Predictors and effects of duration in youth mentoring relationships. *American Journal of Community Psychology, 30*, 199–219.

Guralnick, M. (2005). *The developmental systems approach to early intervention*. Baltimore, MD: Paul Brookes.

Hairston, C., & Oliver, W. (2006). *Safe return: Domestic violence and prisoner reentry: Experiences of Black women and men*. New York, NY: Vera Institute of Justice. Retrieved from http://www.vera.org/content/domestic-violence-and-prisoner-reentry-experiences-african-american-women-and-men

Hagan, J., & Coleman, J. P. (2001). Returning captives of the American war on drugs: Issues of community and family reentry. *Crime and Delinquency, 47*, 352–367.

Hagan, J., & Dinovitzer, R. (1999). Collateral consequences of imprisonment for children, communities, and prisoners. *Crime and Justice, 26*, 121–142.

Hagedorn, J. (1995). *Forsaking our children: Bureaucracy and reform in the child welfare system*. Chicago, IL: Lake View Press.

Hairston, C. F. (1991). Mothers in jail: Parent-child separation and jail visitation. *Affilia, 6*, 9–27.

Hairston, C. F. (1998). The forgotten parent: Understanding the forces that influence incarcerated fathers' relationships with their children. *Child Welfare, 77*, 617–639.

Hairston, C. F. (2001). Fathers in prison: Responsible fatherhood and responsible public policy. *Marriage and Family Review, 32*, 111–135.

Hairston, C. F. (2007, October). *Focus on children with incarcerated parents: An overview of the research literature*. Retrieved from the Annie Casey Foundation website: http://www.aecf.org

Hairston, C. F., Rollin, J., & Jo, H. (2004). *Children, families, and the criminal justice system* (Research Brief, Jane Adams Center for Social Policy and Research). Chicago, IL: University of Illinois.

Haney, C. (2002, January). *The psychological impact of incarceration: Implications for post-prison adjustment.* Retrieved from the Urban Institute website: http://www.urban.org/CraigHaney

Hanlon, T., Blatchley, R., Bennett-Sears, T., O'Grady, K., Rose, M., & Callaman, J. (2005). Vulnerability of children of incarcerated addict mothers: Implications for preventive intervention. *Children and Youth Services Review, 27,* 67–84.

Hanlon, T., Carswell, S., & Rose, M. (2007). Research on caretaking of children of incarcerated parents: Findings and their service delivery implications. *Children and Youth Services Review, 29,* 348–362.

Hanlon, T., O'Grady, K., Bennett-Sears, T., & Callaman, J. (2005). Incarcerated drug-abusing mothers: Their characteristics and vulnerability. *American Journal of Drug and Alcohol Abuse, 1,* 59–77.

Harm, N., & Thompson, P. (1995) *Children of incarcerated mothers and their caregivers: A needs assessment.* Little Rock, AR: Centers for Youth and Families.

Harrison, P. M., & Beck, A. J. (2006). Prisoners in 2005. *Bureau of Justice Statistics, US Department of Justice,* 1–13.

Harvey, J. H. (2002). *Perspectives on loss and trauma: Assaults on the self.* Thousand Oaks, CA: Sage.

Hathaway, A. (2001). Shortcomings of harm reduction: Toward a morally invested drug reform strategy. *International Journal of Drug Policy, 12,* 125–137.

Helms, H., Walls, J., & Demo, D. (2010). Everyday hassles and family stress. In S. Price, C. Price, & P. McKenry (Eds.), *Families and change: Coping with stressful events and transitions* (pp. 357–379). Thousand Oaks, CA: Sage.

Herman-Stahl, M., Kan, M., & McKay, T. (2008, September). *Incarceration and the family: A review of research and promising approaches for serving fathers and families.* Retrieved from http://aspe.hhs.gov/hsp/08/MFS-IP/Incarceration&Family/index.shtml

Hester, R. (2010, May). *Spotlight: The center for young women's development.* Retrieved from the National Resource Center on Children and Families of the Incarcerated at Family and Corrections Network website: http://fcnetwork.org/spotlight.php#more-188

Hillis, S., Anda, R., Dube, S., Felitti, V., Marchbanks, P., Macaluso, M., & Marks, J. (2010). The protective effect of family strengths in childhood against adolescent pregnancy and its long-term psychosocial consequences. *Permanente Journal, 14*(3), 18–27. Retrieved from http://www.thepermanentejournal.org/issues/2010/fall/304-teen-pregnancy.html

Hochstetler, A., Murphy, D., & Simons, R. (2004). Damaged goods: Exploring predictors of distress in prison inmates. *Crime and Delinquency, 50,* 436-457.

Hoffmann, H. C., Dickenson, G. E., & Dunn, C. L. (2007, Jan/Feb). State facilities for women and men: A comparison of communication and visitation policies. *Corrections Compendium.* Retrieved from http://findarticles.com/p/articles/mi_hb5706/is_200701/ai_n32225461/

Hoghughi, M. (2004). Parenting: An introduction. In M. Hoghughi & N. Long (Eds.), *Handbook of parenting: Theory and research for practice* (pp. 1–18). Thousand Oaks, CA: Sage.

Holzer, H., Raphael, S., & Stoll, M. (2002, March). *Can employers play a more positive role in prisoner reentry*? Paper prepared for the Urban Institute Reentry Roundtable: Prisoner Reentry and the Institutions of Civil Society, Washington DC. Retrieved from *http://www.urban.org/uploadedPDF/410803_PositiveRole.pdf*

Hooks, B. (1984). *Feminist theory from margin to center*. Boston, MA: South End Press.

Houck, K. D. F., & Loper, A. B. (2002). The relationship of parenting stress to adjustment among mothers in prison. *American Journal of Orthopsychiatry, 72*, 548–558.

Huebner, B. M., & Gustafson, R. (2007). The effect to maternal incarceration on adult off-spring involvement in the criminal justice system. *Journal of Criminal Justice, 35*, 283–296.

Hungerford, G. (1996). Caregivers of children whose mothers are incarcerated: A study of the kinship placement system. *Children Today, 24*, 23–34.

Ihinger-Tallman, M., Paisley, K., & Beuhler, C. (1993). Developing a middle-range theory of father involvement postdivorce. *Journal of Family Issues, 14*, 550–571.

Irwin, J. (2005). *The warehouse prison: Disposal of the new dangerous class*. Los Angeles, CA: Roxbury.

Jacobsen, L. K., Southwick, S. M., & Kosten, T. R. (2001). Substance use disorders in patients with posttraumatic stress disorder: A review of the literature. *American Journal of Psychiatry, 158*, 1184–1190.

Jaffee, S. R., Moffitt, T. E., Caspi, A., & Taylor, A. (2003). Life with (or without) father: The benefits of living with two biological parents depend on the father's antisocial behavior. *Child Development, 74*, 109–26.

James, D., & Glaze, L. (2006, September). *Mental health problems of prison and jail inmates* (Bureau of Justice Statistics Special Report NCJ 213600). Washington, DC: US Department of Justice, Office of Justice Programs.

Jarrett, R. L. (2010, May). *Building strong families and communities: Lessons from the field*. Research presentation at the meeting of Children, Youth and Families at Risk Annual Conference, San Diego, CA.

Jayakody, R., Danziger S., & Pollack H. (2000). Welfare reform, substance use and mental health. *Journal of Health Politics, Policy and Law, 25*, 623–651.

Johnson, E., & Waldfogel, J. (2004). Children of incarcerated parents: Multiple risks and children's living arrangements. In M. Patillo, D. Weiman & B. Western (Eds.), *Imprisoning America: The social effects of mass incarceration* (pp. 97–131). New York, NY: Russell Sage Foundation.

Johnson, H. D., & Young, D. S. (2002). Addiction, abuse and family relationships: Childhood experiences of five incarcerated African American women. *Journal of Ethnicity in Substance Abuse, 1*, 29–48.

Johnson, R. C. (2009). Ever-increasing levels of parental incarceration and the consequences for children. In S. Raphael & M. Stoll (Eds.), *Do prisons make us safer? The benefits and costs of the prison boom* (pp. 177–206). New York, NY: Russell Sage Foundation.

Johnston, D. (1992). *Children of criminal offenders*. Pasadena, CA.: Pacific Oaks Center for Children of Incarcerated Parents.

Johnston, D., & Gabel, K. (1995). Incarcerated parents. In K. Gabel & D. Johnston (Eds.), *Children of incarcerated parents* (pp. 3–20). New York, NY: Lexington.

Joplin, L., Bogue, B., Campbell, N., Carey, M., Clawson, E., Faust, F., ... Woodward, W. (2004). *Using an integrated model to implement evidence-based practices in corrections* (Publication of the International Community Corrections Association and American Correctional Association). Retrieved from http://www.cjinstitute.org/files/NICCJI_Project_ICCA_2.pdf

Jucovy, L. (2003). *Amachi: Mentoring children of prisoners in Philadelphia*. Philadelphia, PA: University of Pennsylvania, Public/Private Ventures and the Center for Research, Religion and Civil Society.

Jussim, L., & Harber, K. (2005). Teacher expectations and self-fulfilling prophecies: Knowns and unknowns, resolved and unresolved controversies. *Personality and Social Psychology Review, 9*, 131–155.

Justice Policy Institute. (2009). *Pruning prisons: How cutting corrections can save money and protect public safety*. Retrieved from http://www.justicepolicy.org/research/1928

Kagan, R., Reid, W., Roberts, S., & Silverman-Pollow, J. (1987). Engaging families of court-mandated youths in an alternative to institutional placement. *Child Welfare, 66*, 365–376.

Kampfner, C. J. (1995). Post-traumatic stress reactions in children of imprisoned mothers. In K. Gabel & D. Johnston (Eds.), *Children of incarcerated parents* (pp. 89–100). New York, NY: Lexington Books.

Kaslow, N., Kaslow, F., & Farber, E. (1999). Theories and techniques of marital and family therapy. In M. Sussman, S. Steinmetz, & G. Peterson (Eds.), *Handbook of marriage and the family* (pp. 767–792). New York, NY: Plenum.

Katz, L., & Low, S. M. (2004). Marital violence, co-parenting, and family-level processes in relation to children's adjustment. *Journal of Family Psychology, 18*, 372–382.

Katzenstein, M. F., & Shanley, M. L. (2008). *No further harm: What we owe to incarcerated fathers* (Boston Review). Retrieved from http://bostonreview.net/BR33.4/katzenstein.php

Keating, L., Tomishima, M., Foster, S., & Alessandri, M. (2002). The effects of a mentoring program on at-risk youth. *Adolescence, 37*, 717–734.

Kell, V., & Price, J. (2006). Externalizing behavior disorders in child welfare settings: Definition, prevalence, and implications for assessment and treatment. *Children and Youth Services Review, 28*, 761–779.

Kennon, S., Mackintosh, V., & Meyers, B. (2009). Parenting education for incarcerated mothers. *Journal of Correctional Education, 60*, 10–30.

Kerr, T. (2006). Reconsidering the public health failings of the criminal justice system: A reflection on the case of Scott Ortiz. *Harm Reduction Journal. 3(25)*. Retrieved from http://www.harmreductionjournal.com/content/3/1/25

King, R. (2008). *Expanding the vote: State felony disenfranchisement reform, 1997–2008*. Retrieved from the Sentencing Project website: http://www.sentencingproject.org/doc/publications/fd_statedisenfranchisement.pdf

King, R., Mauer, M., & Young, M. (2005). *Incarceration and crime: A complex relationship*. Retrieved from the Sentencing Project website: http://www.sentencingproject.org/doc/publications/inc_iandc_complex.pdf

Kinner, S., Alati, R., Najman, J., & Williams, G. (2007). Do paternal arrest and imprisonment lead to child behavior problems and substance use? A longitudinal analysis. *Journal of Child Psychology and Psychiatry, 48*, 1148–1156.

Kinsman, A., & Wildman, B. (2001). Mother and child perceptions of child functioning: Relationship to maternal distress. *Family Process, 40,* 163–172.

Klebanov, P. K., Brooks-Gunn, J., & McCormick, M. C. (2001). Maternal coping strategies and emotional distress: Results of an early intervention program for low birth weight young children. *Developmental Psychology, 37,* 654–667.

Klee, H. (2002). Women, family and drugs. In H. Klee, M. Jackson, & S. Lewis (Eds.), *Drug misuse and motherhood* (pp. 3–14). New York, NY: Routledge.

Kotchick, B. A., Dorsey, S., & Heller, L. (2005). Predictors of parenting among African American single mothers: Personal and contextual factors. *Journal of Marriage and Family, 67,* 448–460.

Kupers, T. (1999). *Prison madness: The mental health crisis behind bars and what we must do about it.* San Francisco, CA: Jossey-Bass.

Lamb, M. E. (2000). The history of research on father involvement: An overview. In E. Peters & R. Day (Eds.), *Fatherhood: Research, interventions and policies* (pp. 23–42). New York, NY: Hawthorn Press.

Landreth, G. L., & Lobaugh, A. F. (1998). Filial therapy with incarcerated fathers: Effects on parental acceptance of child, parental stress, and child adjustment. *Journal of Counseling and Development, 76,* 157–165.

Langan, P. A., & Levin, D. J. (2002). *Recidivism of prisoners released in 1994* (NCJ 193427). Washington, DC: U.S. Department of Justice, Bureau of Justice Statistics. Retrieved from http://www.bjs.ojp.usdoj.gov/content/pub/pdf/rpr94.pdf

Lanier, C. S. (1993). Affective states of fathers in prison. *Justice Quarterly, 10,* 49–66.

Latessa, E. (2008) What science says about designing effective prisoner reentry programs. In H. Normandin & K. Bogenshneider (Eds.), *Looking beyond the prison gate: New directions in prisoner reentry* (pp. 13–20). Wisconsin Family Impact Seminar. Retrieved from http://familyimpactseminars.org/doc.asp?d=s_wifis26c02.pdf

Lattimore, P. K., Steffey, D. M., & Visher, C. (2009, December). *Prisoner reentry experiences of adult males: Characteristics, service receipt, and outcomes of participants in the SVORI Multi-Site Evaluation.* The Multi-Site Evaluation of the Serious and Violent Offender Reentry Initiative. Retrieved from the U.S. Department of Justice, National Criminal Justice Reference Service website: http://Ncjrs.Gov/Pdfiles1/Nij/Grants/230419

Laub, J., & Sampson, R. (2003). *Shared beginnings, divergent lives: Delinquent boys to age 70.* Cambridge, MA: Harvard University Press.

LaVigne, N., Naser, R., Brooks, L., & Castro, J. (2005). Examining the effects of incarceration and family contact on prisoners' family relationships. *Journal of Contemporary Criminal Justice, 21,* 314–355.

LaVigne, N., Visher, C., & Castro, J. (2005). *Chicago prisoners' experiences returning home.* Washington, DC: Urban Institute.

Little, L., & Kantor, G. K. (2002). Using ecological theory to understand intimate partner violence and child maltreatment. *Journal of Community Health Nursing, 19,* 133–145.

Lerner, J. (1993). The influence of child temperamental characteristics on parent behaviors. In T. Luster & L. Okagaki (Eds.), *Parenting: An ecological perspective.* Hillsdale, NJ: Erlbaum.

Lerner, R. (1998). Theories of human development: Contemporary perspectives. In W. Damon & R. Lerner (Eds.), *Handbook of child psychology: Vol. 1. Theoretical models of human development* (5th ed., pp. 1–24). New York, NY: Wiley.

Lerner, R., Brennan, A. L., Noh, E. R., & Wilson, C. (1998). The parenting of adolescents and adolescents as parents: A developmental contextual perspective. *Parenthood in America*. Retrieved from http://parenthood.library.wisc.edu/Lerner/Lerner.html

Lerner, R., & Castellino, D. (2002). Contemporary developmental theory and adolescence: Developmental systems and applied developmental science. *Journal of Adolescent Health, 31*, 122–135.

Lerner, R., Fisher, C., & Weinberg, R. (2000). Toward a science for and of the people: Promoting civil society through the application of developmental science. *Child Development, 71*, 11–20.

Lerner, R., Sparks, E. E., & McCubbin, L. D. (1999). Developmental contextualism and the developmental systems perspective. In R. Lerner, E. Sparks, & L. McCubbin (Eds.), *Family diversity and family policy: Strengthening families for America's children* (pp. 213–221). Norwell, MA: Kluwer.

Levinger, G. (1992). Close relationship loss as a set of inkblots. In T. Orbuch (Ed.), *Close relationship loss: Theoretical approaches* (pp. 213–221). New York, NY: Springer-Verlag.

Levitt, S. (2004). Understanding why crime fell in the 1990's: Four factors that explain the decline and six that do not. *Journal of Economic Perspectives, 18*, 163–190.

Lee, A., Genty, P., & Laver, M. (2005). *The impact of the adoption and safe families act on children of incarcerated parents.* Washington, DC: Child Welfare League of America.

Lewis, S. (2002). Concepts of motherhood. In H. Klee, M. Jackson, & S. Lewis (Eds.), *Drug misuse and motherhood* (pp. 32–44). New York, NY: Routledge.

Logan, C., Manlove, J., Ikramullah, E., & Cottingham, S. (2006). *Men who father children with more than one woman: A contemporary portrait of multiple-partner fertility.* Child Trends Research Brief (2006-10). Washington, DC.

London, A., & Parker, W. (2009). Incarceration and living arrangements: Findings from the national health and social life survey. *Journal of Family Issues, 30*, 787–812.

Loopoo, L. M., & Western, B. (2005). Incarceration and the formation and stability of marital unions. *Journal of Marriage and Family, 67*, 721–734.

Loper, A., & Novero, C. (2010). Parenting programs for prisoners. In J. Poehlmann & M. Eddy (Eds.) *Children of incarcerated parents: A handbook for researchers and practitioners* (pp. 189–215). Washington, DC: Urban Institute Press.

Loper, A., & Tuerk, E. (2006). Parenting programs for incarcerated parents: Current research and future directions. *Criminal Justice Policy Review, 17*, 407–427.

Loper, A. E., & Tuerk, E. H. (2011). Improving the emotional adjustment and communication patterns of incarcerated mothers: Effectiveness of a prison parenting intervention. *Journal of Child and Family Studies, 20*, 89–101.

Lopez, M., & Light, M. (2009). A rising share: Hispanics and federal crime. Washington, DC: Pew Research Center. Retrieved from http://pewhispanic.org

Lopez, V., Katsulis, Y., & Robillard, A. (2009). Drug use with parents as a relational strategy for incarcerated female adolescents. *Family Relations, 58*, 135–147.

Loury, G. C. (2010, Summer). Crime, inequality & social justice. *Daedalus*, 134–140.

Lowenstein, A. (1986). Temporary single parenthood: The case of prisoners' families. *Family Relations, 35*, 79–85.

Luthar, S. S. (Ed.). (2003). *Resilience and vulnerability: Adaptation in the context of childhood adversities.* New York, NY: Cambridge University Press.

Luthar, S. S. (2006). Resilience in development: A synthesis of research across five decades. In D. Cicchetti & D. Cohen (Eds.), *Developmental psychopathology* (2nd ed., Vol. 3., pp. 739–795). Hoboken, NJ: Wiley.

Luthar, S. S., & Brown, P. J. (2007). Maximizing resilience through diverse levels of inquiry: Prevailing paradigms, possibilities, and priorities for the future. *Developmental Psychopathology, 19*, 931–955.

Luthar, S. S., Cicchetti, D., Becker, B. (2000). The construct of resilience: A critical evaluation and guidelines for future work. *Child Development, 71*, 543–562.

Lynch, J., & Sabol, W. (2001, September). *Prisoner reentry in perspective* (Crime Policy Report Vol. 3). Retrieved from the Urban Institute website: www.urban.org/pdfs/410213_reentry.pdf

Maccoby, E., & Mnookin, R. (1990). *Dividing the child.* Cambridge, MA: Harvard University Press.

MacCoun, R. J. (1998). Toward a psychology of harm reduction. *American Psychologist, 53*, 1199–1208.

MacDonald, H. (2008, Spring). Is the criminal-justice system racist? *City Journal, 18.* Retrieved from the *City Journal* website: http://www.city-journal.org/2008/18_2_criminal_justice_system.html

Mackintosh, V., Myers, B., & Kennon, S. (2006). Children of incarcerated mothers and their caregivers: Factors affecting the quality of their relationship. *Journal of Child and Family Studies, 15*, 579–594.

Mancini, J. A., & Roberto, K. A., (Eds.). (2009). *Pathways of human development: Explorations of change.* Lanham, MD: Lexington Books.

Mandatory Minimum Sentences. (2011). *Drug Policy Alliance.* Retrieved from http://www.drugpolicy.org/drugwar/mandatorymin/

Manning, W. D., & Smock, P. J. (1999). New families and nonresident father-child visitation. *Social Forces, 78*, 87–116.

Marcussen, K., & Large, M. (2003). Using identity discrepancy theory to predict psychological distress. In P. Burke, T. Owens, R. Serpe, & P. Thoits (Eds.), *Advances in identity theory and research* (pp. 151–164). New York, NY: Kluwer.

Markus, H., & Nurius, P. (1986). Possible selves. *American Psychologist, 41*, 954–969.

Marlatt, G. A. (Ed.). (2002). *Harm reduction: Pragmatic strategies for managing high-risk behaviors.* New York, NY: Guilford Press.

Marshall, S., & Lambert, J. D. (2006). Parental mattering: A qualitative inquiry into the tendency to evaluate the self as significant to one's children. *Journal of Family Issues, 27*, 1561–1582.

Martin, M., & Hesselbrock, M. (2001). Women prisoners' mental health: Vulnerabilities, risks and resilience. *Journal of Offender Rehabilitation, 34*, 25–44.

Martinez, D. J. (2009). *Rekindling family support: Former prisoners and their families, social roles, and informal supports.* Paper presented at the annual meeting of the American Society of Criminology (ASC). Retrieved from http://www.allacademic.com/meta/p127251_index.html

Maruna, S. (2001). *Making good: How ex-convicts reform and build their lives.* Washington, DC: American Psychological Association.

Maruna, S. & Lebel, T. (2003). Welcome home? Examining the "reentry court" concept from a strengths-based perspective. *Western Criminology Review, 4*, 91–107.

Maruna, S., & Roy, K. (2007). Amputation or reconstruction? Notes on the concept of "knifing off" and desistance from crime. *Journal of Contemporary Criminal Justice, 23,* 104–124.

Masten, A. S. (2001). Ordinary magic: Resilience processes in development. *American Psychologist, 56,* 227–238.

Masten, A. S., & Powell, J. (2003). A resilience framework for research, policy, and practice. In S. Luthar (Ed.) *Resilience and vulnerability: Adaptation in the context of childhood adversities* (pp. 1–26). New York, NY: Cambridge University Press.

Mauer, M. (2003, May/June). *Invisible punishment: Block housing, education, counterproductive* (Focus, 3). Retrieved from the Sentencing Project website: http://www.sentencingproject.org

Mauer, M. (2006). *Race to incarcerate.* Washington, DC: Sentencing Project.

Mauer, M. (2010, July/August). Viewpoint: The impact of mandatory minimum penalties in federal sentencing. *Judicature, 94 (1).* Retrieved from the Sentencing Project website: http://sentencingproject.org/doc/publications/s_Viewpoint.pdf

Mauer, M., & Chesney-Lind, M. (2002). Introduction. In M. Mauer & M. Chesney-Lind (Eds.), *Invisible punishment: The collateral consequences of mass imprisonment* (pp. 1–12). New York, NY: New Press.

Maybin, J. (2000). Death row penfriends: Some effects of letter writing on identity and relationships. In D. Barton & N. Hall (Eds.), *Letter writing as a social practice* (pp. 151–178). Philadelphia, PA: John Benjamins.

Mays, G. L., & Winfree, T. (2009). *Essentials of corrections* (4th ed.). Belmont, CA: Wadsworth.

McBride, B. A., Brown, G. L., Bost, K. K., Shin, N., Vaughn, B., & Korth, B. (2005). Paternal identity, maternal gatekeeping, and father involvement. *Family Relations, 54,* 360–372.

McCulloch, J., & Scraton, P. (2008). The violence of incarceration: An introduction. In. P. Scraton, & J. McCulloch (Eds.), *The violence of incarceration* (pp. 1–18). New York, NY: Routledge.

McDaniel, A., & Morgan, A. (1996). Racial differences in mother-child coresidence in the past. *Journal of Marriage and Family, 58,* 1011–1017.

McHale, J. P. (1997). Overt and covert co-parenting processes in the family. *Family Process, 36,* 183–201.

McKeganey, N. (2006). *The lure and the loss of harm reduction in UK drug policy and practice.* Retrieved from the University of Glasgow, Institute for Global Drug Policy, Centre for Drug Misuse Research website: http://www.blaivus.lt/linaso7/prevpolitika/533lure.pdf

McLoyd, V., Aikens, N., & Burton, L. (2006).Childhood poverty, policy, and practice. In W. Damon, R. Lerner, K. A. Renninger, & I. Sigel (Eds.), *Handbook of child psychology: Child psychology in practice* (pp. 700–775). Thousand Oaks, CA: Sage.

McLoyd, V. C., & Wilson, L. (1991). The strain of living poor: Parenting, social support, and child mental health. In A. C. Huston (Ed.), *Children in poverty* (pp. 105–135). Cambridge, UK: Cambridge University Press.

Meek, R. (2007). The parenting possible selves of young fathers in prison. *Psychology, Crime and Law, 13,* 371–382.

Meierhoefer, B. S. (1992). *The general effect of mandatory minimum prison terms: A longitudinal study of federal sentences imposed.* Washington, DC: Federal Judicial Center.

Meyerson, J., & Otteson, C. (2009). *Strengthening families impacted by incarceration: A review of current research and practice.* Saint Paul, MN: Wilder Research. Retrieved from http://www.wilder.org/download.o.html?report=2180

Miller, A. (1998). Child fosterage in the United States: Signs of an African heritage. *History of the Family, 3,* 35–62.

Miller, K. (2007). Risk and resilience among African American children of incarcerated parents. *Journal of Human Behavior in the Social Environment, 15,* 25–37.

Miller, R. L. (1996). *Drug warriors and their prey: From police power to police state.* Westport, CT: Praeger.

Minton, T. (2010, June). *Jail inmates at midyear 2009—Statistical tables* (Bureau of Justice Statistics Report NCJ230122). Retrieved from the U.S. Department of Justice, Office of Justice Programs website: http://bjs.ojp.usdoj.gov/index.cfm?ty=pbdetail&iid=2195

Minuchin, S. (1974). *Families and family therapy.* Cambridge, MA: Harvard University Press.

Modecki, K. L., & Wilson, M. N. (2009). Associations between individual and family level characteristics and parenting practices in incarcerated African American fathers. *Journal of Child and Family Studies, 18,* 530–540.

Moore, S. (2009, February 10). The prison overcrowding fix. *The New York Times,* Retrieved from http://www.nytimes.com/2009/02/11/us/11prisons.html

Moras, A., Shehan, C., & Berardo, F. (2007). African American families: Historical and contemporary forces shaping family life and studies. In H. Vera & J. Feagin (Eds.), *Handbook of the sociology of racial and ethnic relations* (pp. 145–160). New York, NY: Springer.

Mumola, C. (2000). *Incarcerated parents and their children* (Bureau of Justice Statistics Special Report NCJ 182335). Washington, DC: U.S. Department of Justice, Office of Justice Programs.

Mumola, C., & Karberg, J. (2006). *Drug use and dependence, state and federal prisoners, 2004* (Bureau of Justice Statistics Special Report NCJ 213530). Washington, DC: U.S. Department of Justice, Office of Justice Programs.

Murray, J. (2005). The effects of imprisonment on families and children. In A. Liebling & S. Maruna (Eds.), *The effects of imprisonment* (pp. 442–462). Cambridge, UK: Willan.

Murray, J., & Farrington, D. P. (2008). Parental imprisonment: Long-lasting effects on boys' internalizing problems through the life-course. *Development and Psychopathology, 20,* 273–290.

Murray, J., Farrington, D. P., Sekol, I., & Olsen, R. F. (2009). Effects of parental imprisonment on child antisocial behaviour and mental health: A systematic review. *Campbell Systematic Reviews, 4,* 1–105.

Myers, B., Smarsh, T., Amlund-Hagen, K., & Kennon, S. (1999). Children of incarcerated mothers. *Journal of Child and Family Studies, 8,* 11–25.

Nadelman, Ethan A. (1998). Common sense drug policy. *Foreign Affairs, 77,* 111–126.

Najavits, L. M., Weiss, R. D., & Shaw, S. R. (1997). The link between substance abuse and posttraumatic stress disorder in women: A research review. *American Journal on Addictions, 6,* 273–283.

Naser, R., & Visher, C. (2006). Family members' experiences with incarceration and reentry. *Western Criminology Review, 7,* 20–31.

National Association for the Advancement of Colored People (NAACP). (2011, April). *Misplaced priorities: Over incarcerate, under educate*. Retrieved from http://www.naacp.org/pages/misplaced-priorities

National Center on Addiction and Substance Abuse. (2003). *Crossing the bridge: An evaluation of the drug treatment alternative-to-prison (DTAP) program* (ACASA White Paper). New York, NY: National Center on Addiction and Substance Abuse, Columbia University.

National Center on Addiction and Substance Abuse at Columbia University. (2006). *Women under the influence*. Baltimore, MD: John Hopkins University Press.

National Institute on Drug Abuse. (2005). *Prescription drugs: Abuse and prevention*. Retrieved from http://www.drugabuse.gov/ResearchReports/Prescription/Prescription.html

Nesmith, A., & Ruhland, E. (2008). Children of incarcerated parents: Challenges and resiliency, in their own words. *Child and Youth Services Review, 30*, 1119–1130.

Nesmith, A., Ruhland, E., & Krueger, S. (2006, January). *Children of incarcerated parents* (Council on Crime and Justice). Retrieved from the Department of Justice website: http://www.racialdisparity.org/.../CCJ%20CIP%20FINAL%20REPORT.pdf

Nickel, J., Garland, C., & Kane, L. (2009). *Children of incarcerated parents: An action plan for federal policymakers*. Retrieved from the Council of State Governments, Justice Center website: http://www.justicecenter.csg.org/files/CIP_final_release.pdf

Nolan, C. M. (2003, July). *Children of arrested parents: Strategies to improve their safety and well-being* (California Research Bureau 03-011). Retrieved from the California State Library website: http://www.library.ca.gov/crb/03/11/03-011.pdf

Nodine, E. (2006). *Harm reduction: Policies in public health*. Retrieved from http://www.cwru.edu/med/epidbio/mphp439/Harm_Reduction_Policies.htm

Nurse, A. M. (2002). *Fatherhood arrested: Parenting from within the juvenile justice system*. Nashville, TN: Vanderbilt University Press.

Nuttbrock, L., & Freudiger, P. (1991). Identity salience and motherhood: A test of Stryker's theory. *Social Psychology Quarterly, 54*, 146–157.

Oberman, M., & Meyer, C. (2008). *When mothers kill*. New York, NY: NYU Press.

O'Brien, P. (2001). Just like baking a cake: Women describe the successful ingredients for successful reentry after incarceration. *Families in Society, 82*, 287–295.

Open Society Institute (for the Global Campaign for Pretrial Justice). (2010a). *Collateral Consequences: How pretrial detention stunts socioeconomic development* (report summary). Retrieved from http://www.soros.org/.../summary-pretrial-detention-socioeconomic.20100409.pdf

Open Society Institute (for the International Harm Reduction Development Program). (2007). *Harm reduction: Public health and public order* (Public Health Fact Sheet). Retrieved from http://www.soros.org/initiatives/health/focus/ihrd/articles_publications/publications/fact_20070927

Open Society Institute (for the United Nations Rule of Law; UNROL) (2010b). *The socioeconomic impact of pretrial detention*. Retrieved from http://www.unrol.org/.../Socioeconomic%20impact%20of%20PTD_Sept%2010%202010_Final.pdf

Osborne, C., & McClanahan, S. (2007). Partnership instability and child wellbeing. *Journal of Marriage and Family, 69*, 1065–1083.

Oyserman, D., Brickman, D., & Rhodes, M. (2007). School success, possible selves, and parent school involvement. *Family Relations, 56,* 479–489.

Pager, D. (2003). The mark of a criminal record. *American Journal of Sociology, 108,* 937–975.

Parental incarceration and child well-being in fragile families. (2008, April). *Fragile Families Research Brief, 42,* 1–4.

Parke, R. D. (2002). Fathers and families. In M. Bornstein (Ed.), *Handbook of parenting: Vol. 3. Being and becoming a parent* (2nd ed., pp. 27–73). Hillsdale, NJ: Erlbaum.

Parke, R. D., & Clarke-Stewart, K. A. (2001). *Effects of parental incarceration on young children.* Prepared for the From Prison to Home: The Effect of Incarceration and Reentry on Children, Families and Communities Conference (January 30–31, 2002). U.S. Department of Health and Human Services, Urban Institute. Retrieved from http:// aspe.hhs.gov/hsp/prison2home02/parke-stewart.htm

Parke, R. D., & Clarke-Stewart, K. A. (2003). Effects of parental incarceration on children: Perspectives, promises, and policies. In J. Travis & M. Waul (Eds.), *Prisoners once removed: The impact of incarceration and reentry on children, families, and communities* (pp. 189–232). Washington, DC: Urban Institute Press.

Parkman, T. (2009). *The transition to adulthood and prisoner reentry: Investigating the experiences of young adult men and their caregivers* (Doctoral dissertation, Virginia Tech, 2009, etd-04172009-123438).

Paternoster, R., & Bushway, S. (2009). Desistance and the "feared self": Toward an identity theory of criminal desistance. *Journal of Criminal Law and Criminology, 9(4).* Retrieved from http://www.thefreelibrary.com/Desistance and the "feared self": toward an identity theory of...-a0219589000

Patton, M. Q. (2002). *Qualitative research and evaluation methods.* Thousand Oaks, CA: Sage.

Petersilia, J. (2003). *When prisoners come home.* New York, NY: Oxford University Press.

Pettit, B., & Western, B. (2004). Mass imprisonment and the life course: Race and class inequality in U.S. Incarceration. *American Sociological Review, 69,* 151–169.

Pew Center on States. (2010, April). *Prison count 2010* (Issue Brief). Retrieved from the Pew Charitable Trusts website: http://www.pewcenteronthestates.org/report_detail. aspx?id=57653

Phillips, J. (2001). Cultural construction of manhood in prison. *Psychology of Men and Masculinity, 2,* 13–23.

Phillips, L., & Votey, H. L. (1984). Black women, economic disadvantage, and incentives to crime. *American Economic Review, 74,* 293–297.

Phillips, S., Burns, B. J., Wagner, H. R., & Barth, R. (2004). Parental arrest and children involved with child welfare services agencies. *American Journal of Orthopsychiatry, 74,* 174–186.

Phillips, S. D., Burns, B. J., Wagner, H. R., Kramer, T. L., & Robbins, J. M. (2002). Parental incarceration among adolescents receiving mental health services. *Journal of Child and Family Studies, 11,* 385–399.

Phillips, S., Dettlaff, A., & Baldwin, M. (2010). An exploratory study of the range of implications of families' criminal justice system involvement in child welfare cases. *Children and Youth Service Review, 32,* 544–550.

Phillips, S., Erkanli, A., Keeler, G., Costello, J., & Angold, A. (2006). Disentangling the risks: Parent criminal justice involvement and children's exposure to family risks. *Criminology and Public Policy, 5,* 677–702.

Phillips, S., & Gates, T. (2010). A conceptual framework for understanding the stigmatization of children of incarcerated parents. *Journal of Child and Family Studies, 20,* 286–294.

Phillips, S., & Zhao, J. (2010). The relationship between witnessing arrests and elevated symptoms of posttraumatic stress: Findings from a national study of children involved in the child welfare system. *Children and Youth Services Review, 32,* 1246–1254.

Pinderhughes, E., Dodge, K., Bates, J., Pettit, G., & Zelli, A. (2000). Discipline responses: Influences of parents' socioeconomic status, ethnicity, beliefs about parenting, stress, and cognitive-emotional processes. *Journal of Family Psychology, 14,* 380–400.

Pleck, J. H. (1997). Paternal involvement: Levels, sources, and consequences. In M. E. Lamb (Ed.), *The role of the father in child development* (3rd ed., pp. 66–103). New York, NY: Wiley.

Poehlmann, J. (2005a). Children's family environments and intellectual outcomes during maternal incarceration. *Journal of Marriage and Family, 67,* 1275–1285.

Poehlmann, J. (2005b). Incarcerated mothers' contact with children, perceived family relationships, and depressive symptoms. *Journal of Family Psychology, 19,* 350–357.

Poehlmann, J. (2005c). Representations of attachment relationships in children of incarcerated mothers. *Child Development, 76,* 679–696.

Poehlmann, J. (2010). Attachment in infants and children of incarcerated parents. In J. Poehlmann & M. Eddy (Eds.), *Children of incarcerated parents: A handbook for researchers and practitioners* (pp. 75–100). Washington, DC: Urban Institute Press.

Poehlmann, J., Dallaire, D., Loper, A., & Shear, L. (2010). Children's contact with their incarcerated parents: Research findings and recommendations. *American Psychologist, 65,* 575–598.

Poehlmann, J., & Eddy, J. M. (2010). A research and intervention agenda for children and incarcerated parents. In J. Poehlmann & M. Eddy (Eds.), *Children of incarcerated parents: A handbook for researchers and practitioners* (pp. 319–341). Washington, DC: Urban Institute Press.

Poehlmann, J., Shlafer, R., Maes, E., & Hanneman, A. (2008). Factors associated with young children's opportunities for maintaining family relationships during maternal incarceration. *Family Relations, 57,* 267–280.

Pollock, J. (2002). Parenting programs in women's prisons. *Women & Criminal Justice, 14,* 131–154.

Pope, C., Lovell, R., & Brandl, S. (2001). Introductions: Foundations of criminal justice research. In C. Pope, R. Lovell, & S. Brandl (Eds.), *Voices from the field: Readings in criminal justice research* (pp. 1–16). Belmont, CA: Wadsworth.

Porter, N. (2010). *The state of sentencing 2009: Developments in policy and practice.* Retrieved from the Sentencing Project website: http://www.sentencingproject.org

Powers, M., & Faden, R. (2006). *Social justice: The moral foundations of public health and health policy.* New York, NY: Oxford University Press.

Prison and beyond: A stigma that never fades. (2002, August 10). *The Economist,* 25–27.

Pynoos, R. S. (1993). Traumatic stress and developmental psychopathology in children and adolescents. In J. M. Oldham, M. B. Riba, & A. Tasman (Eds.), *Review of psychiatry* (Vol. 12, pp. 205–238). Washington, DC: American Psychiatric Press.

Radhakrishna, A., Bou-Saada, I., Hunter, W., Catellier, D., & Kotch, J. (2001). Are father surrogates a risk factor for child maltreatment. *Child Maltreatment, 6,* 281–289.

Ramirez, J. (2009, March 12). The ripple effect: Get out of jail free. *Newsweek.* Retrieved from http://www.newsweek.com/id/188944

Rane, T. R., & McBride, B. A. (2000). Identity theory as a guide to understanding fathers' involvement with their children. *Journal of Family Issues, 21,* 347–366.

Rapp, C. A., Saleebey, D., & Sullivan, W. P. (2005). The future of strengths-based social work. *Advances in Social Work, 6,* 79–90.

Ratcliffe, C., & McKernan, S. (2010, June). *Child poverty persistence: Facts and consequences* (Brief 14). Retrieved from Urban Institute website: http://www.urban.org/ uploadedpdf/412126-child-poverty-persistence.pdf

Reed, D. F., & Reed, E. L. (1997). Children of incarcerated parents. *Social Justice, 24,* 152–169.

Richie, B. (2001). Challenges incarcerated women face as they return to their communities: Findings from life history interviews. *Crime and Delinquency, 47,* 368–389.

Richie, B. (2002). The social impact of mass incarceration on women. In M. Mauer & M. Chesney-Lind (Eds.), *Invisible punishment* (pp. 136–149). New York, NY: New Press.

Riveland, C. (1999). Prison management trends. In M. Tonry & J. Petersillia (Eds.), *Prisons* (pp. 163–203). New York, NY: Russell Sage Foundation.

Roberts, D. (2004). The social and moral costs of mass incarceration in African American communities. *Stanford Law Review, 56,* 1271–1305.

Roe, G. (2005). Harm reduction as paradigm: Is better than bad good enough? The origins of harm reduction. *Critical Public Health, 15,* 243–250.

Rose, D., & Clear, T. (1998). Incarceration, social capital, and crime: Implications for social disorganization theory. *Criminology, 35,* 1–39.

Ross, J., & Richards, S. (2002). *Behind bars: Surviving prison.* Indianapolis, IN: Alpha Books.

Roy, K. (2005). "Nobody can be a father in here": Identity construction and institutional constraints on incarcerated fatherhood. In W. Marsiglio, K. Roy, & G. L. Fox (Eds.), *Situated fathering: A focus on physical and social spaces* (pp. 163–187). Oxford, UK: Rowman and Littlefield.

Roy, K., & Dyson, O. (2005). Gatekeeping in context: Babymama drama and the involvement of incarcerated fathers. *Fathering, 3,* 289–310.

Russell, A., Mize, J., & Bissaker, K. (2002). Parent-child relationships. In P. Smith & C. Hart (Eds.), *Blackwell handbook of child social development* (pp. 205–222). Walden, MA: Wiley-Blackwell.

Rutter, M. (1990). Psychosocial resilience and protective mechanisms. In J. Rolf, A. Masten, D. Cicchetti, K. Nuechterlein, & S. Weintraub (Eds.), *Risk and protective factors in the development of psychopathology* (pp. 181–214). New York, NY: Cambridge University Press.

Sabol, W., & Couture, H. (2008). *Prison inmates at midyear 2007.* Washington, DC: U.S. Department of Justice, Bureau of Justice Statistics Bulletin.

Sabol, W., Couture, H., & Harrison, P. (2007, December). *Prisoners in 2006.* (Bureau of Justice Statistics Bulletin NCJ 219416). Washington, DC: Office of Justice Programs.

Sack, W., & Seidler, J. (1978). Should children visit their parents in prison? *Law and Human Behavior, 2,* 261–266.

Sameroff, A., Seifer, R., Barocas, R., Zax, M., & Greenspan, S. (1987). Intellectual quotient scores of 4-year old children: Social-environmental risk factors. *Pediatrics, 79,* 343–350.

Sampson, R., & Laub, J. (1997). A life course theory of cumulative disadvantage. In T. Thornberry (Ed.), *Developmental theories of crime and delinquency* (pp. 133–161). New Brunswick, NJ: Transaction Publishers.

Sampson, R., & Laub, J. (2003). Life course desisters? Trajectories of crime among delinquent boys followed to age 70. *Criminology, 41,* 301–309.

Sampson, R., & Loeffler, C. (2010, Summer). Punishment's place: The local concentration of mass incarceration. *Daedalus,* 20–31.

Sands, R., Goldberg-Glen, R., & Shin, H. (2009). The voices of grandchildren of grandparent caregivers: A strengths-resilience perspective. *Child Welfare, 88,* 25–45.

Sano, Y. (2005). The unanticipated consequences of promoting father involvement: A feminist perspective. In V. Bengston, A. Acock, K. Allen, P. Dilworth-Anderson, & D. Klein (Eds.), *Sourcebook of family theory and research* (pp. 355–356). Thousand Oaks, CA: Sage.

Schlesinger, T. (2005). Racial and ethnic disparity in pretrial criminal processing. *Justice Quarterly, 22,* 170–192.

Schmid, T. J., & Jones, R. S. (1991). Suspended identity: Identity transformation in a maximum security prison. In D. H. Kelly (Ed.), *Deviant behavior* (pp. 427–443). New York, NY: St. Martin's Press.

Schmitt, J., Warner, K., & Gupta, S. (2010, June). *The high budgetary cost of incarceration.* Retrieved from the Center for Economic and Policy Research website: http://www.cepr. net

Schneider, A., & Ingram, H. (1993). Social construction of target populations: Implications for politics and policy. *American Political Science Review, 87,* 334–347.

Schoenbauer, L. J. (1986). Incarcerated parents and their children: Forgotten families. *Law and Inequality, 4,* 579–601.

Scott, M. M. (2005). A powerful theory and a paradox: Ecological psychologists after Barker. *Environment and Behavior, 37,* 295–329.

Shahar G. (2001). Maternal personality and distress as predictors of child neglect. *Journal of Research in Personality, 35,* 537–545.

Shapiro, C. (1998, April). La Bodega de la Familia: Reaching out to the forgotten victims of substance abuse (*Bureau of Justice Bulletin* NCJ-170595). Retrieved from the U.S. Department of Justice, Office of Justice Programs, Bureau of Justice Assistance website: http:// www.ncjrs.gov/pdffiles/170595.pdf

Shelden, R. G. (2000). *Controlling the dangerous classes: A critical introduction to the history of criminal justice.* Boston, MA: Allyn and Bacon.

Shlafer, R. J., & Poehlmann, J. (2010). Attachment and caregiving relationships in families affected by parental incarceration. *Attachment and Human Development, 12,* 395–415.

Shlafer, R. J., Poehlmann, J., Coffino, B., & Hanneman, A. (2009). Mentoring children with incarcerated parents: Implications for research, practice, and policy. *Family Relations, 58,* 507–519.

Seidman, E., & Peterson, S. (2003). Holistic contextual perspectives on risk, protection and competence among low-income adolescents. In S. Luthar (Ed.), *Resilience and vulnerability, adaptation in the context of childhood adversities* (pp. 318–342). Cambridge, UK: Cambridge University Press.

Sentencing Project (2008). *Reducing Racial Disparity in the Criminal Justice System.* Retrieved from http://www.sentencingproject.org

Simon, R. (1992). Parental role strains, salience of parental identity and gender differences in psychological distress. *Journal of Health and Social Behavior, 33,* 25–35.

Smith, D., & Gibson, J. (2006). The use of outsider-witnessing in a prison setting. *International Journal of Narrative Therapy and Community Work, 3,* 46–51.

Snell-Johns, J., Mendez, J., & Smith, B. (2004). Evidence-based solutions for overcoming access barriers, decreasing attrition, and promoting change with underserved families. *Journal of Family Psychology, 18,* 19–35.

Snyder, Z. K., Carlo, T. A., & Mullins, M. M. (2001). Parenting from prison: An examination of a children's visitation program at a women's correctional facility. *Marriage and Family Review, 32,* 33–61.

Sobolewski, J., & King, V. (2005). The importance of the coparental relationship for nonresident fathers' ties to children. *Journal of Marriage and Family, 67,* 1196–1212.

Solomon, A. L., Johnson, K. D., Travis, J., & McBride, E. C. (2004). *From prison to work: The employment dimensions of prisoner reentry: A report of the reentry roundtable.* New York, NY: Urban Institute Justice Policy Center.

Spitzer, C., Dudeck, M., Liss, H., Orlob, S., Gillner, M., & Freyberger, H. J. (2001). Posttraumatic stress disorder in forensic inpatients. *Journal of Forensic Psychiatry and Psychology, 17,* 63–77.

Spohn, C. (2000). Thirty years of sentencing reform: The quest for a racially neutral sentencing process. *Criminal Justice, 3,* 427–501. Retrieved from the National Institute of Justice website: http://www.nij.ncjrs.gov

Stiles, M. (2010, April). *Texas prisoners spent $95 million at commissaries* (Texas Tribune). Retrieved from http://www.texastribune.org/texas-dept-criminal-justice/texas-department-of-criminal-justice/texas-prisoners-spent-95-million-at-commissaries/

Stover, H., Weilandt, C., Zurhold, H., Hartwig, C., & Thane, K. (2008). *Final report on prevention, treatment, and harm reduction services in prison, on reintegration services on release from prison and methods to monitor/analyse drug use among prisoners* (Directorate General for Health and Consumers). Retrieved from http://ec.europa.eu/health/ph_determinants/life_style/drug/.../drug_frep1.pdf

Stryker, S. (1968). Identity salience and role performance. *Journal of Marriage and the Family, 30,* 558–564.

Stryker, S. (1980). *Symbolic interactionism: A social structural version.* Menlo Park, CA: Benjamin Cummings.

Substance Abuse and Mental Health Services Administration. (2009). *Results from the 2008 National Survey on Drug Use and Health: National Findings* (Office of Applied Studies, NSDUH Series H-36, HHS Publication No. SMA 09-4434). Rockville, MD.

Suchman, N., Pajulo, M., DeCoste, C., & Mayes, L. (2006). Parenting interventions for drug-dependent mothers and their young children: The case for an attachment-based approach. *Family Relations, 55,* 211–226.

Sudnow, D. (1967). *Passing on: The social organization of dying.* Englewood Cliffs, NJ: Prentice-Hall.

Sullivan, E., Mino, M., Nelson, K., & Pope, J. (2002). *Families as a resource in recovery from drug abuse: An evaluation of La Bodega de la Familia.* Retrieved from the Vera Institute of Justice website: http://www.vera.org

Sullivan, L. (2010, October 28). Prison economics help drive Arizona immigration law. *National Public Radio* [Written article and Audio podcast]. Retrieved from http://www. npr.org/templates/story/story.php?storyId=130833741

Susman, E. J., Dorn, L. D., & Schiefelbein, V. L. (2003). Puberty, sexuality, and health. In R. M. Lerner & M. A. Easterbrooks (Eds.), *Handbook of psychology: Developmental psychology* (Vol. 6, pp. 295–324). New York, NY: Wiley.

Suter, J., Byrne, M., Byrne, S., Howells, K., & Day, A. (2002). Anger in prisoners: Women are different from men. *Personality and Individual Differences, 32*, 1087–1100.

Swisher, R. R., & Waller, M. (2008). Confining fatherhood: Incarceration and paternal involvement among nonresident White, African American, and Latino fathers. *Journal of Family Issues, 29*, 1067–1088.

Sykes, G. M. (1958). *The society of captives*. Princeton, NJ: Princeton University Press.

Teplin, L., Abram, K., & McClelland, G. (1997). Mentally disordered women in jail: Who receives services? *American Journal of Public Health, 87*, 604–609.

Terry, C. (2003). *The fellas: Overcoming prison and addiction*. Belmont, CA: Wadsworth.

Tesser, A., & Schwarz, N. (2002). *Blackwell handbook of social psychology: Intraindividual processes*. Hoboken, NJ: Wiley-Blackwell.

Testimony of the United States Department of Justice. (2010, May). Retrieved from http:// ftp.ussc.gov/AGENDAS/20100527/Testimony_Yates_DOJ.pdf

Thoits, P. A. (1991). On merging identity theory and stress research. *Social Psychology Quarterly, 54*, 101–112.

Thompson, P. J., & Harm, N. J. (2000). Parenting from prison: Helping children and mothers. *Issues in Comprehensive Pediatric Nursing, 23*, 61–81.

Thornberry, T., & Call, J. (1983). Constitutional challenges of prison overcrowding: The scientific evidence of harmful effects. *Hastings Law Journal, 35*, 313–351.

Todis, B., Bullis, M., Waintrup, M., Schultz, R., & D'Ambrosio, R. (2001). Overcoming the odds: Qualitative examination of resilience among formerly incarcerated adolescents. *Exceptional Children, 68*, 119–139.

Tonry, M. (1996). *Sentencing matters*. New York, NY: Oxford University Press.

Tonry, M. (2005). The functions of sentencing and sentencing reform. *Stanford Law Review, 58*, 37–66.

Tonry, M., & Hatlestad, K. (1997). Race and sentencing. In M. Tonry & K. Hatlestad (Eds.), *Sentencing reform in overcrowded times: A comparative perspective* (pp. 217–218). New York, NY: Oxford University Press.

Travis, J. (2002). Invisible punishment: An instrument of social exclusion. In M. Mauer & M. Chesney-Lind (Eds.), *Invisible punishment: The collateral consequences of mass imprisonment* (pp. 15–36). New York, NY: New Press.

Travis, J. (2005). *But they all come back: Facing the challenges of prisoner reentry*. Washington, DC: Urban Institute.

Travis, J., McBride, E., & Solomon, A. (2005). *Families left behind: The hidden costs of incarceration and reentry*. Washington, DC: Urban Institute.

Travis, J., Solomon, A., & Waul, M. (2001). *From prison to home: The dimension and consequences of prisoner reentry*. Washington, DC: Urban Institute.

Travis, J., & Waul, M. (2003). *Prisoners once removed: The impact of incarceration and reentry on children, families, and communities*. Washington, DC: Urban Institute Press.

Treadwell, H., & Kingsbury, E. (2009, December 17). Ex-felons denied foodstamps, other assistance. *Black Star News*. Retrieved from http://www.blackstarnews.com/news/135/ARTICLE/6163/2009-12-17.html

Trice, A. D., & Brewster, J. (2004). The effects of maternal incarceration on adolescent children. *Journal of Policy and Criminal Psychology, 19*, 27–35.

Tripp, B. (2009). Fathers in jail: Managing dual identities. *Applied Psychology in Criminal Justice, 5*, 26–56.

Tsushima, T., & Burke, P. J. (1999). Levels, agency, and control in the parent identity. *Social Psychology Quarterly, 62*, 173–189.

Tuerk, E. H., & Loper, A. B. (2006). Contact between incarcerated mothers and their children: Assessing parenting stress. *Journal of Offender Rehabilitation, 43*, 23–43.

2009 Criminal Justice Transition Coalition. (2008, November 5). *Smart on crime: Recommendations for the next administration and Congress*. Retrieved from http://2009transition.org/criminaljustice/index.php?option=com_docman&task=details&gid=42&Itemid=

Uggen, C., & Inderbitzin, M. (2009). The price and promise of citizenship: Extending the vote to non-incarcerated felons. *American Society of Criminology Policy Essay*. Retrieved from http://www.soc.umn.edu/~uggen/uggen_inderbitzin_asc_09.pdf

Uggen, C., & Wakefield, S. (2005). Young adults reentering the community from the criminal justice system: The challenge of becoming an adult. In D. W. Osgood, E. M. Foster, C. Flanagan, & G. Ruth (Eds.), *On your own without a net: The transition to adulthood for vulnerable populations* (pp. 114–144). Chicago, IL: University of Chicago Press.

Ungar, M. (2008). *Nurturing hidden resilience in troubled youth*. Toronto, Canada: University of Toronto Press.

United Nations Development Fund for Women (UNIFEM). (2010, April). *Women and drugs: From hard realities to hard solutions* (UNIFEM Fact Sheet No. 6). Retrieved from http://www.docstoc.com/.../UNIFEM-BANGKOK-GENDER-ISSUE-FACT-SHEET-No

U.S. Department of Health and Human Services, Administration for Children and Families. (2008, December). *Mentoring children of prisoners program: More than 100,000 matches*. Retrieved from http://www.acf.hhs.gov/programs/fbci/progs/fbci_mcp.html

U.S. Department of Justice, Office of the Inspector General, Evaluations and Inspections Division. (2009, September). *The Department of Justice's efforts to prevent staff sexual abuse of federal inmates*. Retrieved from http://www.justice.gov/oig/reports/plus/e0904.pdf

van Olphen, J., Eliason, J., Freudenberg, N., & Barnes, M. (2009). Nowhere to go: How stigma limits the options of female drug users after release from jail. *Substance Abuse Treatment, Prevention, and Policy, 4*, 1–10.

Van Wormer, K. (1999). Harm induction vs. harm reduction: Comparing American and British approaches to drug use. *Journal of Offender Rehabilitation, 29*, 35–48.

Vendlinski, T. (2003). Prison letter. In R. Shelton (Ed.), *Walking Rain Review IX* (p. 32). Tucson, AZ: Post Litho Printing.

Visher, C., LaVigne, N., & Travis, J. (2004). *Returning home: Understanding the challenges of prisoner reentry: Maryland pilot study: Findings from Baltimore*. Washington, DC: Urban Institute Press.

Visher, C., & Travis, J. (2003). Transitions from prison to community: Understanding individual pathways. *Annual Review of Sociology, 29*, 89–113.

Wacquant, L. (2001). Deadly symbiosis: When ghetto and prison meet and mesh. *Punishment and Society, 3,* 95–133.

Wacquant, L. (2010, Summer). Class, race & hyperincarceration in revanchist America. *Daedalus,* 74–90.

Waller, M., & Plotnick, R. (1999). *Child support and low-income families: Perceptions, practices, and policy.* San Francisco, CA: Public Policy Institute of California.

Walsh, F. (2006). *Strengthening family resilience* (2nd ed.). New York, NY: Guilford Press.

Walters, G. D. (2003). Changes in criminal thinking and identity in novice and experienced inmates: Prisonization revisited. *Criminal Justice and Behavior, 30,* 399–421.

Warren, J. (2008). *One in 100: Behind bars in 2008.* Retrieved from the Pew Center on States website: http://www.pewcenteronthestates.org/uploadedFiles/One%20in%20100.pdf

Warren, R. (2007). *Evidence-based practice to reduce recidivism: Implications for state judiciaries.* The Crime and Justice Institute. Retrieved from the Nation Center State Court website: http://www.ncsconline.org/csi/analysis.html

Watts, H., & Nightengale, D. S. (1996). Adding it up: The economic impact of incarceration on individuals, families, and communities. *Journal of the Oklahoma Criminal Justice Research Consortium, 3.* Retrieved from http://www.doc.state.ok.us/DOCS/OCJRC/Ocjrc96/Ocjrc55.htm

Webb's National Criminal Justice Commission Act of 2011. (2011, February). Senator Webb reintroduces national criminal justice act. Retrieved from http://webb.senate.gov/newsroom/pressreleases/02-08-2011-02.cfm

Werner-Lin, A., & Moro, T. (2004). Unacknowledged and stigmatized losses. In F. Walsh & M. McGoldrick (Eds.), *Living beyond loss* (pp. 247–271). New York, NY: Norton.

West, H. C., W. Sabol, & M. Cooper. (2009). *Prisoners in 2008* (NCJ 228417). Retrieved from the U.S. Department of Justice, Bureau of Justice Statistics website: http://www.bjs.ojp.usdoj.gov/content/pub/pdf/p08.pdf

Western, B. (2004). *Incarceration, marriage, and family life.* Princeton, NJ: Princeton University.

Western, B. (2006). *Punishment and inequality in America.* New York, NY: Russell Sage Foundation.

Western, B., Loopoo, L., & McLanahan, S. (2004). Incarceration and the bonds between parents in fragile families. In M. Patillo, D. Weiman, & B. Western (Eds.), *Imprisoning America: The social effects of mass incarceration* (pp. 21–45). New York, NY: Russell Sage.

Western, B., & McLanahan, S. (2000). Fathers behind bars: The impact of incarceration on family formation. *Contemporary Perspectives in Family Research, 2,* 309–324.

Western, B., & Pettit, B. (2010a, Summer). Incarceration and social inequality. *Daedalus,* 8–19.

Western, B., & Pettit, B. (2010b). *Collateral costs: Incarceration's effect on economic mobility.* The Pew Charitable Trusts. Retrieved from the Pew Center on States website: http://www.pewcenteronthestates.org/report_detail.aspx?id=60919

White, M. (1995). *Re-authoring lives: Interviews and essays.* Adelaide, Australia: Dulwich Centre Publications.

Whitehead, T. L., Peterson, J., & Kaljee, L. (1994). The "hustle": Socioeconomic deprivation, urban drug trafficking, and low-income, African-American male gender identity. *Pediatrics, 93,* 1050–1054.

Wilbur, M., Marani, J., Appugliese, D., Woods, R., Siegel, J., Cabral, H., & Frank, E. (2007). Socioemotional effects of fathers' incarceration on low-income, urban, school-aged children. *Pediatrics, 120,* 678–685.

Wilson, J. (2007, June). Habilation or harm: Project Greenlight and the potential consequences of correctional programming. *NIJ Journal, 257.* Retrieved from http://www.ojp.usdoj.gov/nij/journals/257/habilitation-or-harm.html

Wilson, J., & Davis, R. (2006). Hard realities meet good intentions: An evaluation of the Project Greenlight reentry program. *Criminology and Public Policy, 5,* 303–338.

Wolf, M. (1992). *A thrice-told tale: Feminism, postmodernism, and ethnographic responsibility.* Stanford, CA: Stanford University Press.

Wonders, N. A. (1996). Determinate sentencing: A feminist and postmodern story. *Justice Quarterly, 13,* 613–648.

World Health Organization (WHO). (2005, May). *Status paper on prisons, drugs and harm reduction.* Copenhagen, Denmark: WHO Regional Office for Europe. Retrieved from http://www.euro.who.int/__data/assets/pdf_file/0006/78549/E85877.pdf

Wright, K. E., & Lewin, P. M. (1998, September). *Drug war facts.* Washington, DC: Common Sense for Drug Policy Foundation.

Young, I. M. (1990). *Justice and the politics of difference.* Princeton, NJ: Princeton University Press.

Young, V., & Reviere, R. (2006). *Women behind bars: Gender and race in US prisons.* Boulder, CO: Reinner.

Zafirovski, M. (2007). *The protestant ethic and spirit of authoritarianism: Puritanism versus democracy and the free civil society.* Denton, TX: University of North Texas.

Zlotnick, C. (1997). Posttraumatic stress disorder (PTSD) comorbidity, and childhood abuse among incarcerated women. *Journal of Nervous and Mental Disease, 185,* 761–763.

Zwiebach, L., Rhodes, J., & Rappaport, C. (2010). Mentoring interventions for children of incarcerated parents. In J. Poehlmann & M. Eddy (Eds.), *Children of incarcerated parents: A handbook for researchers and practitioners* (pp. 217–236). Washington, DC: Urban Institute Press.

Index

2009 Criminal Justice Transition
  Coalition, 149
4-H Living Interaction Family Education,
  174

Abram, K., 30
ACF, 169
Acock, A., 6, 78, 81
addiction, 3, 50, 75, 129, 154, 162–165
Administration of Children and Families,
  169
African American families, resilience,
  128–129
African American fathers, concentration
  in prisons, 73
African American men: inmate identity,
  75; length of sentence, 72
African Americans: caregiver
  responsibilities, 113; impact of
  incarceration on electoral process,
  149; incarceration rates, 145; invisible
  punishments, 148; mothers, 68; women
  and intersectionality, 65
agency, 10, 16, 35–36, 143, 166
Ahrons, C., 41
Alati, R., 98
Albuquerque's Youth Diagnostic and
  Development Center, 36
Alessandri, M., 168
Allen, K., 85–86, 160
Altshuler, S. J., 28
ambiguous loss, 37, 97, 102–107, 126–127,
  134–135, 170; definition, 102; types of,
  103
antisocial behavior, in children, 8

Applegate, B. K., 117
Arditti, J., 2, 6–7, 10, 12, 14–17, 21, 26–32,
  34–37, 40, 42–43, 47–48, 56–66, 68,
  72–74, 76–82, 85–90, 101–102, 104, 108–
  113, 117, 121, 123–126, 135–136, 150–151,
  153, 161, 174, 177–179
Arizona Senate Bill 1070, 159
Armstrong, A., 90
Arriola, K. R. J., 46
Asay, S., 179
attachment, and weakened parent-child
  bond, 110
Austin, J., 2, 5, 8, 18, 32, 76, 155

Bahr, S. J., 6, 78, 90, 92
Baker, J., 41
Bakken, T., 120
Baldwin, M., 115
Bales, W. D., 39, 119, 122, 124–125
Barak, G., 25, 32–33
Barclay, L. M., 60
Barnes, M., 30
Barocas, R., 17
Bates, F., 28, 76
Baum, S. D., 149
Beck, A., 29, 31, 43, 46, 50, 59, 112
Becker, B., 164
Beckmeyer, J., 174
Beddoes, P. V., 151
Belsky, J., 34
Bennett-Sears, T., 30
Berardo, F., 129
Bernstein, N., 6, 106, 115, 167, 173
Berry, P., 31, 34
Beuhler, C., 84

mandatory minimum sentencing, 50–51, 157, 160; definition, 50; families, 161; increase in prison growth, 160; racial disparities, 160; social inequality, 161

Manlove, J., 78

Manning, W. D., 78

Marcussen, K., 34

marginalization, 144. *See also* stigma

marital status, 26–27, 49, 52, 79

Markus, H., 81

Marlatt, G. A., 153

Marshall, S., 35

Martina, S., 39, 176, 177

Martinez, 39, 172

Maruna, S., 39, 91–93, 176–178, 181

Maruschak, L., 4, 72–73, 114, 117–121

masculinity, inmate identity, 76

mass imprisonment, 3, 6, 25, 153

mass incarceration, 6, 22, 26, 139, 152, 155

Masten, A. S., 128, 131

maternal distress, 15, 28, 59–61, 112, 164; definition, 60

maternal gatekeeping, 86; definition, 86; paternal incarceration, 86

maternal incarceration: child outcome, 59, 68; grandmother caregiver responsibilities, 113; intergenerational incarceration, 118; negative child outcomes, 118; substance use, 46

maternal substance use, 55–57

Mauer, M., 4–5, 148–149, 155, 161

Maybin, J., 177

Mayes, L., 57

McBride, E., 65, 84–86, 91

McCall, P., 5

McClanahan, S., 6, 10, 31–32, 84, 101, 112

McClelland, G., 30

McClintock, C., 29, 153, 161

McCubbin, L. D., 12

McCulloch, J., 10, 37

McDaniel, A., 129

McHale, J. P., 41

McKay, T., 6

McKeganey, N., 155

McKernan, S., 145

McLoyd, 9, 60

Mears, D. P., 39, 119, 122–125

Meek, R., 37, 81

Mendez, J., 178

mental health, 3, 8, 15–19, 24, 28–38, 57, 64–67, 101- 102, 111–115, 150, 166, 171; anxiety, 37, 41, 47–49, 60, 68, 98, 102, 108, 134; co-occurring substance use, 30; depression, 23, 29, 37, 43–47, 58–60, 67, 98, 101, 106–108, 125, 150; effects of incarceration, 36; family history, 30; gender differences, 64; sentence length, 30

Mentoring Children of Prisoners, 165, 169, 182

Mentoring Connections, 171

mentoring programs, 168–172; ambiguous loss, 170; benefits for children, 168; effects on children, 170; for children with incarcerated parents, 168; mental health and drug use, 171; reduced drug use in children, 170; statistics, 168; termination, 171

mesosystem, 9

methodology, 19; challenges of conducting research in corrections settings, 19

Meyer, C., 60, 62

Meyers, B., 174

Meyerson, J., 179, 181

microlevel, 6

microsystem, 9

Miller, R. L., 128–129, 161

Mincy, R., 19, 100

Mino, M., 180

Minton, T., 4

Minuchin, S., 41

Mnookin, R., 41

Modecki, K. L., 78, 79

modifiers, definition, 116

Moffitt, T. E., 116

Moore, S., 162

Moras, A., 129

Morgan, A., 129

Moro, 104

mother-child relationship, 37, 59; during incarceration, 37, 61

mother-daughter bonds, 167

mothers: history of child victimization, 56; more contact with children, 119; reentry, 62

Mullins, M. M., 28

Mulrow, C., 20

Multidimensional Trauma Resilience and Recovery Interview, 137–138

multiple contexts, 10

multiple risk factors, 18

Multisystemic Parenting Programs, 172

Mumola, C., 25-26, 29–30, 45, 47, 59, 61, 68, 72–73, 117, 120

Murray, J., 8, 17–18, 27, 32, 59, 97–102

Myers, B., 42, 105

Nadelman, E. A., 154

Najavits, L. M., 47

Najman, J., 98

narrative therapy, 175–176

Naser, R., 30–31, 33, 39–40, 62, 74, 122, 124

National Association for the Advancement of Colored People, 146, 151, 158

National Center on Addiction and Substance Abuse, 47, 162

National Council on Crime and Delinquency, 114

National Criminal Justice Commission Act, 149

National Institute on Drug Abuse, 47

National Public Radio, 159

negative parenting, maternal distress, 112

Nelson, T., 20, 180

Nesmith, A., 91, 116, 124–125, 129–132, 136

New York's Drug Treatment Alternative to Prison, 162

Newton, R., 172

Nickel, J., 149, 174

Nightengale, D. S., 12

no-contact visiting rules, child trauma and, 109

Nodine, E., 152

Nolan, C. M., 106

nonviolent drug offenders, 147, 153, 160

Novero, C., 168, 173

Nurius, P., 81

Nurse, A. M., 32–35, 40, 73–76, 81, 87–89

O'Brien, P., 42, 74

O'Grady, K., 30, 55–57, 61

Oberman, M., 60, 62

offender behavior while incarcerated, effects of visitation, 122

offender resilience, 137

Olsen, S., 8, 27

Open Society Institute, 146, 147, 153

oppression, definition, 145

Osborne, C., 101, 112

Otteson, C., 179, 181

outcomes, 9, 12–19, 21, 33, 42, 60, 101, 137, 139, 143, 163–164, 172–173, 181; children, 41; incarcerated mothers, 46; parental incarceration, 182

Owen, B., 20

Oyserman, D., 81

Pager, D., 65, 156

Paisley, K., 84

Pajulo, M., 57

Panel Study of Income Dynamics, 110

Paranal, R., 20

parent education, with visitation, 174

parental agency, 36

parental arrest, poor child outcomes, 99

parental capital, 69

parental distress, 31, 33, 36–37, 40, 60, 122; effects of visitation, 122

parental functioning, 9

parental identity, 16, 33, 35–36, 39, 165, 180; coparenting, 42; definition, 34; during incarceration, 76

parental incapacitation, 43

parental incarceration: ambiguous loss, 103–104; behavior problems in children, 101; caregivers' loss of employment, 111; children and prisoner reentry, 153; children's adjustment, 7, 59, 100–101, 118, 138, 165, 173; children's aggression, 101; children's depression, 101; children's experience of traumatic events, 99, 101; children's mental health, 101; children's poor school performance, 101; children's posttraumatic stress disorder, 106–107; children's stigmatization,

Treadwell, H., 46, 148
Trice, A. D., 101, 122
Tripp, B., 74, 76, 77
Tsushima, T., 34–36
Tuerk, E. H., 31, 37, 39–40, 62, 122, 172–173

U.S. Sentencing Commission, 160
Uggen, C., 14–15, 33, 149
undocumented immigrants, incarceration rates, 145
Ungar, M., 175
United Nations Development Fund for Women, 51

van Olphen, J., 30–32, 36
Van Wormer, K., 153, 155, 157
Visher, C., 6, 15, 17, 29–31, 42, 73–74, 90, 120
visitation, 25, 40, 174; ambiguous loss, 126; as a key moderator for child adjustment, 118; benefits, 39, 121, 122; child trauma, 102, 109; conditions, 127; difficulties, 120, 122, 124–126; effects on children, 122; emotional pain, 126; environment, 14; facilitates social reintegration, 119; factors influencing frequency, 121; family-friendly visitation, 40; family-friendly intervention programs, 122; fathers, 26; institutional practices, 31; institutional restrictions precluding physical contact, 31; mail contact, 119; negative effects for maternal offenders, 125; negative effects on children, 123–124; parenting programs, 167; poor conditions, 123; programs to support, 167; protective factor, 119; proximal traumatic reminder, 118; recidivism, 124; secondary prisonization, 127; traumatic separation, 108
visitation trends, 119
voluntary paternal separation during incarceration, 82
Votey, H. L., 52
Voth, E. A., 154
vulnerability, maternal, 69

Wacquant, L., 145, 148, 152, 158
Wagner, H. R., 27, 112
Waintrup, M., 137
Wakefield, S., 14–15, 33
Waldfogel, J., 27, 30
Walker, L., 2
Waller, M., 7, 25, 27, 39, 79
Walsh, F., 128–129, 178
Wardle, B., 74
Warner, K., 160
Warren, J., 64, 159, 162
Watts, H., 12, 110
Waul, M., 18, 68, 105
Webb's National Criminal Justice Commission Act, 149
Weilandt, C., 153
Weinberg, R., 164
Weiss, R. D., 47
welfare. See Temporary Assistance for Needy Families
welfare reform, impact of drug charges on benefit eligibility, 148–150
Werner-Lin, A., 104
West, H. C., 4, 90
Western, N., 6, 10, 18, 25–29, 31–33, 38, 43, 72, 145, 154
Whitehead, T. L., 75–76
Wilbur, M., 19, 101
Williams, E., 98
Wilson, L., 9, 78–79, 106, 124, 132, 171–172, 181
women of circumstance, 51, 55; define, 51
Wonders, N. A., 3
Wood, J., 32
World Health Organization, 152
Wright, K. E., 161

Young, 5, 33–34, 58, 64, 122, 144–145

Zafirovski, M., 155
Zax, M., 17
Zhao, J., 106
Zurhold, H., 153
Zwiebach, L., 169–171

About the Author

Joyce A. Arditti is Professor of Human Development, Virginia Polytechnic Institute and State University, and author of numerous articles on incarcerated parents and their reentry into family life.